THE TIGRESS IN THE SNOW
Motherhood and Literature in
Twentieth-Century Italy

The Tigress in the Snow explores how literature was influenced by and helped to shape notions of motherhood in twentieth-century Italy. From late-nineteenth-century religious iconography, to the Fascist regime's campaign to boost Italy's birthrate, to more recent feminist challenges to traditional gender roles, this study demonstrates that concepts of motherhood and the social status associated with mothers were subject to constant negotiation. Examining how this negotiation came to be represented in literature, Laura Benedetti looks at four generations of women writers, stressing their similarities and differences, as well as their complex interactions with their male counterparts and their reactions to changes in Italian soceity.

Drawing on examples from a wide range of novels, plays, poems, and short stories as well as from critical and public debate, the book highlights literature's role in the formation of cultural discourses up to the dawn of the twenty-first century. An intriguing look at the changing nature of the maternal role in a culture that has always put strong emphasis on the institution of motherhood, this volume goes further to show how literature investigates, shapes, and envisions social models for the present and future.

(Toronto Italian Studies)

LAURA BENEDETTI is the Laura and Gaetano De Sole Associate Professor in Contemporary Italian Culture at Georgetown University.

The Tigress in the Snow

Motherhood and Literature in Twentieth-Century Italy

Laura Benedetti

UNIVERSITY OF TORONTO PRESS
Toronto Buffalo London

© University of Toronto Press 2007
Toronto Buffalo London
utorontopress.com

Reprinted in paperback 2009

ISBN 978-0-8020-9744-6 (cloth)
ISBN 978-1-4426-1086-6 (paper)

Toronto Italian Studies

Library and Archives Canada Cataloguing in Publication

Benedetti, Laura, 1962–
The tigress in the snow : motherhood and literature in twentieth-century
Italy / Laura Benedetti.

(Toronto Italian Studies)
Includes bibliographical references and index.
ISBN 978-0-8020-9744-6 (bound). –ISBN 978-1-4426-1086-6 (pbk.)

1. Italian literature – 20th century – History and criticism.   2. Motherhood
in literature.   3. Mothers in literature.   4. Social change in literature.
5. Motherhood – Italy – History – 20th century.   I. Title.   II. Series:
Toronto Italian Studies.

PQ4088.B385 2007   850.9'352520904   C2008-903509-4

Publication of this book was made possible by the Georgetown University
Graduate School Competitive Grant-in-Aid Award.

University of Toronto Press acknowledges the finanical assistance to its
publishing program of the Canada Council for the Arts and the Ontario Arts
Council.

University of Toronto Press acknowledges the financial support for its pu -
lishing activities of the Government of Canada through the Book Publishing
Industry Development Program (BPIDP).

Cover illustration: Käthe Kollwitz, *Woman with Dead Child (Frau mit Totem
Kind)*. Gift of Philip and Lynn Straus. Courtesy of the Board of Trustees,
National Gallery of Art, Washington, DC.

To Martina:

... Gaudentque tuentes
Dardanidae, veterumque agnoscunt ora parentum.
(Virgil, *Aeneid* V, 575–6)

Contents

Acknowledgments ix

Introduction 3

1 Mothers at the Dawn of the Twentieth Century 12
 The New Mother 12
 From Mother to Daughter: Annie Vivanti's *The Devourers* 23
 The Mother as Artist: Luigi Pirandello's *Suo marito* 25
 A Revolution Named Sibilla 28
 Self-Sacrifice and Marian Imagery 32
 The Invisible Working Woman 39

2 Resilience and Resistance: The Fascist Years 43
 From Benevolence to Dominance 43
 Literature and the Escape from History 45
 Mothers without a Name and the Search for Women's Identity 47
 Mothers at War 52
 'Like War Is to Men' 58
 Future as a Revised Version of the Past 60
 No Turning Back 67

3 Questioning Motherhood 74
 Slow Changes 74
 The Tigress in the Snow 78
 'Una Maternità Sociale': The Upheaval of the 1970s 84
 Too Close, Too Far: Motherhood as a Dialogue with the Self 89

4 Struggling with the Mother   94
   Through the Daughters' Voices   94
   The Mother and the City   102
   Daughter *and* Mother   110

5 Mothers without Children   114
   From Flesh to Phantom   114
   The Symbolic Order of the Mother   116
   A World of Mothers   119

Notes   123

Works Cited   149

Index   161

Acknowledgments

The writing of this book has accompanied me for a long time and through different times. My heartfelt gratitude and respect go to those who have believed in it, and in me. Patrizia Bettella, Claude Cazalé Bérard, Carol Dover, Franco Fido, Pietro Frassica, Tommasina Gabriele, Mary Gaylord, Albert Mancini, Enrico Musacchio, Daria Perocco, Cosetta Seno Reed, Roberto Severino, and Diego Zancani offered suggestions, encouragement, and support in various ways and at different stages.

My thoughts go to the late Bob Dombroski, who with his distinctive generosity read parts of the manuscript and was the first to think it would make a fitting addition to the catalogue of the University of Toronto Press. Following his suggestion, I came to know the competent thoughtfulness of my editor, Ron Schoeffel, the insightful judgment of the anonymous readers, and the unerring attention of my copyeditor, Barbara Czarnecki. They all assisted me in bringing this book to light.

Georgetown University provided a summer research fellowship and, more important, a congenial environment to write and grow. Domenico De Sole and Sara Hager proved tireless in their support of the humanities, while students in my 'Bella Ciao!' classes helped me to elaborate my thoughts on motherhood and writing. Thanks to the Georgetown Undergraduate Research Opportunities Program, I was able to discuss my ideas and refine my style with Emily Langer, a bright young scholar of exceptional promise. The final revisions were facilitated by Michael Brown's sharp eyes. The responsibility for any mistakes and omissions is, of course, entirely mine.

Finally, although it has been said before, a special thanks to Brad Marshall, without whom I would have finished this book much earlier.

THE TIGRESS IN THE SNOW

Motherhood and Literature in
Twentieth-Century Italy

Introduction

Desired or feared, accepted or denied, cherished as a privilege or stigmatized as a biblical curse, motherhood has a capital influence on women's lives. The century that has just ended witnessed radical redefinitions of the maternal role in the Western world. The stereotypical figure of the married woman with child (or, more often, with children) is now accompanied by a growing number of women raising children out of wedlock, without a male companion, or alone. The ever-increasing number of adoptions have separated the nurturing side of mothering from the biological, while new reproductive technologies have challenged deeply ingrained notions of lineage and parenting.

In few countries have these changes been so dramatic as in Italy. In 1900 Italian women bore an average of 5 children each, but by 1950 that figure had dropped to 1.88, making Italy the country with the lowest birth rate in Europe.[1] By 1998 the rate had declined further, to 1.19 children per woman – one of the lowest in the world.[2] This is the most striking in a series of shifts that Italian motherhood underwent during the twentieth century and that literature has investigated, reflected upon, supported, or resisted. From the turn-of-the-century rhetorical celebration of the mother as Madonna (a celebration that often ignored the very real lives of mothers working in factories and rice fields) to the Fascist regime's demographic campaign and the feminist revisions of the maternal role, the institution of motherhood has been the site of constant negotiation.

This book was born from the conviction that the theme of motherhood as elaborated by poets, playwrights, and novelists is crucial to the understanding of twentieth-century Italian culture as a whole. At its core lies the belief that literature does not merely reflect but also anticipates, corrects, challenges, and shapes social forces. Neither entirely absorbed in a hermetic dialogue with tradition nor reducible to predictable commentaries on a reality that has existed before and independently of them, literary texts can be seen as part of a field of forces upon which they draw and to which they contribute.³

As well as dealing with the symbolic value of motherhood or the mother-child relationship, this book explores motherhood as a concrete experience in women's lives, as reflected in and shaped by literature. This particular angle of investigation led to a discovery, which in turn produced an unintended consequence. Considering the emphasis placed on motherhood in the Italian cultural landscape, it was surprising to discover the limited space literature has devoted to mothers *as subjects*. Worshipped in its manifestation as the sacrificial mother of Christ and feared in its representation as Medea's annihilating power, the image of the mother seems to be trapped in a web of symbolic associations curiously distant from women's daily lives.⁴ *Maria, Medea, e le altre* (*Mary, Medea, and the Others*) was, appropriately, the title of a 1982 anthology of articles on motherhood. While taking into account the inescapable influence of Mary and Medea in the construction of motherhood, this book looks for the literary emergence and manifestations of the 'altre,' of women of human – rather than mythical – stature, who offer insights on their conditions as individuals endowed with the specifically female prerogative of bringing another being into life.

The representations of motherhood found in Italian literature are, almost invariably, images of the mother seen through the eyes of her son. With only a few exceptions, these loving mothers are reduced to a single emotion: unconditional devotion to their offspring. They are capable of overcoming even fear and pain in the face of death, as exemplified in this poem by Giovanni Pascoli, which describes a dying mother's reaction upon seeing her son:

'Non parla, non vede – a la porta
mi dicono – piú! né baciarla
puoi piú che in un viso di morta
già freddo!'

M'accosto al suo letto: ella un poco
li occhi alza: ella vede, ella parla:
'Oh, povero bimbo! ... del fuoco,
che ha freddo!'⁵

'She no longer speaks, she no longer sees!' I am told at the door. 'You can only kiss the already cold face of a dead woman!' I approach her bed. She opens her eyes a little. She sees, she speaks: 'Oh, poor baby! ... Make a fire, he is cold!')[6]

The ideal mother-child relationship glorified by religion, encouraged by family structure, and sanctioned by psychoanalysis is indeed the one that unites a mother to her son. Locked in this self-effacing and one-dimensional role, the mother hardly seems a suitable topic for literary creativity. Isabella Nardi attributes the rare occurrence of the theme of motherhood in nineteenth-century literature to the absence of an appropriate narrative structure. Too weak socially to act as a positive role model, and at the same time too closely linked to her biological role, the mother proves incapable of posing a challenge to society. Therefore, the critic concludes, motherhood remains strictly subordinate to the themes of marriage and adultery.[7]

The difficulty of seeing motherhood from the point of view of the mother, and thus of endowing her with individuality, is certainly not limited to the nineteenth century nor to literature written by men.[8] Women writers who have reflected on motherhood have done so almost exclusively as daughters. Even for them, the condition of mother and that of subject seem often to be mutually exclusive. It is difficult to imagine how it could have been otherwise. One could argue that, before becoming a daughter or a son – that is, before becoming aware of sex differences – every infant experiences a relationship in which the mother is the object. Furthermore, as Jessica Benjamin has suggested, 'Independence from the mother as object rather than recognition of her as a subject constitutes the essence of individuation [...] To the extent that until recently "man" and "individual" were synonymous, the male experience of differentiation has stamped the image of individuality.'[9]

Crucial in a psychoanalytical framework and endorsed by the organization of society, the objectification of the mother has proven a resilient and long-lasting construction. Benjamin eloquently denounced the persistence of this model and the dangers it entailed:

> It must be acknowledged that we have only just begun to think about the mother as a subject in her own right, principally because of contemporary feminism, which made us aware of the disastrous results for women of being reduced to the mere extension of a two-month-old. Psychology in general and psychoanalysis in particular too often partake of this distorted

view of the mother, which is so deeply embedded in the culture as a whole. No psychological theory has adequately articulated the mother's independent existence.[10]

This lack of adequate theoretical models helps explain women's difficulty in combining motherhood and subjectivity – i.e., 'the ability to assume a position of enunciation, of saying "I."'[11] Yet, even if the mother cannot break free from her role as an object, the subject's gender is not irrelevant, and a woman's representation of motherhood does bring specific concerns to the foreground. Even if we could imagine a daughter in the same predicament as the son in Pascoli's poem, she would not be able to receive the mother's sacrifice as an unconditional gift. This imaginary daughter would know that, by accepting her mother's love, she would one day be expected to offer in turn the same unconditional love to her own children, honouring an implicit but nevertheless binding agreement. It was only in the 1980s that the complexity deriving from women's position as both daughters *and* (at least potentially) mothers became the focus of attention. A woman's relationship to her mother was then defined as inextricably linked to the conceptualization of her own reproductive capacity. And yet, in spite of this historical delay, the idea of motherhood as a complex and often conflictual experience had already surfaced in the work of a few pioneers. From Sibilla Aleramo's visionary and thought-provoking definition of motherhood as a set of chains passed on from mother to daughter, to Alba De Céspedes's candid portrayal of the ambivalent feelings of a single mother in Fascist Italy, to the radical *remise en jeu* of the feminist movement, motherhood has proven to be an event that calls into question a woman's notion of self, her place in society, her relation to others.

The choice to focus on motherhood as an experience led not only to the discovery of the limited place granted to mothers as subjects in Italian literature, but also to an unforeseen consequence, immediately apparent to anyone who may peruse the index of this book, where women writers are disproportionally over-represented. Perhaps not surprisingly, women were the authors who throughout the century, albeit within the limitations indicated above, offered the most complex representations of mothering, developing a critique that has gained in profundity and intensity over the last twenty-five years.

The chronological organization of the chapters of this book allows for an analysis of the role played by literature in the cultural discourse of each of the periods considered. It also highlights, however, literature's prerogative to bring to the fore issues seemingly remote from the concerns of its time. René Wellek's remarks on artists' ability to reach into their past 'or into the remotest past of humanity'[12] can be expanded to encompass the future as well. Literature's undeniable contributions to the cultural discourses of its time should not overshadow its capacity to reach outside its chronological boundaries, bringing into focus issues that may not seem immediately relevant but that will become pertinent and fully understandable at a later time and in another context. Antonia Pozzi, who in the 1930s addressed a heart-wrenching poem to her 'fake baby,' and Elsa Morante, who, ostensibly oblivious to literary trends and historical changes, developed a reflection on motherhood as a mythical force offer a reminder of literature's power to rise above the concerns of its time.

Just as women writers have provided most of the material discussed in the following pages, so too has international gender criticism offered the most pertinent analytical tools. In particular, the reflection on motherhood initiated by Adrienne Rich and Nancy Chodorow, along with Marianne Hirsch's and Sara Ruddick's crucial contributions, and the philosophical revisions of the Diotima group have provided the theoretical framework for this analysis. I have combined their insights with the attention to issues of narrative construction, style, and intertextuality that is indispensable when dealing with literary texts. As a history of twentieth-century Italian motherhood seen through a literary lens, this book aims to be faithful to history, sensitive to the complexity of its topic, and keenly aware of the specificity of literature, its visionary quality, and its enduring power.

The starting point in chapter 1 is an analysis of the notion of motherhood that developed in the second half of the nineteenth century. In the early 1900s, the experience of motherhood was divided among several roles (procreation, nursing, education), all of which were played by different individuals, sometimes in different places. Around 1850 those functions were combined into a single figure: that of the mother giving birth, raising, and educating her children in the family home.[13] This new, comprehensive, and powerful figure found its counterpart in the increasingly widespread cult of the Virgin Mary, which reached its climax in 1854 with the dogma of the Immaculate Conception.[14] This concurrence constitutes a revealing example of the inescapable influence of Catholicism on the Italian notion of motherhood.[15] While representing an abstract, timeless, and powerful model, this ideal entailed serious consequences for women who refused to (or could not) fulfil it.

At the turn of the century, a number of authors investigated the contradictions implicit in this new role. In *L'indomani* (*The Next Day*, 1889) Neera (Anna Radius Zuccari) saw motherhood as the crucial event in a woman's life, a miracle that could save her from the awkwardness and confusion of a conjugal relationship. On the other hand Sibilla Aleramo, in her controversial *Una donna* (*A Woman*, 1906), investigated the sacrifices that motherhood imposed upon the rights of a woman as an individual. Her novel, in which the protagonist eventually decides to leave her son behind in order to start a new life alone, caused a scandal; the pages in which Aleramo describes motherhood as a legacy of slavery passed from mother to daughter horrified critics. In Ada Negri's poems, the topic is explored in its social and political implications: motherhood links all women, and the unattainable ideal proposed by religion and society gives way to the real stories of the *Dolorose*, working women who labour in the malaria-infested rice fields, passing on to their children their 'guasto sangue [...] e il peso [delle loro] catene' (sick blood [...] and the weight of [their] chains).[16]

Chapter 2 examines the ways in which the Fascist regime tried to exert close control over reproduction, seeking to shape a society in which the bearing of children would be the only suitable destiny for women. In his 'Speech of the Ascension' on 26 May 1927, Mussolini outlined the demographic goal of Fascist Italy: the country needed to reach a population of sixty million by the middle of the twentieth century (from forty million in the 1920s). Women were called to the front line of this battle. During the following years, special laws reduced their salaries to half those of men and doubled their college tuition fees.[17] While women studying and working outside the home faced this hostile discrimination, those who fully conformed to the maternal role and bore seven or more children (the *prolifiche*) received generous financial rewards in public ceremonies. Once again, the price for the glorification of the mother was the humiliation of the woman.

Fascist critics sought to extend these restrictions to literature[18] and declared writing to be incompatible with a woman's true vocation as a mother.[19] And yet, as the laws aimed at barring women from the workforce achieved mixed results (lower wages ultimately increased the demand for female workers, who were also called to replace the men who had left for the war front), attempts to prevent women's cultural participation had only limited success. Some of the most popular novels of the Fascist era were in fact written by women. Most books, whether written by men or women, sold no more than 2,000 copies, and only five or six books reached sales of 20,000. Nevertheless, Annie Vivanti's 1927 *Mea culpa!* sold 100,000 copies and Alba De Céspedes's 1938 *Nessuno torna indietro* sold 150,000.[20] Short stories were also published in journals and magazines, frequently on the *terza pagina* (the cultural page) of daily papers such as *Il Corriere della Sera, Il Giornale d'Italia*, and *La Stampa*.[21] Chapter 2 focuses on novels, poems, and short stories in which writers such as Grazia Deledda (winner of the 1926 Nobel Prize), Gianna Manzini, and Paola Drigo, who were perceived as transgressive for the simple fact of their writing, portray the figure of the mother - the glorified ideal that the Fascist regime wanted all women to embody.

Chapter 3 focuses on the years from the aftermath of the Second World War to the end of the 1970s, a time during which Italy underwent radical transformations. Industrialization, internal migration, student movements, and the affirmation of feminism altered the traditional relationships between the sexes in society and within the family. Divorce became legal in 1970, and in 1975 the new family law assured greater equality between husband and wife. Finally, the 1978 abortion law provided women with a new means to control their reproduction. The feminist movement of the 1970s was marked by a rejection of motherhood, perceived as a dangerous force able to draw independent and socially engaged women back into domestic oppression and a limited world. The mother was considered 'everything one did not want to become in life'; ecological concerns reinforced the refusal to procreate, which was perceived in some cases as a form of 'personal morality.'[22] In 1975 Oriana Fallaci explored the ambivalent feelings of a prospective mother in her powerful *Lettera a un bambino mai nato* (*Letter to a Child Never Born*), dedicated 'a chi si pone il problema di dare la vita o negarla' (to those who face the challenge of giving life or denying it). A similar dilemma faces Angela, the protagonist of Gina Lagorio's *La spiaggia del lupo* (*The Wolf Beach*, 1977), who in the novel's last chapter boards a train with her child to begin a new life independent of the baby's father. While these works capture the new challenges facing women (paradoxically linked with the new opportunities available to them), others depict motherhood in a timeless, almost mythical dimension. Elsa Morante, undoubtedly one of the greatest authors of twentieth-century Italy, put the figure of the mother at the center of her work, notably in her masterpiece *La Storia: Romanzo (History: A Novel*, 1974), in which Iduzza Ramundo fights against 'History and all the Nations of the world' to keep her son Useppe alive, finally giving in to madness when he dies. Morante's work provides a useful reminder of the web of symbolic associations spun around the figure of the mother, and a warning against simplistic interpretations of literature as a mirror of social phenomena.

The fourth chapter explores a particular facet of the debate on motherhood: the mother-daughter relationship, as portrayed in several novels written in the 1980s. An analysis of these works makes it clear that an understanding of the 'mother-daughter knot' – to borrow from Marianne Hirsch's momentous 1989 volume – is essential not only to the well-being of both but also to the daughter's acceptance or refusal of her own potential as a mother. In Fabrizia Ramondino's *Althénopis* (1981), a mother on the verge of death manages to send a sign that, however enigmatic, frees her daughter from the ghosts of the past, so that 'ved[ano] la luce altri nati di donna'[23] (others, born of woman, may see the light). More often, however, time works against reconciliation. When the daughter overcomes her rejection and begins to understand the inescapable influence of her mother on her life, the mother has already disappeared.[24] The daughter then must take on the task of reconstructing their relationship through recordings (Carla Cerati's *La cattiva figlia* [*The Bad Daughter*, 1990]), memories and dreams (Francesca Sanvitale's *Madre e figlia* [*Mother and Daughter*, 1980] and Elena Ferrante's *L'amore molesto* [*Harassing Love*, 1992]).

Chapter 5 concludes this exploration of the meanings of motherhood with an analysis of the last twenty years, a time marked by the consequences of the pronounced decline in birth rates discussed above. Not only is motherhood no longer every woman's destiny; for a considerable percentage of Italian women, it is not even a life experience.[25] Nevertheless, the relationship with motherhood continues to be of crucial importance. In feminist thought, the illusion of equality has given way to the acknowledgment of the differences between women, which in turn has inspired the practice of *affidamento* (a system of fostering and mentorship)[26] as well as a philosophical reflection on the figure of the mother.[27] Novels of this most recent period often portray relationships that mirror those between mothers and their children. In Valeria Viganò's *Prove di vite separate* (*Attempts at Separate Lives*, 1992), Mabel develops a strong attachment to a little girl, Matilde, and dreams of being her mother. Dacia Maraini's *Dolce per sé* (*Sweet in Itself*, 1996) describes a similar bond: the novel is laid out in a series of letters that a fifty-year-old woman addresses to a little girl in the hope of overcoming the generational barrier.

This new model significantly reverses the paradigm prevalent in the early nineteenth century. While in those times the biological experience of motherhood did not necessarily entail the sentimental implications we now associate with the figure of the mother, some late twentieth-century novels depict relationships that mirror the intense attachment of a maternal bond but lack a biological component. This model of 'nonprocreative motherhood'[28] has just begun to receive attention in an Anglo-Saxon context and has been largely ignored in the analysis of Italian fiction.

The title of this book was inspired by Elsa Morante's *La Storia: Romanzo*, where the image of the tigress in the snow is introduced to describe Ida Ramundo's desperate attempt to keep her son Useppe alive:

> A lei stessa niente faceva gola, perfino la secrezione della saliva le si era prosciugata: tutti i suoi stimoli vitali si erano trasferiti su Useppe. Si racconta di una tigre che, in una solitudine gelata, si sostenne assieme ai propri nati leccando, per parte sua, la neve; e distribuendo ai piccoli dei brandelli di carne che lei stessa si strappava dal proprio corpo coi denti.[29]

> She did not crave anything for herself. Even her saliva had dried up. All her vital instincts had been transferred to Useppe. It is said that a tigress, in a frozen solitude, survived with her cubs by licking the snow to sustain herself; and she administered to her little ones pieces of flesh that she tore from her body with her teeth.

It is a powerful, haunting image that conveys two seemingly conflicting notions, merging authority with self-immolation. The animal believed to sacrifice its flesh to nourish its young is, in fact, the pelican, which for this reason became a symbol of Christ in religious iconography. The implicit comparison raises humble, unassuming Ida Ramundo to an almost supernatural level. Yet her strength as a tigress coincides with her indifference to her own pain. Her power is inseparable from her tendency towards self-annihilation. This image effectively captures the risks and the rewards of motherhood, as experienced and feared by so many characters in this study, and it provided the guiding metaphor of this work.

chapter 1

Mothers at the Dawn of the Twentieth Century

The New Mother

In Carolina Invernizio's best-seller *Il bacio di una morta* (*The Kiss of a Dead Woman*, 1886), the protagonist, Clara, reveals to her husband, Guido, that she is pregnant, and expresses her firm intention to nurse the baby herself ('Io stessa l'allatterò'). Guido, overcome with joy, supports her decision, pledging not to entrust the child to strangers ('Non lo lasceremo nelle mani di estranei').[1] Awkward as such a dialogue may sound to modern readers, it also serves as a reminder that the family to which we have grown accustomed (with mothers who nurse, and children who live with their parents) was in those times a young institution. Clara's decision was not the only one possible for an upper-middle-class woman of the late nineteenth century and may even have seemed unusual.

The figure of the mother that emerges at the end of the nineteenth century, as exemplified by Invernizio's Clara, is in fact radically different from that of the early 1800s. At the beginning of the century, motherhood was a fragmented responsibility, and the functions of procreation, nursing, and upbringing were fulfilled by different individuals, often in different places. About fifty years later, those functions were combined into a single figure – that of the mother, who gave birth and raised and educated her children in the home.[2]

This phenomenon was not limited to Italy and can be attributed to a variety of economic and cultural factors. As the Industrial Revolution separated the home from the workplace, mothers became increasingly associated, in theory if not always in practice, with the domestic sphere. This division, of course, directly contradicted the economic realities faced by many working-class families that depended on women's salaries for their subsistence. It therefore imposed upon working mothers two irreconcilable demands, as the final part of this chapter will investigate. A growing emphasis on the emotional aspects of family ties accompanied these socio-economic changes, as mothers took on primary responsibility for their children's upbringing.

Elisabeth Badinter, who has studied the evolution of motherhood in France, stresses the importance of Rousseau's *Émile* (1762) as the text that 'donne le véritable coup d'envoi à la famille moderne, c'est-à-dire à la famille fondée sur l'amour maternel'[3] (marks the true beginning of the modern family, namely the family based on maternal love). She also points out, however, that this new model took many years to establish itself, in a process that neared completion only towards the end of the nineteenth century. The psychologist Marcello Marcellini notes how the twentieth century was marked by the strong attention paid to children's psychology and needs, and concludes: 'La dimensione emotiva che oggi osserviamo così chiaramente nella generalità delle madri è in effetti un prodotto storico-evolutivo, una modalità relazionale madre-figlio così nuova che ci è difficile ritrovarla così trasparente nei secoli passati'[4] (The emotional dimension that today manifests itself so clearly in most mothers is the result of historical evolution, a relationship between mother and child so new that it is difficult to find its precise equivalent in past centuries). Thus, at the end of the nineteenth and the beginning of the twentieth centuries, Italian mothers took on the daunting task of assuming full responsibility for the emotional development of their children.

The end of the nineteenth century also witnessed the entrance of numerous women onto the Italian literary stage – a truly revolutionary event for the peninsula. Only in the late Renaissance had there been signs of a similar phenomenon, albeit on a much smaller scale. This development, linked to the emergence of a vast female reading public, is among the most remarkable results of the 1859 Casati law, which had made elementary education mandatory for children of both sexes. The consequences of the new policies for the female population were particularly remarkable: while in 1861 a staggering 81 per cent of Italian women were illiterate, by 1901 that percentage had dropped to 54 per cent, and by 1911 to 42 per cent.[5] The Casati law, however, was strangely silent about women's secondary education,[6] and in practice female education was often restricted to the lowest grades.

An additional and perhaps unforeseen consequence of the new legislation was an increased demand for educators. Because the salary of elementary school teachers was extremely low, in spite of the years of education required to qualify for such positions, men's presence in the field declined and for the first time in history women as a group gained access to a formal intellectual profession. Popular writers such as Ada Negri and Marchesa Colombi (Maria Antonietta Torriani) started their careers working as teachers, and Matilde Serao left a powerful representation of prospective teachers in her short story 'Scuola Normale Femminile.' In practice, teaching was one of the few professions available to women.[7] Forced to travel alone and work in an often hostile environment in exchange for a stipend always inferior to the already meagre salary received by their male colleagues, the *maestrine* can be considered unwilling pioneers of women's emancipation.[8] The tragic case of Italia Donati, driven to suicide by slander, is emblematic.[9]

The persecution undergone by female teachers was due more to the unconventional lifestyle they were forced to lead than to their profession. Teaching, in fact, did seem a logical occupation for women, as it was considered in line with their maternal instincts and duties. In addition to being educators, female teachers were supposed to function as mothers to their students. Ida Baccini, a successful author of children's books, went as far as lecturing her audience on how teaching could fulfil one's maternal desires. She even discouraged teachers from having children of their own, as such 'supreme joy' would prevent them from 'mothering' their little pupils ('non si può far da madre ai figliuoli degli altri quando Iddio ci ha concesso la gioia suprema di un figliuolo nostro').[10] Ostensibly persuaded by this logic, the jury awarded her the gold medal for the best paper presented at the conference.

Although extremely popular at the time, turn-of-the-century women writers were neglected until the publication of Giuliana Morandini's *La voce che è in lei* (*The Voice inside Her*, 1980), a groundbreaking anthology that also included a brief account of the life and work of each author. Morandini's compilation recognized and gave credit to the remarkable, unconventional, sometimes tragic lives of these women. It included authors such as Cristina Trivulzio di Belgioioso, who visited the oriental harems so many male writers had dreamed of, denouncing the squalour and dirt in which women lived; and Contessa Lara, who was killed by her lover; not to mention the cosmopolitan Anne Vivanti, whose work will receive closer scrutiny later in this chapter.[11]

Scholars have highlighted the importance of love in many of these books and have often criticized the unrealistic, sentimental view of life they portray. However, some of these authors, while investigating love and its effects, also delineate complex social realities. For them, love becomes a key element in the struggle between ideals and reality, one of the compromises adult women are forced to make. It is in this context that the theme of motherhood acquires its specific meaning: for many characters, the initial experience of pregnancy coincides with the loss of the sentimental dreams of their youth and with the discovery of a more profound form of love.

Nowhere is this clearer than in Neera's *L'indomani* (*The Day After*, 1889).[12] When the protagonist, Marta, marries the thirty-seven-year-old Alberto, she is 'already' twenty-three,[13] and her only glimpse of love dates back to her adolescence:

> A quindici anni Marta aveva avuta la prima preoccupazione d'amore: null'altro che un fremito, una lunga stretta di mano, uno sguardo che la fece trasalire; e poi molte notti d'insomnia, molte ore di tristezza, molte lagrime sparse in segreto; nessuna ebbrezza amorosa, ma l'intuizione di tutte le ebbrezze.
>
> Ed era finito così.[14]

> When she was fifteen, Marta had had her first experience with love: nothing more than a shiver, a long handshake, a glance that unsettled her; and then many nights of insomnia, many hours of sadness, many tears wept in secrecy; no ecstasy of love, but the intuition of all ecstasies.
>
> And so it ended.

The novel begins when Marta awakes for the first time in her marital bedroom (in what could already be an explanation of the title). Far from her family, Marta starts a new life in the village where her husband has always lived. Alberto is in no way harsh towards his young wife (we are very far indeed from the brutality described in other novels of the time, such as Sibilla Aleramo's *Una donna* or Anna Franchi's *Avanti il divorzio!*), but this allows Neera to investigate even more subtly the incompatibility between two human beings whose gendered upbringing has led them to cherish different values.[15] Marta is dumbfounded when she learns that her husband finds it normal to separate sex and emotional attachment. The discovery of Alberto's past affairs leaves her torn between jealousy and a very different feeling: the fear that the love and commitment his former lovers had revealed in their passionate letters had not been reciprocated, and thus that Alberto may be intrinsically incapable of loving. In the climactic final chapter of the novel, Marta witnesses the embrace between a young mother and her husband, but that glimpse at the possibility of love and communion in marriage is soon obliterated by the simultaneous discovery that she too will soon become a mother:

> Marta aveva soffocato un grido, come colpita al cuore; e nello stesso momento aveva sentito le sue viscere sollevarsi, muoversi nel suo grembo un essere, e per le sue vene, per la sua carne correva il palpito atteso, la rivelazione di un'altra vita scoppiata colla rivelazione stessa dell'amore.
> Ogni velo era tolto, sciolto ogni dubbio, la sua verginità cadeva in quel punto, ella era fatta donna.[16]

> Marta suffocated a scream, as if struck in the heart; at the same moment she felt her insides rise, a being move in her womb, and in her veins the awaited throb, the revelation of another life exploded with the revelation of love itself.
> All veils dropped, all doubts disappeared. Her virginity was lost at that moment. She had become a woman.

Back at home, Marta has an animated discussion with her mother about marriage and love. Love, the older woman says, is such an ambiguous word that everybody finds a different meaning in it.[17] But Marta dissents: 'Love exists,' she says, before the new life inside her makes itself felt once again, reinforcing her new awareness:

> Ma intanto la piccola mano ripeteva con insistenza: Apri, io sono l'amore e la verità.
> E Marta rivedeva in una specie di visione magnetica la bella campagna estiva, gli alberi frondosi ramificanti sopra lo sfondo azzurro e un meschino insetto che tendeva i suoi fili d'argento. Spezzato un filo gettava l'altro, e un altro ancora e ancora, sempre avanti, la tela prendeva proporzioni gigantesche, i fili abbracciavano tutto il creato, salivano ad altezze verginose, toccavano il cielo.
> Era la vasta tela della vita umana, il lavoro ogni giorno rinnovato di chi soffre e combatte; il lavoro temerario che poggia nel vuoto guardando arditamente la luce; lo sforzo immane di milioni di esseri, intelligenze torturate, cuori spasimanti, schiavi in pena, tutti sorgenti dalle loro catene, tutti lanciando il loro filo d'argento al misterioso Ignoto. E i fili si spezzano e la tela si strappa e la felicità dondola sempre sospesa all'impalpabile bava di un aracnide. Che importa? Tutto muore, tutto nasce, tutto cambia, tutto

si rinnova, le tombe scoperchiate servono di culla, i cuori insanguinati e piangenti danno nuovo sangue e nuove lagrime alla vita.
Avanti, coraggio![18]

But in the meantime, the little hand insistently repeated: 'Open, I am love and truth.'
And Marta saw again, in a kind of magnetic vision, the beautiful summer countryside, the leafy trees stretching their branches against the azure background, and a humble insect spinning its silver threads. Once a thread was broken, it spun another one, then another and another. The web took on gigantic proportions, the threads extended all over creation, rose to lofty heights, touched the sky.
It was the vast web of human life, the everyday work renewed by those who suffer and fight; the daring work perched on the void as it bravely looks at the light; the colossal effort of millions of beings, tortured intelligence, suffering hearts, slaves in sorrow, all rising from their chains, tossing their silver thread to the mysterious Unknown. And the threads break and the web is lacerated and happiness swings, always attached to the impalpable saliva of a spider. What does it matter? Everything dies, everything is born, everything changes, all is renewed, open graves serve as cradles, bloody and tearful hearts give new blood and new tears to life.
Move on, be brave!

In this epilogue, the tone turns from realistic to visionary, revealing the true, deeper meaning of the title: the subject of the book is not simply the 'day after' of a married woman who awakens to the uneasiness and boredom of her new condition, but the future of life and the perpetuation of the species. Disenchanted with a romantic passion that had revealed itself to be an impossible dream, Marta discovers a more profound kind of love in the humble acceptance of a role that gives her a place in the arcane order of the universe.
L'indomani concludes Neera's 'ciclo di una fanciulla' (cycle of the maiden). After *Teresa* (1886) and *Lydia* (1887), which portray respectively a woman who does not marry and one who yields to passion and ends her life in suicide, the author created in *L'indomani* a character who saves herself through the discovery that existential fulfilment does not lie in that which her literary predecessors (and she herself) had struggled to attain. The importance of this conclusion, not simply for *L'indomani* but for the entire cycle, is confirmed by Neera's refusal to alter it, even if that refusal meant losing her chance to be translated and

published in one of the most prestigious European magazines of the time, the *Revue des Deux Mondes*. Antonia Arslan, in a seminal essay on the author, reconstructed the tormented relationship between Neera, her translator Hérelle, and Brunetière, director of the *Revue*, persuasively showing the reasons behind Neera's steadfast refusal to eliminate the last chapter, in which the story reveals its true meaning. Hérelle objected that 'le dernier chapitre [...] a le défaut d'être beaucoup moins un "hymne à la maternité" qu'une dissertation écrite dans une langue abstraite, un article de journal mis en dialogue' (the last chapter [...], far from being a "hymn to maternity," is a dissertation written in an abstract language, a newspaper article turned into dialogue). Neera, however, firmly opposed the mutilation of a book so dear to her ('ce livre si chéri, si vécu, si pleuré'),[19] even if the decision resulted in her losing 'Parigi per pochi fogli di stampa'[20] (Paris for a few sheets of paper).

The protagonist of Carola Prosperi's *L'estranea* (*The Stranger*, 1915) reaches conclusions remarkably similar to Marta's. By the end of the novel, Francesca has attained everything she had ever longed for. She has been reinstated in the family to which she belonged by birth and has married Guido, the man she loves. Yet she experiences a lingering feeling of dissatisfaction and uneasiness:

> Quando Guido esce, ella sospira, lo guarda con occhi tristi e gelosi, lo lascia andare in silenzio, senza cercare di trattenerlo, e rimasta sola si sente fredda, stanca e vuota, come non lo fu mai. Ma dunque ora che è ricca, sposata, servita e tranquilla, è meno contenta di quando andava pel mondo, come un'affamata, in cerca di pane?[21]

> When Guido goes out, she sighs, looks at him with sad and jealous eyes, lets him go in silence, without trying to keep him, and when she is left alone she feels cold, tired, and empty, like never before. How is it possible, now that she is rich, married, comfortable, and calm, that she feels less happy than when she travelled the world, like someone hungry, looking for bread?

In this context, the presence of her unborn child is the only sign of consolation and hope for the future:

> Verrà tempo in cui la storia della sua giovinezza le parrà lontana e vaga come un sogno; tempo in cui i tormenti dell'amore e le agitazioni della

passione avranno ceduto interamente il posto ai tormenti e alle agitazioni degli affetti familiari. Altre saranno le gioie del suo cuore, altre le tempeste. Avanti dunque, con la vita. Ancora china il capo sul petto, con gli occhi chiusi a guardare ansiosamente dentro se stessa: ed ecco, ciò che pareva grigio di crepuscolo della sua vita di donna si tinge d'un roseo d'alba. E la cara manina ignota batte al suo povero cuore con battito amoroso e soave, e la piccola voce, non viva ancora, le parla del misterioso futuro.[22]

A time will come when the story of her youth will seem to her vague and far away, like a dream; a time when the sorrows of love and the turmoil of passion will have given way entirely to the sorrows and agitation of family relationships. Her heart will have other joys, other turmoil. Let's move on, then, with life. With her head to her chest, her eyes closed to look anxiously within herself. Suddenly, what looked grey like the sunset of her life turns pink, like the dawn. And the dear unknown hand knocks at her poor heart with a loving and tender beat, and a little voice, not yet alive, speaks to her of a mysterious future.

The similarities between this conclusion and that of *L'indomani* confirm Neera's importance as a model for turn-of-the-century women writers.[23] Apart from achieving considerable recognition for her novels (especially for *Teresa*), Neera was an opinion maker and even collaborated with the anthropologist Paolo Mantegazza in compiling the popular *Dizionario d'igiene per le famiglie* (1901). The split between Neera the artist and Neera the thinker has often been commented on by critics. The same writer who investigated the oppression of the female condition in her novels firmly opposed all advancement of women in society in her theoretical work, going so far as to condemn education as being not only useless but even harmful to women. These ideas are repeated, more than elaborated upon, in a pamphlet entitled *Le idee di una donna* (*The Ideas of a Woman*, 1903). Neera's aversion to feminism rests on the notion of a profound difference between the sexes, which obliges women to fulfil the 'splendid and wonderful mission' for which they were created:

Se gli uomini fossero migliori delle donne, oh! di certo queste dovrebbero fare il possibile per eguagliarli, ma poiché sono semplicemente diversi ed in tale differenza sta la legge armonica della natura che a tutto ciò che è vitale assegna una particolare funzione, nessuna nobile meta può raggiungere la donna nella concorrenza [...] Rimanga la donna al suo posto da cui ha fatto tanto bene all'umanità, da cui ne farà ancora col resistere allo spirito volgare che ne circonda da ogni lato e che tenta anche lei, vestendo, naturalmente, le bianche forme di un angelo liberatore. La vera schiavitú dalla quale ella deve liberarsi sta nel concetto materialista della felicità, sta nel credere che il suo ingegno produrrebbe migliori frutti e maggiori soddisfazioni le darebbe in cattedra anziché in casa; e credere ch'ella sarebbe piú utile a se stessa ed all'uomo guadagnando del denaro; e non capire e non sapere ed aver dimenticato di quale delicatezza, di quale ardore misterioso sia circondata la sua missione sulla terra, così splendida e meravigliosa che ella potrà, sì, degenerando, esercitare i lavori maschili, ma nessun uomo saprebbe mai nella piú grande elevazione preparare i miracoli che ella compie nel silenzio del suo amore.[24]

If men were better than women, women would have to do their best to be like them. But men are simply different, and in this difference lies the harmonic law of nature that gives a specific function to everything that is vital; women cannot, therefore, reach any noble goal by competing with men [...] Women should keep playing their role, in which they have benefited humankind immensely, as they will in the future if they resist the vulgar spirit that surrounds them on all sides and tempts them, while wearing the white gown of a liberating angel. The real slavery from which a woman must free herself consists of the materialistic notion of happiness, of the belief that her intelligence would produce better results and would be of greater satisfaction to her if used for public speaking rather than in the home, the belief that she would be more useful to herself and to men by making money; the real slavery is to fail to understand or to forget how precious, how mysteriously vibrant her mission on earth is. It is so splendid and wonderful that, while she could lower herself to take on manly jobs, no man could elevate himself to the point of achieving the miracles she performs in the silence of her love.

It is tempting to attribute such a conservative stance to a form of caution and to speculate that the woman writer, aware of her new and potentially transgressive role, may have consciously chosen to reassure her audience and critics. But this view is unnecessarily optimistic: the hypothesis of a progressive Neera is not confirmed by any of her public writings or actions, and the vehemence of her antifeminist pronouncements appears as heartfelt and visceral today as it did to her contemporaries. Sibilla Aleramo noticed:

Piú che l'intelletto, piú che l'anima, sembra siano i nervi della vibrante Neera che si sentono urtati atrocemente da questo movimento [il femminismo] che osa atteggiarsi ad 'ideale umano.' Piú che il raziocinio, è il sentimento misoneista, stranamente accentuato in lei, che la spinge a gettare con invidiabile calore il ridicolo e l'anatema alla nova crociata che il mondo va bandendo in pro della donna: e la scrittrice ch'è orgoglio ed affetto dell'Italia odierna, e che pur essendo madre amorosissima e cosciente volle e seppe trovar il tempo per darci una quantità di libri attestanti l'alto valore dell'ingegno muliebre, si mostra in quest'occasione [...] deficiente di serie argomentazioni in sostegno della sua tesi.[25]

More than her intelligence, more than her soul, it seems that the nerves of the fervent Neera are atrociously struck by feminism, a movement that dares to portray itself as a 'human ideal.' More than her reason, it is her strangely intense misoneism that incites her, with enviable passion, to condemn as ridiculous the new crusade that the world has announced in support of women. A writer who is regarded with pride and affection by modern Italians and who, although a loving and thoughtful mother, found the time to give us many books that prove the high value of women's intelligence is in this instance [...] incapable of providing serious evidence to support her argument.

By striving to advance themselves as human beings, women were abdicating, according to Neera, their true mission and nature in the name of 'the materialistic concept of happiness.' This opposition to feminism in the name of the spiritual values of life was a common theme among Catholics, and it is documented as early as 1855 in an exchange between Madame D'Héricourt and Giulia Molino Colombini. To D'Héricourt, who in an article entitled 'L'avenir des femmes' ('Women's Future') had called for equal electoral and professional rights for women, Molino Colombini replied by disparaging the importance of material goods and of political participation.[26] Neera's aversion to the women's movement, however, is made stronger by her perception of the alliance between socialism and feminism that had been developing around the turn of the century.[27] In his widely read *La donna e il socialismo* (*Woman and Socialism*, 1879), August Bebel equated the condition of women to that of workers, and proposed socialism as the solution to the problems of both groups. According to Bebel, the abolition of private property would necessarily entail radical reforms of both marriage and family in regard to the transmission of wealth and property. Attempting to construct a more solid platform for rejecting this theory, Neera puts forth a pseudoscientific explanation:

> L'uomo, genio creatore, quanto piú ha creato in opere, tanto meno trasmette al figlio, per naturale legge di equilibrio [...] La parte della trasmissione è invece affidata alla donna che, a sua volta, tanto piú trasmetterà l'ingegno, quanto meno ne avrà impiegato. È dunque desiderabile che la donna abbia ingegno, e molto, ma nello stesso modo che le vestali avevano il fuoco; per custodirlo e conservarlo all'altare.[28]

> The more that man, the creative genius, produces with his work, the less he can pass on to his children, because of a natural law of compensation [...] It is the woman who is in charge of that transmission: the less she uses her talent, the more she can pass on to her children. It is therefore advisable that woman have talent, and lots of it, but in the same way that the Vestals had fire: in order to guard it and keep it for the altar.

We can perceive in this statement a distorted echo of the theory put forth by Cesare Lombroso and Guglielmo Ferrero in *La donna delinquente, la prostituta e la donna normale* (*The Female Offender, the Prostitute, and the Normal Woman*, 1893). The two scientists, after spending many pages explaining the inferiority of female animals in general and of women in particular, concluded that the fundamental reason for that inferiority lies in the importance of reproduction to the female organism:

> Al pari che per la struttura organica, per l'intelligenza, il maschio ha una potenzialità primitiva di sviluppo superiore alla femmina, grazie alla parte minore che ha nella riproduzione della specie [...] La intelligenza in tutto il regno animale varia in ragione inversa della fecondità; c'è un antagonismo tra le funzioni di riproduzione e le intellettuali [...] Ora, essendo il lavoro della riproduzione in gran parte devoluto alla donna, per questa cagione biologica essa è rimasta indietro nello sviluppo intellettuale.[29]

> Males, more than females, have the potential to develop not only their bodies, but also their intelligence, thanks to the small role they play in the reproduction of the species [...] All over the animal kingdom, intelligence is inversely proportional to fecundity; there is an antagonism between intellectual and reproductive functions [...] Therefore, given that the reproductive work is assigned mainly to the woman, she has, for this biological reason, stayed behind in intellectual development.

Maternity, defined earlier in the treatise as a woman's primary quality,[30] is thus turned into the mark of her inferiority.

Neera seems to adapt Lombroso and Ferrero's theory by changing its status and transforming it from an immutable law to a contingent phenomenon occurring in certain circumstances. She does not go as far as saying, like the two scientists, that women are inferior to men because of the importance of their role in reproduction. She does advise, however, keeping hidden and latent whatever talent a mother may possess, for the benefit of her children.

It is remarkable that Neera never alludes to herself as a woman writer in her pamphlet. The modern edition of *Le idee di una donna*, published together with *Confessioni letterarie* (*Literary Confessions*) – an 1891 literary biography and an artistic manifesto in the form of a letter to Luigi Capuana – makes the split between the two sides of her personality all the more striking. Neera talks about literature only in the *Confessioni letterarie*. In *Le idee di una donna*, on the contrary, she manages not to mention her profession at all – not even when addressing prospective women writers.[31] Had she done so, it would have been difficult to reconcile the theory of the split between genius and motherhood with the concrete example of herself as a successful author *and* a mother. Despite her strategic omission, the contradiction lurks below the surface.

From Mother to Daughter: Annie Vivanti's *The Devourers*

An artistic rendition of Neera's law (namely, that mothers can pass on their talent to children only by stifling it in themselves) is the central thesis of Annie Vivanti's *I divoratori* (1910), first published in English as *The Devourers*. The daughter of a German mother and an Italian father who had followed Mazzini in his exile to England, Vivanti had a cosmopolitan upbringing that greatly influenced her adult life as an actress, singer, poet, novelist, and war correspondent. The success her novels enjoyed, however, did not spare her from confinement and poverty during the Second World War, when her identity as an English-born Jew made her an easy target for discrimination.[32] The reasons for the popularity of Vivanti's books, as well as the limits of their narrative construction, are apparent in *I divoratori*: ever-changing international settings are bound to hold readers' attention, and improbable revelations come to the rescue of the plot at crucial moments, providing new, unexpected twists.[33] More than any other of Vivanti's novels, *I divoratori* is a *roman à thèse*: a woman's talent is bound to disappear when she becomes a mother, as it is devoured by the child. Valeria lives only for her daughter, Nancy, a promising young poet: 'Valeria non era piú Valeria. Era la madre di Nancy. Il giovane Genio è un'aquila, che balza inatteso dal nido di una colomba; e, sbattendo le ali noncuranti e devastatrici, per vivere distrugge, per nutrirsi divora, per creare annienta'[34] (Valeria was no longer Valeria. She was Nancy's mother. A young genius is an eagle that unexpectedly jumps out of a dove's nest and, flipping its careless and devastating wings, destroys in order to live, devours to feed itself, annihilates in order to create).

After enjoying early success as a poet, Nancy marries the handsome but inept Aldo Della Rocca and gives birth to a daughter. After initial resistance, Nancy acquires Aldo's compulsive passion for gambling, to the point that the family, reduced to poverty, is obliged to leave Monte Carlo for New York. It is in New York that Anne-Marie reveals her prodigious talent as a violinist and Nancy begins devoting herself entirely to developing her daughter's gift, as her mother had done with her. In a moment of introspection, Nancy interprets her personal experience as one example of a universal law:

> Io sono una delle "divorate." La mia piccola Anne-Marie mi ha divorata. Ed è giusto, ed è bello, ed è santo che sia così. Essa mi ha consumata, e io ne sono lieta. Essa mi ha annichilita e io ne sono riconoscente. Poiché è questa l'eterna legge, inesorabile e magnifica: che a queste vite date a noi, la nostra vita deve essere data. Ed io – come tutte le madri – estasiata e a ginocchi, dò la mia vita alla creatura inconscia che la esige. Ecco: io ricado nell'ombra: la mia corsa non finita, la mia mèta non raggiunta, la mia missione non compiuta. Che importa? Ciò che a me fu negato, sarà dato a Anne-Marie. Mia figlia raggiungerà le vette ch'io non ascesi. Per lei sarà la Gloria ch'io non conquistai.[35]

> I am one of the 'Devoured.' My little Anne-Marie devoured me. It is right, beautiful, and holy that it be this way. She consumed me, and I am happy. She annihilated me, and I am grateful. This is the eternal, inexorable, and magnificent law: our life must be given to these lives that are given to us. And I – like all mothers –ecstatic and on my knees, give my life to the unconscious creature that demands it. I fall back in the shade: my race is not over, my goal has not been reached, my mission has not been accomplished. What does it matter? What I have been denied will be given to Anne-Marie. My daughter will conquer the summits I did not climb. The Glory I did not reach will be for her.

But Nancy's dream will never become reality. The last chapter shows Anne-Marie recovering after giving birth. The novel's last lines ('La creaturina nella culla aprì gli occhi e pianse: — *Ho fame!*' [The little creature in the cradle opened her eyes and cried: *I am hungry!*']) are identical to the first, suggesting that Anne-Marie's destiny will not be different from Valeria's. She too will obliterate herself to nourish the talent of a child who will in turn sacrifice everything when she becomes a mother. 'Certaines femmes [...] souhaitent ou accueillent une fille avec l'amer plaisir de se retrouver en une autre victime' (Certain women [...] desire or welcome a daughter with the bitter pleasure of recognizing themselves in another victim), Simone de Beauvoir would ponder years later.[36] In Vivanti's novel, a daughter constitutes a double of her mother, and as such is destined to repeat the mother's life choices. Vivanti's all-female lineage leaves readers curious to know what would happen if the child in question were a boy: In this case, would *he* be able to develop his talents? Would the chain of abnegation and sacrifice be broken?

In his portrayal of Annie Vivanti, Valentino Brosio provides interesting documents that suggest that *I divoratori* is inspired by events from the author's life. Like Nancy, Vivanti put her artistic career on hold to support her daughter Vivien, who was an extremely talented in music as child. A pupil of the renowned violinist and teacher Otakar Ševčík, Vivien performed in concerts all over Europe until she married and stopped her public career in order to devote herself to her two children.[37] However superficial it might seem at a first glance, Vivanti's central thesis in *I divoratori* had been inspired by a close scrutiny of the author's own life, by the need to find a structural law that could explain her experience, and perhaps also by the desire to disprove this law with evidence from real life: *I divoratori* marked in fact Vivanti's triumphal return to the literary scene and her definitive conversion from poetry to the novel, the genre that would make her famous.

The Mother as Artist: Luigi Pirandello's *Suo marito*

While Vivanti described three generations of women relinquishing their professional ambitions for the well-being of their children, Luigi Pirandello focused on the other side of the coin and analysed the consequences of a mother's reluctance (or inability) to sacrifice her talent. *Suo marito* (*Her Husband*, 1911) is an unusual novel in that its protagonist is a woman writer, Silvia Roncella, who exalts the timeless, mythical value of motherhood in her plays.[38] The work that grants her fame is none other than *La nuova colonia* (*The New Colony*), Pirandello's own play about the redeeming value of motherhood in a prostitute's life. Silvia, however, cannot be present at the first performance of the play that will make her famous because that night she is in labour, giving birth to a son. But motherhood never becomes a full-time commitment for her. Her son, Rino, is entrusted to a nurse, while Silvia continues her artistic career under the watchful eye of her husband and manager, Giustino.[39] In spite of Silvia's superficial and limited relationship with her son (or perhaps precisely because of that, as a form of compensation), she continues to extol the power of motherhood in her plays. Her second great success is again a work that Pirandello himself authored, *Se non così* (*If Not So*), and it is also centred on the importance of children in one's life. This time Silvia is able to attend the opening night of the play and even receives a standing ovation. But there is a terrible price to pay. While she is able to enjoy the results of her talent, she is also forced to face the consequences of having placed art above maternal duty. At the very moment when her career has reached its peak, her child is dying of a sudden illness. Informed of the situation, Silvia rushes to his side only to find him dead.

Suo marito is an intriguing, ambiguous novel. Its critical importance is probably destined to increase with time, as the scandal surrounding its initial publication is forgotten.[40] Pirandello's contemporaries read this work as an allusion to the relationship between Grazia Deledda and her husband, Palmiro Madesani. Their unconventional marital arrangement, in which the husband's work was a function of the wife's, must have been the object of derision and criticism in literary circles. Pirandello, yielding to a less than noble instinct, decided to recreate that relationship in this novel, which in its original title sarcastically alluded to the demasculinization of a man in such circumstances: *Giustino Roncella, nato Boggiòlo* (*Giustino Roncella, Born Boggiòlo*). But sarcasm and petty rivalry alone could not have taken the novel very far. In developing the initial situation, Pirandello seems to have behaved like the 'demonietto' (little devil) he portrayed in his essay 'L'umorismo' ('On Humor,' 1908), who 'smonta il congegno d'ogni immagine [...] per veder com'è fatto; scaricarne la molla, e tutto il congegno striderne, convulso' ('takes apart the mechanism of each image [...] in order to see how it is made [...]; releases the mainspring, and the whole mechanism squeaks convulsively').[41] His investigation of this particular marital relationship took on new complexity, as he alternately identified with and divorced himself from Silvia, a woman, but also a writer who at the beginning of the novel turns from narrative fiction to drama (as Pirandello himself had just done).

Pirandello drastically separates the creative and institutional sides of artistic production by attributing them to two separate characters. Silvia is a creator who needs only to follow her instinct to make art of the highest quality, while Giustino is totally oblivious to artistic concerns and considers his wife's plays as ordinary material goods. Their relationship, Robert Dombroski has argued, is therefore similar to that between a proletarian and a capitalist.[42] Silvia's plight as a writer is depicted sympathetically by Pirandello, who lends her not only his plays but also the benefit of his own experience.[43] Certainly, *Suo marito* goes much farther than *I divoratori* in representing the struggle to break free from social and economic constraints in order to follow one's artistic inclinations. Silvia's ambition, however, is revealed in the end to be totally inappropriate for a woman and is therefore deserving of terrible punishment. As Lucienne Kroha writes, 'The childbirth metaphor is often used to describe the artistic process, but here it is used at a first level to designate *difference* as well as affinity. It reminds us that, in the life of a woman, mind and body, creativity and procreativity, books and babies, have historically been mutually exclusive.'[44]

Kroha incisively formulates the 'either/or' theory that for centuries has channelled women's energies and talent towards procreation, at the expense of all forms of intellectual activity.[45] Just a few years after the publication of *Suo marito*, Gina Lombroso (daughter of the famous criminal anthropologist Cesare Lombroso) wrote a successful slim volume, *L'anima della donna* (*The Soul of Woman*), that endorsed this rigid dichotomy. She claimed that given that every human being strives to leave an imprint on the world, there are two distinct ways to achieve that goal. One can either follow 'love, which makes us unconsciously tend with our flesh and blood toward the flesh and blood which will prolong us throughout time,' or 'ambition, which makes us strive to create, with our brain, something palpable, moral or ideal that will be greater than ourselves, that will prolong our being in space and in time and leave an imprint of us in the infinite.'[46] Her warning against the dangers of generalizations does not prevent her from concluding that 'as a general rule it cannot be denied that love gives woman, much more than man, the opportunity to attain the goal of her life,'[47] and that motherhood is therefore for women the equivalent of what creative and intellectual production is for men. Lombroso's discussion helps explain the theory that underlies the protagonist's tragic story in *Suo marito*. Silvia Roncella's sin, in Pirandello's construction, is to have pursued eternity not only by the means appropriate to her gender but also by those reserved for men. The loss of her child is presented as the logical punishment for her immoderate ambition.

Suo marito can be read as an expression of Pirandello's anxiety at a time when an increasing number of women writers were challenging men's traditional supremacy in the literary arena, and the allusions to Grazia Deledda seemed transparent to contemporary readers. The critic Chiara Frenquellucci, however, has recently been able to show striking similarities between the character of Silvia Roncella and another important writer of the time: Sibilla Aleramo.

A Revolution Named Sibilla

By the time Vivanti and Pirandello had published their novels, their central thesis, so similar to that put forth by Neera in *Le idee di una donna*, had already received a powerful rebuttal. In *Una donna* (*A Woman*, 1906), Sibilla Aleramo had rejected the belief that a woman's sacrifice in the name of motherhood was good for herself, her children, and society. Aleramo's novel is remarkable in many respects: the protagonist's plea for her sexual rights, her lucid analysis of the ills of the middle-class family and the resulting social problems (chief among them, prostitution), and even her criticism of the national literary tradition, which she accuses of having failed to grasp women's nature and needs, are nothing short of revolutionary for turn-of-the-century Italy. Detractors and supporters alike drew parallels between Aleramo's nameless character and Nora, the protagonist of Ibsen's *Casa di bambola*; Alfredo Gargiulo declared *Una donna* a foundational text, the Genesis in the Bible of feminism.[48] Nothing, however, attracted more public attention than the protagonist's decision to leave her abusive husband, even when she knew that this exposed her to the risk of never seeing her son again. In motivating herself to go, the central character develops a powerful critique not of motherhood itself but of what it has become in a patriarchal society. The distinction between motherhood as potential and as institution elaborated in the 1970s by Adrienne Rich[49] is already implicit in Aleramo's stance. It can be found in the 'nucleo generatore di *Una donna*' (generating core of *Una donna*), as the author titled a handwritten note dated 'giugno 1901, dopo una notte insonne'[50] (June 1901, after a sleepless night). With minimal changes, this note would appear in a crucial chapter of the novel, strengthening the protagonist's decision to leave her family:

Perché nella maternità adoriamo il sacrifizio? Donde è scesa a noi questa inumana idea dell'immolazione materna? Di madre in figlia, da secoli, si tramanda il servaggio. È una mostruosa catena. Tutte abbiamo, a un certo punto della vita, la coscienza di quel che fece pel nostro bene chi ci generò; e con la coscienza il rimorso di non aver compensato adeguatamente l'olocausto della persona diletta. Allora riversiamo sui nostri figli quanto non demmo alle madri, rinnegando noi stesse e offrendo un nuovo esempio di mortificazione, di annientamento. Se una buona volta la fatale catena si spezzasse, e una madre non sopprimesse in sé la donna, e un figlio apprendesse dalla vita di lei un esempio di dignità?[51]

Why do we adore mothers as martyrs? From where did we receive this inhuman idea of maternal sacrifice? Servitude has been handed down from mother to daughter for centuries. It is a monstrous chain. As women, we all realize, at some point in our lives, how much we owe the woman who generated us. With that recognition comes remorse for not having adequately compensated the sacrifice made by that beloved person. So we give our children what we did not give to our mothers, betraying ourselves and offering a new example of mortification and annihilation. What if, once and for all, the fateful chain broke, and a mother did not kill the woman in her, and a child saw her life as an example of dignity?

About sixty years after the publication of *Una donna*, Nancy Chodorow, in her influential and controversial *The Reproduction of Mothering*, argued that women's need to be their children's primary caregivers derives from 'social structurally induced psychological processes.'[52] The fact that women, rather than men, mother has consequences for the children's psycho-sexual development: girls, unlike boys, grow into adults who 'come to want and need primary relationship with children.'[53] This means that mothering is an inherently female prerogative that tends to reproduce itself in each generation. Writing in Italy at the beginning of the twentieth century, Aleramo could not ask Chodorow's revolutionary question: Why do women mother? That women should find their fulfilment in caring for children was considered natural, intrinsic to humankind and therefore immutable. Her question is, rather, Why do women mother *in a certain way*, a way that turns out to be destructive for themselves as well as detrimental to their children? Like Chodorow, Aleramo focuses on the legacy of motherhood and on how it tends to perpetuate itself, conditioning women's lives, generation after generation.

The subversive nature of *Una donna* did not escape its first critics. The novel received positive reviews from influential writers such as Arturo Graf, Alfredo Panzini, and Luigi Pirandello, but also elicited some visceral reactions. Gina Lombroso pointedly commented on the novel shortly after its publication: 'Il dramma della vita che Sibilla Aleramo ci tratteggia non è già dato dalla lotta tra quest'uomo e questa donna [...] ma dalla lotta che la donna combatte contro la madre'[54] (The tragedy of the life depicted by Sibilla Aleramo does not consist of the struggle between this man and this woman [...] but in the struggle the woman fights against the mother).

Depiction of the struggle between being a woman and being a mother, to adopt Lombroso's terminology, were not new in Italian literature. The outcome, however, had traditionally been in favor of the latter. In Giuseppe Giacosa's 1887 play *Tristi amori* (*Sad Loves*), for instance, Emma refuses to run away with her lover because she is afraid that by doing so she will lose her five-year-old daughter. Her husband understands Emma's struggle without her saying anything and praises her decision: 'Ho creduto che tu andassi ... e non te lo avrei impedito ... perché impedirtelo? Ma sei rimasta ... eh ... sei madre ... e questo è un sentimento che non si vince'[55] (I thought you were leaving ... I would not have stopped you ... why should I have? But you stayed ... you are a mother ... and this feeling cannot be overcome).

The unexpected outcome of Aleramo's novel took critics by surprise. Adelaide Bernardini, one of the first reviewers, found the protagonist's decision unjustifiable because of her motivations. She argued that women who in the past had left their families had done it 'per un amante, travolte dalla passione cui hanno sacrificato la pace, l'onore, pronte a sacrificarle anche la vita!' (for a lover, swept away by the passion to which they had sacrificed their honour, their peace, and to which they would even sacrifice their life!). Their passionate instinct, Bernardini concludes, places them above Aleramo's heroine: 'L'anonima protagonista, invece, commette quella viltà per egoismo; e commette quasi un infanticidio, lasciando il bambino in un ambiente da cui lei, cosciente e forte, fugge come da una galera'[56] (The anonymous protagonist, on the contrary, commits such a cowardly act for her selfish interest; she comes close to committing infanticide, leaving her child in an environment from which she, being strong and aware, escapes as if it were a prison).

What Aleramo's protagonist had painfully acknowledged and defined as human dignity is downgraded, in Bernardini's analysis, to simple egoism. It would be easy to dismiss this opinion as merely reactionary, were there not additional evidence that Aleramo's novel had indeed hit a nerve. An epistolary exchange between the writer and Ersilia Majno is revealing in this regard. The letters preserved in Majno's archive attest to her active interest in the women's movement, which culminated in the founding of the Unione Femminile in 1899. This involvement had made her a point of reference for women of different social classes throughout the peninsula.[57] A personal friend of Aleramo's, she wrote her affectionate and encouraging letters during the 'supreme struggle' that the writer, as well as her fictional counterpart in the novel, had sustained in order to escape from an abusive relationship.[58] Majno could very well be, then, the ideal reader of *Una donna* – the one who could fully understand the tragedy the novel depicts. Clearly, it was with this hope that Aleramo had sent her a copy of the novel. She received a devastating answer. Majno accused the author of exposing herself in front of her public because of her 'orgoglio sconfinato' (boundless pride), and reminded her of the limits imposed by maternal duty on even the most sincere confession:

> V'è però una misura anche per certe confessioni. La misura che dovrebbe importi il dovere verso il figlio [...] pel quale se non hai creduto di poter sacrificare i tuoi istinti, i tuoi desideri di donna, potresti, dovresti sacrificare il desiderio di farti un posto fra le scrittrici gettando a piene mani il fango su tutto quanto e quanti saranno i ricordi della sua vita infantile.[59]

> There is, however, a limit, even for this kind of confessions. This limit should be dictated by your duties towards your son [...] Although you did not think you could sacrifice your womanly instincts and desires for him, you could and should sacrifice your desire to have a place among women writers, if this means throwing mud all over his childhood memories.

Although Aleramo replied by denying that ambition had played a role in her decision to write the novel, another harsh letter from Majno made clear that no further communication on this topic was possible.

The reactions that Aleramo elicited even from a progressive reader like Majno demonstrate just how radical her position was: forced to decide between the conflicting identities of woman and mother, her anonymous protagonist chose to sacrifice the latter. Motherhood had thus been defined as an obstacle in a woman's path towards individuality and dignity. It is impossible at this point, for Aleramo and her heroine, not only to experience but even to imagine motherhood as separate from its social institution. While the protagonist's story concludes only one year after her escape, at which time it is not clear whether and when she will be allowed to see her son again, a historical reconstruction of Aleramo's life reveals that, despite her legal and personal efforts, she was denied any contact with the boy. She finally managed to see him again in 1933, when he was a thirty-eight-year-old man, and his mother little more than a stranger to him.[60] Aleramo personally experienced the paradoxical nature of being a mother in early twentieth-century Italy: the institution of motherhood could turn into a form of oppression, and yet motherhood was possible only within its institution. Later on, however, she linked her maternal capacity with her own artistic potential. In an essay titled 'La pensierosa' ('The Pensive Woman') she expressed the belief that a woman artist like herself had the potential to create forms of art radically different from those created by men. Closer to life, she could take upon herself, and upon the 'sensibilità delle [...] fibre materne' (sensibility of [...] maternal fibres), the task of 'intensifying and purifying reality' through art.[61] However enticing for contemporary feminist thought centred on the notion of female spiritual and psychological difference, this reflection remained at an embryonic stage.[62] Its importance in this context lies in Aleramo's attempt to move beyond the acceptance/rejection dichotomy that had marked *Una donna*, and to envision motherhood no longer as an institution but as a potential that lies at the source of women's creativity.

Self-Sacrifice and Marian Imagery

The impact made by Aleramo's novel is also confirmed by the publication of an antidote in the form of Maria di Borio's *Una moglie* (*A Wife*, 1909). Mina, the protagonist, shares many of the experiences of the anonymous woman in Aleramo's novel but comes to a very different conclusion: humiliated by her husband's betrayals, she resorts to leaving him, attaching herself even more to their son Mario. The discovery of her vocation as a writer does not prompt social and intellectual enquiries, as in the case of *Una donna*. Under the pseudonym of Ciprietta, Mina uses her talent to publish an article on the life and deeds of her beloved husband, a composer. He, in turn, develops an infatuation for this unknown admirer, and the discovery of her true identity brings him back to his wife. Deservedly forgotten, *Una moglie* is, however, much more representative of the turn-of-the-century conception of wifehood and motherhood than *Una donna*.

Intense portrayals of the self-sacrificing mother can also be found in some of the most accomplished works produced by Grazia Deledda, recipient of the 1926 Nobel Prize in literature. These novels often portray a close-knit community threatened by transgression of sexual morals. With remarkable frequency, a tragic sacrifice is required in order to restore social harmony. This tension is in full display in *Elias Portolu*, in which the protagonist, disgusted for having a child with his brother's wife, seeks refuge by entering the priesthood. Yet his moral purification is not complete, as he still feels strongly attracted to the child's mother. The culmination of Elias's process of regeneration coincides with his son's death, which causes him to relinquish his earthly passions.[63]

The same pattern is present in *Annalena Bilsini*, where the ordered life of the Bilsini family is threatened by the return of one of the sons from his military service. Bored and dissatisfied with the family routine, Pietro first attempts to seduce his brother's wife, 'al di fuori di ogni legge divina e umana'[64] (outside of every divine and human law), and then tries to secure a prosperous financial future by pursuing Lia, his wealthy landlord's daughter. When the young woman fails to return home, everybody in the family believes that Pietro is somewhat responsible for her mysterious disappearance. In a crucial scene, Uncle Dionisio, the only male authority figure in the family, confronts Pietro, who reacts with irony and contempt and does not deny the accusations brought against him. The altercation deeply upsets the old man, who spends a restless night, falls gravely ill, and dies soon after. This new, tragic event sets the stage for a general reconciliation. The priest who is called to the uncle's deathbed brings the news that in fact Lia had run away to become a nun and has been found in a nearby convent. Pietro is therefore discovered to be innocent, and the family's unity is restored.

A similar mechanism is at work in both novels, whereby a tragic event leads to social healing. In *La violence et le sacré* (*Violence and the Sacred*), René Girard stresses the importance of sacrifice as a means of diverting to a designated victim the violence that otherwise would threaten an entire society.[65] Ideally, the victim is from outside to the community but could also very well be a child, who does not fully belong to the group because of his or her age.[66] The model proposed by Girard can be useful in this context only if we take into account both its similarities to and differences from the situations described in Deledda's novels. Her characters, in fact, do not consciously or unconsciously resort to sacrifice in order to placate tensions in the community. The death of the protagonist's son in *Elias Portolu*, as well as that of the old uncle in *Annalena Bil-*

sini, can be described as accidental. And yet it is through these tragic events that the family is brought back together and a central male character overcomes, at least momentarily, his destructive impulses. At the opposite ends of the spectrum, in terms of age and authority, a child and an old man die, drawing attention to an unseen supernatural force whose power is never explicitly acknowledged but becomes apparent in the outcome of the stories.

These examples show that ritual sacrifices in Deledda's works are not always linked to female characters. It can be argued, however, that this peculiar way of resolving interpersonal conflict takes on a stronger symbolic meaning when a mother sacrifices herself to benefit her son. In *Cenere* (*Ashes*, 1903), self-immolation is explicitly and consciously chosen. Rosalia prefers to kill herself rather than endanger her son Anania's happiness. The gruesomeness of the scene (the old woman cuts her own throat and bleeds to death) and the violation of the taboo of suicide make the novel unusual among Deledda's works. With her death, Rosalia gives birth to her son for the second time, allowing him to move on with his life, attain maturity, and marry the woman he loves.

A more famous (and subtle) example of abnegation taken to the extreme can be found in *La madre* (*The Mother*, 1920). Agnese, the mother of a young priest, partakes in her son's struggle against earthly temptations to such an extent that she falls dead at the end of a religious service, in what is probably the most celebrated scene Deledda ever created. It would be a mistake, however, to interpret self-destruction exclusively as a form of weakness or subjection. On the contrary, sacrifice is a means for mothers to reaffirm their symbolic power. As Maria Giovanna Piano states, in Deledda's novels 'l'autorità delle madri presenta tratti assoluti e regali, esse sono dotate di grande forza simbolica e archetipa, di una forza primordiale'[67] (mothers' authority takes on absolute, regal characteristics; mothers are endowed with great symbolic and archetypal force, a primordial force). Through sacrifice, mothers are thus able to perpetuate their authority.

This is better perceived in a character who does not have to resort to extreme means to assert her strength. The protagonist of *Annalena Bilsini* (1927) is the memorable figure of a matriarch who represses all instincts in order to maintain her control over an all-male family (five sons and their uncle): 'Ella non si abbandonava al suo istinto; non per paura del peccato, ma per sostenere il suo dominio su sé stessa e gli altri'[68] (She never yielded to instinct; she was not afraid of sinning, but rather she wanted to keep her power over herself and the others). Her superhuman control allows her to conclude, on the last page of the novel, that 'servi o padroni, i miei figliuoli saranno sempre sottoposti alla madre'[69] (servants or masters, my sons will always be under their mother). This example makes clear how the price for the triumph of the mother as a symbolic and almost mythic figure is the sacrifice of the mother as a real human being, as a woman. Elena Gianini Belotti has observed how

> la condizione di madre sembra riassumere il più alto grado di onnipotenza e di impotenza: idealizzata ed esaltata come salvatrice del genere umano, purché offra amore senza limiti, la madre è vittima in quanto donna di uno status sociale di inferiorità che non le consente di determinare il modo in cui vivere la propria maternità.[70]

> the condition of the mother seems to combine the highest degree of omnipotence and impotence: idealized and exalted as the saviour of the human race, as long as she provides unlimited love, the mother, as a woman, is the victim of an inferior social status that does not allow her to determine how to live her maternity.

The model behind this representation of the self-sacrificing and yet powerful mother is clearly a religious one. The cult of the Virgin had been powerfully revamped in the second half of the nineteenth century. The dogma of the Immaculate Conception was proclaimed in 1854; the Catholic Church readily and enthusiastically endorsed the reported apparitions of the Virgin at Lourdes in 1858 and even proclaimed a special jubilee to celebrate the twenty-fifth anniversary of the first manifestation; and Leo XIII (1878–1903) started a wave of canonizations of female saints that would continue throughout the papacy of Pius XII (1939–58).[71]

The close link between religion and the model of motherhood prevalent in the literature of this time is apparent in *Vae Victis!* (1917), undoubtedly Vivanti's most tragic novel. On the night of her eighteenth birthday, Chérie and her sister-in-law Luisa are raped by German soldiers who are invading Belgium, while Luisa's daughter Mirella is strapped to the railing and forced to watch. Mirella becomes mute as a result of the trauma, while Chérie loses all memory of the event and thus cannot interpret the feelings she experiences a few months later in England, where the three have found refuge:

> Era una sensazione indefinita di gioia – di gioia morale e fisica, era ... che

cosa era? Era come una pulsazione lieve, un fremito d'una dolcezza impossibile a definire. Ma non appena questo strano senso la scosse, che già era svanito. Allora Chérie si rammentò: ecco ciò che l'aveva svegliata! Sì, era quello stesso palpito strano ch'ella aveva sentito nel sonno – quel lieve tremolio somigliante a un batter d'ali, quasi che un altro cuore pulsasse entro al suo.[72]

It was like an indefinite sensation of joy – of moral and physical joy ... what was it? It was like a soft beat, the flutter of an indefinable sweetness. As soon as this strange sensation startled her, it was already gone. Then Chérie remembered: this was what had woken her! Yes, it was the same strange quiver that she had felt in her sleep - that light flutter resembling the flapping of wings, as if another heart were beating inside hers.

When the entire truth is revealed to her, she is incapable of transferring her anger towards her aggressor to the new life inside her. In spite of Luisa's opposition, she decides to keep the baby, who is born after their return to their Belgian village. Ostracized by her sister-in-law and abandoned by her fiancé, Florian, when he comes back from the front, Chérie decides one night to drown herself in the river together with her baby. However, as she prepares to leave the house, she is seen by Mirella, who, unable to sleep, in fascination and horror has been watching the red curtain that opened once before, during the night of the invasion, to reveal Chérie's rape. Only this time, 'inondata dai raggi della luna, tutta velata di rilucente azzurrità, stava una Madre col suo Bambino. Dietro di lei brillava un gran cerchio di luce'[73] (inundated by the moonlight, veiled by a shining azure light, there was a Mother with her Child. Behind her a large circle of light shone).

Vivanti cleverly orchestrates this crucial moment in her novel. After following Chérie and her baby through the house, she swiftly changes the perspective, causing the reader to stand in the dark with Mirella, before the red curtain. The strong theatrical elements of the scene evoke the original form of the story (which was, in fact, a play before becoming a novel)[74] and stress the visionary element of the event that is about to unfold. The stage that was once the scene of violence and humiliation becomes the setting for supernatural, purifying love. Chérie as a woman disappears behind the icon she is called to represent: a Madonna as she could have been imagined by a medieval painter. Overwhelmed by the sight, Mirella makes a desperate effort to greet the vision, regaining her voice: 'Qualche cosa sembrò spezzarlesi nella gola

[...] ecco dalle sue labbra fluire le parole del saluto immortale: "*Ave Maria!*"'[75] (Something seemed to crack in her throat [...] suddenly the words of the immortal salutation flew from her lips: '*Hail Mary!*'). Maternal love triumphs over violence and becomes miraculous. Hearing her daughter's voice in the dark, Luisa rushes to the scene and in awe repeats the prayer. A second, more subtle, miracle is performed: the three women reunite, overcoming the horror that had once left them powerless and numb.

However moving, the epilogue of *Vae Victis!* reflects only part of the picture of motherhood developed by Vivanti in the novel. Chérie's story is, in fact, complemented by Luisa's. Also pregnant because of the rape, she goes from door to door in London looking for a doctor who is willing to perform an abortion. Unlike Chérie, who has lost memory of that fateful night (and whose experience of maternity thus closely resembles a 'virgin birth'), Luisa cannot separate her pregnancy from 'la faccia convulsa, ubbriaca del nemico china sopra di lei'[76] (the convulsive face of the drunken enemy bending over her). After many physicians refuse to help her, she tells her story in front of a vicar, his wife, and their family doctor. The three serve as a tribunal empowered to sanction the legitimacy of her choice. The vicar argues that victimhood does not give one the right to commit a crime, but Luisa passionately objects, describing the fetus as a cancer and begging the doctor to free her from it. Much to the vicar's surprise, the doctor accepts her pleas:

> Qui si tratta di ubbidire ai sentimenti della piú elementare umanità, che nel caso attuale, coincidono esattamente cogli insegnamenti della scienza. Date le condizioni in cui trovo questa donna, devo tentare di tutto per salvare la sua ragione e la sua vita. E cosí farò [...] La legge divina dà alla donna il diritto di selezione. Essa ha il diritto di scegliere chi sarà il padre delle sue creature. E questo sacrosanto diritto è stato violato.[77]

> It is necessary to follow the most elementary principles of humanity, which in this specific case coincide exactly with scientific teachings. Given the conditions in which I find this woman, I must try everything to save her mind and her life. And I will do it [...] Divine law gives a woman the right to choose. She has the right to select the father of her children. This holy right has been violated.

To the vicar who accuses him of killing a human being, the doctor replies: 'Non è quasi ancora un essere umano ... Per me questa donna è afflitta da un morbo, da una infermità. Porta in sé un male che va estirpato, un male che corrompe ed avvelena le piú profondi sorgenti della vita'[78] (It is not yet a human being ... I believe that this woman is afflicted by a disease, an illness. She bears an evil that must be extirpated, an evil that corrupts and poisons the deepest springs of life).

In spite of its epilogue, *Vae Victis!* does not constitute an unconditional celebration of motherhood. Vivanti does not cast a negative light on Luisa's decision. She portrays sympathetically her character's search for help, follows her as she is questioned sceptically by doctors about the *real* cause of her pregnancy, and witnesses her increasing desperation as time goes by. The vicar himself is portrayed as a hypocritical bon vivant. Before receiving Luisa, he is busy writing an article for the *Northern Ecclesiastical Review* entitled 'Le nostre domeniche peccaminose' ('Our Sinful Sundays'), yet he learned French by studying '*sur place* con benevola attenzione le domeniche peccaminose del Continente.'[79] (the continental sinful Sundays *sur place*, with benevolent attention). This generous tolerance of his own flaws makes his attitude towards Luisa's dilemma seem particularly harsh and inflexible. On the other hand, the vicar's wife, who is portrayed as the devoted mother of a blind girl, approves of the doctor's choice. Vivanti does not endorse Chérie's decision over Luisa's, and neither woman has any regrets. The author leaves readers with the conclusion that motherhood can be either a curse or a blessing, depending on the individual and the circumstances.[80] The social relevance of the theme bravely explored by Vivanti is attested to by the establishment in Portogruaro of the Istituto San Filippo Neri per la Prima Infanzia, whose main objective was to provide shelter, education, and support to children born during the First World War in the territories then controlled by the Austro-Hungarians. *I figli della guerra (Children of War)*, a booklet devoted to the institute, describes situations very similar to the ones found in *Vae Victis!* Vivanti's account of the consequences of war for women's lives provides a sobering counterpoint to the noisy glorification of war staged by the Futurists, and in particular to Valentine de Saint-Point's endorsement of rape as a right of war and as a way for the victorious army to replenish its ranks and 'recreate life.'[81]

The three protagonists of *Vae Victis!* could easily, and perhaps more accurately, be considered collectively as one. The emotions felt by a woman who discovers that she is pregnant in such traumatic circumstances are polarized and divided between Luisa and Chérie. Rachel DuPlessis, who studied the use of collective protagonists in novels written by twentieth-century American women, maintains that: 'these fictions replace individual heroes or sealed couples with groups, which have a sense of purpose and identity, and whose growth occurs in mutual collaboration. The use of a collective protagonist may imply that problems or issues that we see as individually based are in fact social in cause and in cure.'[82] In light of this remark, the scene in which Luisa joins Mirella in her dramatic salutation of the vision takes on a more specific meaning. Victim of a kind of violence that made all women potential targets, the group had reacted by splitting and releasing three alienated individuals. Only a quasi-supernatural expression of maternal love could heal the wounds and restore the unity the war had shattered.

The Invisible Working Woman

What makes *Vae Victis!* unique, however, is not its use of Marian imagery but rather the open discussion of abortion that takes place in the vicar's office. Unwanted pregnancy and the refusal to become a mother were, in fact, rarely portrayed in the literature of the time. Deledda's autobiographical novel *Cosima* (1937) constitutes one of the few exceptions, in its portrayal of the sudden death of the protagonist's sister, Enza. In a dramatic passage, Cosima, alerted by a servant, runs to Enza's house only to find that 'l'infelice giaceva in una pozzanghera di sangue nero e fetente'[83] (the poor woman was lying in a puddle of black and smelly blood). The doctor who arrives at the scene diagnoses an *aborto*, a term that carries a certain ambiguity. Italian does not make a clear lexical difference, as in English, between 'abortion' and 'miscarriage.' *Aborto* refers to any interruption in a pregnancy that occurs before the fetus is viable, and only further specification allows one to distinguish between an *aborto naturale* (a termination of pregnancy by natural causes: a miscarriage) and an *aborto procurato* (a termination of pregnancy induced by medical procedures: an abortion).[84] Obliged to choose between the two meaning of the words, the English translator interpreted *aborto* as 'miscarriage' and translated the passage as 'The doctor came and said she was miscarrying.'[85] Several elements in Deledda's text, however, such as the disagreements between Enza and her husband, and the tragic epilogue of the scene, suggest that Enza's death is the result of her attempt to terminate an unwanted pregnancy. The issue is never fully clarified, however, and the very haste with which the poor woman is abandoned to her destiny by the narrator belies Deledda's audacity and uneasiness in dealing with such a theme.

Another example can be found in Gabriele D'Annunzio's 'Le

vergini,' a short story from the collection *Il libro delle vergini*, where the protagonist Giuliana, a victim of rape, purchases from a *strega* (witch) a potion that kills her. However, the refusal to become a mother was not a common literary theme.[86] Literature of the time shows a pronounced tendency to avoid the description of social situations that made motherhood a daunting task. Representations of the working classes are, in fact, difficult to find in this period, a time when most writers and readers belonged to the middle class and shared common interests and concerns.[87] This supports other evidence of the gap between intellectuals and the working classes so persuasively investigated by Antonio Gramsci in his *Quaderni del carcere* (*Prison Notebooks*). By reading turn-of-the-century novels, one could forget that Italian women in 1881 had a life expectancy of only thirty-four years[88] and that important sectors of the national were based on the work of women and children.[89] The new conception of motherhood, as described thus far, applies only to the bourgeoisie. Far from being asked to devote themselves to their children, women of the working class were forced to leave them alone for a significant part of the day to work at physically demanding and low-paying jobs. Anna Kuliscioff eloquently denounced this paradox in an 1890 article published in *Il fascio operaio*:

> Per la maggioranza del sesso femminile, che è la donna operaia, nessuno parla della famiglia che va di mezzo; qui la donna ha da faticare per 10, 12 e in certe produzioni anche 14 e 16 ore. Qui si calpesta la femminilità, la maternità, l'allevamento dei figli, tutto ciò di cui si fanno arme gli uomini della borghesia quando è la donna del loro ceto che vuol entrare nelle professioni.[90]

> For the majority of the female sex, that is, for the factory workers, nobody speaks of the sacrifice of the family; here women must work 10, 12, and in certain factories even 14 and 16 hours a day. Here it is acceptable to crush femininity, maternity, and children's education. These same ideals become the rhetorical weapons of middle-class men when it is a woman of their same class who wants to enter a profession.

The bourgeois notion of motherhood must have seemed to these women not a golden prison but rather an impossible dream. Holding a naked baby in one arm, the other hand stretched out to question or plead, a mother marches in the foreground of Pellizza da Volpedo's painting *Il quarto stato* (1901).

The few literary works that overcame this general lack of interest in the working classes, however, are indicative of the gap between the idealized notion of motherhood and the actual female condition. The short story 'Nedda' (1874), which marked Giovanni Verga's turn to *Verismo*, ends with the description of a young mother's plight. The eponymous protagonist is a peasant who works to support her sick mother. When the old woman dies, Nedda has a relationship with Janu, who intends to marry her. In order to save some money, Janu, although recovering from malaria, accepts a job as an olive picker, then falls from a ladder and dies. Alone and pregnant, Nedda is ostracized by the community but refuses to abandon her daughter. Only her uncle's charity manages to save her from starvation. Her little girl, however, is born 'rachitica e stenta' (gaunt and with rickets), and Nedda can only helplessly witness her demise.[91] Grazia, a character in 'Vagabondaggio' ('Vagabondage,' another short story by Verga), breaks down under similar pressure. Rejected and alone, she kills her baby one rainy night.

Following the precept of objectivity, Verga depicts Nedda's and Grazia's stories without formulating any explicit social commentary. Ada Negri, on the other hand, endows the protagonists of her poems with class consciousness. In *Maternità* (*Maternity*, 1904), a private dialogue between a pregnant woman and her unborn child leads to a broader social perspective. The section 'Le Dolorose' ('Women in Pain') focuses on working women who go through their pregnancies 'con fatica, con fame e con paura' (in fatigue, hunger, and fear) and give birth to babies with their same 'guasto sangue [...] e il peso [delle loro] catene'[92] (rotten blood and the weight of [their] chains). Once they become mothers, they can rarely see their children, forced as they are to spend most of their days in the fields or at the factory. Martha, one of the portraits in the gallery of the *Dolorose*, works until she goes into labour, and rushes home only to give birth to 'un angioletto morto' (a dead little angel) whom she barely has time to mourn: 'Ma il quarto giorno – e gelido il rovajo / soffiava ancora – volle alzarsi, esangue / come avesse perduto tutto il sangue [...]/ così disfatta, ritornò al telajo'[93] (But the fourth day – while the freezing wind was still blowing – she wanted to get up, colourless as if she had lost all of her blood [...] devastated, she went back to the spinning wheel). And when one of the *Dolorose* abandons her newborn in an alley to die, Negri carefully chooses the target of her polemic fervour: 'Che ferocia di leggi su gli uomini grava / se fame o vergogna può vincer l'istinto materno?'[94] (What cruel law oppresses the human race if hunger or shame can overcome maternal instinct?)

Harshly criticized by Benedetto Croce for the ideological nature of her writings,[95] Negri is the only writer of the time who established such a close link between motherhood and social struggle.

By the time the Fascists came to power in 1922, the ideal of motherhood as a total, self-annihilating experience was already well established. The regime would exploit it to the fullest, replacing persuasion with prescription, and using the carrot of public recognition and the stick of ostracism to limit women's activity to their maternal mission. Fascist propaganda used both traditional and modern means (from public speeches to radio and cinema) to influence private life, infiltrating it to an unprecedented extent. While women who studied and worked outside the house faced hostile discrimination, those who fully conformed to the maternal role and bore seven children or more (the *prolifiche*) received generous financial rewards in public ceremonies. Once again, the price for the glorification of the mother was the humiliation of the woman. Fascist critics sought to extend these restrictions to literature and declared writing incompatible with a woman's true vocation as a mother.[96] And yet scholars have demonstrated how the laws aimed at barring women from the workforce achieved contradictory results. By the same token, as the next chapter will show, the attempts to prevent women's literary production proved far from successful.

chapter 2

Resilience and Resistance: The Fascist Years

From Benevolence to Dominance

It is perhaps the greatest irony in the history of Italian women that after two decades of intense struggle, female suffrage was adopted under the regime of a dictator who would shortly thereafter suppress the electoral rights of all citizens, men and women alike. On 15 May 1925, Mussolini convinced the parliament to adopt the Acerbo resolution, which extended to women the right to vote in administrative elections. His speech is indicative of the ambiguity that marked the first years of the dictatorship. Posing as an advocate of modernity, Il Duce chastised the opposition for behaving as if Italy were still in the Middle Ages, as if women were standing at the balcony, waiting for the return of their knights. He declared female employment a reality brought about by the 'century of capitalism,' a time when financial constraints forced women to become lawyers, professors, and doctors. Mussolini also evoked the great deeds women had performed during the First World War and declared military readiness a priority for the entire nation. This new reality, he maintained, made the exclusion of women from suffrage inconceivable. Finally, in a thinly veiled threat, he reminded his audience that Fascism found its strength in the subordination of the many to the will of one.[1] Perhaps more than the socio-economic analysis and the rhetorical praise of modernity that constituted the focus of the speech, this concluding appeal to party discipline, with its not-too-subtle allusion to the dangers of disobedience, persuaded the previously reluctant assembly to overcome internal dissent and to vote in favour of female suffrage.

The hopes raised by this resolution would soon be shattered.

Women's organizations had barely begun tackling the massive task of registering women to vote[2] when Mussolini, on 2 September 1926, eliminated administrative elections altogether.[3] This sudden turn of events must have made Mussolini's vision of a woman's role in society rather bewildering for his contemporaries. Things soon became clearer, however, when control over women's bodies became an integral part of the social engineeering program adopted by the regime to advance its colonial and bellicose pursuits. In the 'Discorso dell'Ascensione,' given on 26 May 1927, Mussolini equated population with power. Surrounded by 'ninety million Germans and two hundred million Slavs,'[4] Italy could not assert its strength without substantial population growth. It was crucial, in the dictator's view, that the country's population reach sixty million inhabitants by the middle of the twentieth century (from forty million in the 1920s).

Although women were hardly mentioned in the speech, reproductive policies soon made their role in the new demographic battle clear. Founded in 1925, the ONMI (Opera nazionale maternità ed infanzia [National Agency for Maternity and Childhood]) cared for mothers and children who lived outside the traditional family structure. Single women received free medical care and financial compensation for the last trimester of their pregnancy. In some cases, they were allowed to reside in special institutions (Case della madre e del bambino).[5] In 1928 families with more than six children began to receive monetary rewards and loans on advantageous terms. From 1934 on, working women were granted two months of paid maternity leave (one before, one after delivery) and were allowed interruptions during the workday for nursing.[6]

While these measures may seem at first to have been designed to help women balance the responsibilities of work and family, other initiatives make clear that their ultimate goal was to confine women to the domestic sphere. The first of these laws, passed in 1927, reduced women's salaries to half those of men. The same year, women were excluded from teaching literature and philosophy in high schools, and in 1928 they were prohibited from directing middle schools. University education was actively discouraged, as the price of tuition for women was raised to twice that for men. These and other policies culminated in the law of 1 September 1938, which limited women's presence in government offices to a maximum 10 per cent of all personnel.[7]

Aware that laws alone could not bring about the social change Fascism intended to promote, Ferdinando Loffredo saw a possible ally in public opinion:

L'abolizione del lavoro femminile deve essere la risultante di due fattori convergenti: il divieto sancito dalla legge, la riprovazione sancita dall'opinione pubblica. La donna che [...] lascia le pareti domestiche per recarsi al lavoro, la donna che, in promiscuità con l'uomo, gira per le strade, sui trams, sugli autobus, vive nelle officine e negli uffici, deve diventare oggetto di riprovazione, prima e più che di sanzione legale.[8]

The abolition of female labour must be the result of two converging factors: the prohibition established by law and the contempt expressed by public opinion. Women who [...] leave their homes to go to work, women who, mixing with men, wander the streets, on trams, on buses, and who live in factories and offices must be the object of contempt, more than of legal sanctions.

While indicative of a visceral hostility towards working women, Loffredo's call went largely unanswered. Female employment was already on its way to becoming a distinctive feature of twentieth-century Italy (as Mussolini himself had acknowledged in his speech on 25 May 1925), and all attempts to turn back the clock must have seemed not only futile but even suicidal for families that depended on women's salaries. As a matter of fact, the war would not only reinforce women's presence in traditional fields such as teaching, but it would also open many predominantly male professions to women, as men were forced to leave their families for the war.[9]

Literature and the Escape from History

On the whole, literature did not follow the regime in its celebration of the maternal ideal and its rejection of alternative female roles. In this, as in other domains, there was a wide gap between the official propaganda and the concerns of the literary world.[10] As early as 1927, the critic Arnaldo Frateili lamented the absence of true Fascist literature, by which he meant not simply art produced by people affiliated with the party or known for their commitment to the Fascist cause, but art that reflected the goals and ideals of the regime. Frateili's explanation for the phenomenon was a paradox: he concluded that, at the time, there were writers who wrote and writers who did not, and that, generally speaking, the latter were better artists than the former. The article ended with the hope that the change in social climate would, in due time, break the writers' reluctance and inspire them to create true Fascist literature.[11]

A reading of the influential bimonthly *Critica fascista* and other periodicals of the *ventennio*, however, shows that the concerns expressed by Frateili never dissipated. In 1933 an editorial in *Il secolo fascista* lamented that 'il Fascismo non ha conquistato un solo palmo di terreno nel mondo della cultura' (Fascism hasn't gained a single inch in the cultural world);[12] a columnist who signed his pieces in *Critica fascista* with the pseudonym of 'Il doganiere' (The Customs Officer) regularly lamented the distance between the glorious historical moment the country was experiencing and the writers' private, allegedly ahistorical concerns.[13]

This general unwillingness of the literary world to serve as a mouthpiece for the regime explains in part why the prolific mother never became a literary theme. Some writers even tried to remove motherhood from its historical determinants and context altogether. In Gianna Manzini's short story 'The Pomegranate' (1936), Amalia reconstructs her relationship with her son Sandro through the memories of her pregnancy. While waiting for her son's return with the rest of the family, Amalia tries to pinpoint the moment that had interrupted 'her last slow conversation with the baby who was about to be born': 'Inescapably then, life, which is impossible for anyone to control, intervened to break the miracle of those two hearts beating harmoniously together so it could secretly mark the little child inside her [...] Perhaps, even in her womb, the baby was becoming less hers, already a little bit stolen.'[14] Amalia remembers in particular seeing a horse fall in a 'peaceful way,' collapsing gently on its front legs. That episode, she realizes, had marked her child forever, instilling in him a peculiar sense of kindness. When Sandro finally arrives from the city, Amalia has gained a unique insight. Without his saying a word, Amalia is able to understand her son's need to be left alone. Motherhood thus becomes the site of a secret, privileged relationship, unaffected by historical constraints.[15]

Also escaping history, but moving in a different direction, Pirandello made motherhood the principle of a mythical regeneration. In *La nuova colonia* (*The New Colony*, 1928), a group of outcasts find refuge on a island where, amidst tensions and contradictions, they lay the foundations for a new society based on work and solidarity. The only woman among them is La Spera, who had abandoned prostitution after becoming a mother. Throughout the play, she tries to remind the group of the hope for renewal that had drawn them to the secluded island in the first place. And yet, jealousy and greed creep in, endangering the social experiment. The already divided community is shattered by the arrival of a new group of people who bring with them the distorted, materialistic values of the mainland. La Spera refuses to relinquish her ideals and return to her former existence. When Currao, her child's father, tries to take the boy away from her, she climbs a high rock. Soon the earth begins to tremble and the ocean rises to submerge the island, leaving La Spera and her son as the only survivors. The play concludes with the mother's cry, at the same time desperate and defiant: 'Ah Dio, io qua, sola, con te figlio, sulle acque!'[16] (Oh God, here I am, alone with you, my son, on the waters!)

Like the other 'myth plays' (*Lazzaro* and *I giganti della montagna*), *La nuova colonia* has traditionally elicited 'perplexity rather than enthusiasm.'[17] Pirandello's nihilism reaches new depths as he tackles two themes dear to Fascist ideology: colonialism and motherhood.[18] In *La nuova colonia*, the hope of regeneration implicit in the search for a new land is exposed as an escapist dream: human nature only leads the characters to recreate, in a new environment, the same unjust and spiritually inadequate social structure that existed before. By the same token, motherhood, while having a regenerating and redeeming effect on women, proves insufficient as a social force. Even before people from the mainland visit the new colony, short-lived respect for La Spera had begun to give way to jealousy and contempt. A primary, archetypal force defended and upheld in the conclusion of the play by the natural elements, motherhood defines itself as intrinsically 'other' from society. The triumph of motherhood is proclaimed at the very moment in which it severs its ties with a community that had attempted to bring it under its laws and use it for its means.[19] In spite of Pirandello's much publicized endorsement of Fascism in the aftermath of the assassination of the Socialist deputy Giacomo Matteotti (1924), his attitude of ideological distance from the regime would prove, in this and on other occasions, adamant and visceral.[20]

Mothers without a Name and the Search for Women's Identity

Another possible reason why the prolific mother never became a literary theme lies in the fact that Fascist ideologues were the first to attribute to this figure rather unpoetic features. In 1931 Carlalberto Grillenzoni, an expert in statistics, tried to find out whether fertility could be associated with certain physical and social characteristics, only to conclude that prolific mothers tended to be shabby and unattractive.[21] The lack of individuality (and, therefore, the scarce artistic appeal) of such a figure was paradoxically confirmed by the very same ceremonies that were supposed to exalt it. When the 'Giornata della madre e dell'infanzia' (Mother's and Childhood Day) was instituted in 1933, a national rally in Rome gathered the most prolific mothers in the country. The celebration of these women had nothing to do with their identities but rather was based on their fertility alone. This is perhaps best illustrated by the fact that the rally's roll call announced them not by their names but only by the number of each woman's live births.[22] Individuals, be they mothers or children, were bound to disappear behind the sheer power of numbers – the only meaning the regime attached to them. It is therefore not surprising that even popular literature, the infamous 'romanzo rosa,' shied away from celebrating prolific mothers, preferring to focus instead on the protagonists' sentimental turmoil and the triumph of love that inevitably followed.[23]

Almost absent from the Fascist ranks at the beginning of the movement,[24] women seemed sceptical – and, in some cases, openly critical – of their position in the new political scene. The case of Laura Casartelli Cabrini is revealing in this context. A moderate socialist, Casartelli Cabrini wrote for six years (1920–5) the annual 'Rassegna del movimento femminile' ('Review of the Women's Movement'), arguably the most politically committed column in the popular *Almanacco della donna italiana (Italian Women's Almanac)*. After documenting with prudence and detachment, year after year, the changes in the Italian political landscape and its consequences for women's organizations, Casartelli Cabrini used her 1925 column to develop a scathing criticism of Fascist ideology and practices. Abandoning her usually cautious stance, she gave voice to women's disappointment and attitude towards the regime: 'Il permanere della violenza, la corruzione dei giovani [...], la menomazione delle libertà costituzionali non trovano indulgenza presso le donne, le quali nella grande maggioranza, non sono consezienti nella politica fascista'[25] (The persistence of violence, the corruption of the youth [...], and the limitation of constitutional freedom are not condoned by women, the great majority of whom disagree with Fascist politics).

Casartelli Cabrini was blunt and uncompromising in her attack on everything Fascism represented. The fact that this was her last review for the *Almanacco* seems, in hindsight, more than a curious coincidence. The following year, she was replaced by Ester Lombardo, whose allegiance to the regime was well known, and who gave ample space to Fascist women's groups in her column.[26] Yet Lombardo opened her 1928 review with some striking remarks that cryptically convey her uneasiness at the announcement of the death of the Italian women's movement. In a skilful rhetorical move, she did not tackle the issue of women's attitudes towards Fascism directly, but feigned an interview with a naive foreign correspondent. In this imaginary conversation, Lombardo ironically praises the accomplishments of the regime, from the abolition of free elections to the creation of ONMI, and conclude by voicing complete satisfaction. She then ventures to guess her credulous interlocutor's thoughts and reactions: 'L'interlocutore rimane soddisfatto; piglia appunti, ringrazia, saluta e poi scrive sul suo giornale: le donne italiane sono tutte innamorate di Mussolini e non si lagnano se egli ha loro negato i diritti politici. Così si fa la cronaca e forse anche la storia'[27] (The journalist is satisfied. He takes notes, thanks me, bids farewell, and writes in his paper: Italian women are all in love with Mussolini and do not complain that he has denied them their political rights. That's how you make news, and perhaps also history).

This imaginary interview appeared in what would be, significantly, the last review of the activities of the women's movement. From 1929 on, the *Almanacco* devoted its attention exclusively to the activity of the Fasci femminili, the Fascist women's organization.[28] Written at such a crucial historical juncture, Lombardo's words can be interpreted as a plea for future generations to read between the lines and be aware of the limitations imposed by a totalitarian regime. But her warning would go largely unheeded. The acquiescence extorted by Fascism would be interpreted, not only by contemporary witnesses (those who wrote the 'news') but also by more recent and supposedly more objective observers (those charged with interpreting 'history'), as women's wholehearted, uncritical endorsement of Fascist politics. The resulting image of women under Fascism bears a striking resemblance to that of Antonietta, the protagonist of Ettore Scola's 1977 film *Una giornata particolare* (*A Special Day*): a forlorn mother of six children, a household slave, Antonietta is incapable of formulating any criticism of her own condition and harbours a viscerally erotic obsession for Mussolini, the quintessential male, until another and very different male – her charming homosexual neighbour, played by Marcello Mastroianni – stimulates her intellectual and sexual awakening.[29] Only recently have critics begun to question this view. In her influential *How Fascism Ruled Women*, Victoria De Grazia warned that 'to know the intentions of Fascist sexual politics is not necessarily to know its outcome.'[30] A close analysis reveals how women's responses to Fascist demands were 'more complex than the attitudes commonly ascribed to them, namely, passive subordination or delirious enthusiasm.'[31]

Robin Pickering-Iazzi has challenged the well-established notion of women's silence under Fascism, shedding new light on women's literary works. The critic has focused in particular on the short stories published on the *terza pagina* (the cultural page) of newspapers. Paradoxically, as Pickering-Iazzi powerfully states, post-war critics accomplished what Fascism had failed to do – namely, silence women's voices:

> Despite the significant contribution women writers made to Italian life and culture during the dictatorship, their voices have been silenced. Surprisingly, the subject of women's writing produced in the twenties and thirties was repressed not by policies designed to manage culture during Fascism, but by the postwar critical establishment, which either omitted female writers or dismissed them in accounts of culture and literature in the Fascist State, alleging that women merely 'reproduced' conservative ideology. Thus, scholars are faced with the irony that postwar literary criticism managed to accomplish the work of Fascist ideologues: to marginalize women writers who generated sustained attention among prominent critics and the general reading public.[32]

Pickering-Iazzi's groundbreaking work has opened a virtually unexplored field of enquiry. Women's writing in the 1920s and 1930s was, in fact, as abundant and popular as it is neglected now. In 1930, Stanis Ruinas mentioned the existence of a thousand women writers – or 'scribblers,' as he paternalistically defined them. Even in its last issue, published in 1942, the *Annuario* published in the *Almanacco della donna italiana* listed the names and addresses of more than five hundred women writers. To be sure, not all of them are remarkable for their artistic qualities – however loosely one wants to interpret the concept – or unconventional attitudes. Nevertheless, their mere existence complicates the traditional notion of literature during the Fascist years and certainly calls for further scrutiny.

An analysis of the maternal experience in the works of women writers is particularly relevant in this context because motherhood was, as we have seen, the object of intense Fascist propaganda. The representation of the mother thus presented particular risks for women, who were faced with a double bind. The mere fact of portraying a figure that, according to official propaganda, represented women's sole suitable role in society called into question their own act of writing, highlighting its subversive potential. Ruinas's introduction to his catalogue of women writers of the time is revealing in this regard. Ruinas attributes to the

Italian people a certain contempt for women writers, who constitute a danger to the home and to children. He concludes by invoking Mussolini's authority: 'Mettendo all'ordine del giorno della Nazione le famiglie numerose, aiutandole con mezzi validi, il governo Fascista ha inflitto la piú grave delle umiliazioni [...] alle donne di lettere infeconde!'[33] (By putting large families on the national agenda, by helping them with valuable measures, the Fascist government has inflicted the deepest humiliation on the [...] sterile women of letters!).

Most of Ruinas's criticism of individual authors is based not on their artistic accomplishments but on their maternal behaviour. Grazia Deledda is therefore praised for being 'prima d'ogni altra cosa, donna; donna all'antica, tradizionalmente italiana, madre esemplare'[34] (first and foremost, a woman; an old-fashioned woman, in the Italian tradition, an exemplary mother); Benedetta Cappa Marinetti is a 'futurista nata' (born futurist) who 'ha saputo essere donna nel piú bel significato della parola: donna e madre'[35] (managed to be a woman in the most beautiful meaning of the word: woman and mother). Sibilla Aleramo, on the other hand, although recognized as a 'scrittrice di primo ordine' (first-class writer), is condemned because her books 'ripugnano al gusto e al buon senso del virtuoso popolo italiano, amante della casa e adoratore della famiglia'[36] (are offensive to the taste and common sense of the virtuous Italian people, who love the household and adore the family). Sometimes Ruinas quotes passages in which the authors themselves declare their priorities. Edvige Pesce Gorini, a student of Pirandello who enjoyed a certain success as a poet, maintains that she is 'prima di tutto [...] una onesta e tenera mamma. L'arte, che pure mi dà tanta gioia e tanta pena, viene dopo'[37] (first and foremost [...] an honest and tender mom. Art, although it gives me so much joy and so much sorrow, comes after). Maria Luisa Fiumi, a successful author of novels, is quick to admit that 'prima di essere artista mi ricordo di essere madre'[38] (I always remember that I am a mother before being an artist). In his last chapter, significantly titled 'Incremento alla demografia' ('Increase in Population'), Ruinas claims that over half of the thousand women writers he knows have no children and sarcastically recommends that they be forced to abandon their artistic ambitions and be sent to less populated regions, where they could contribute to the demographic mission.

Apart from being inflammatory and misogynistic, Ruinas's attitude was also oddly misplaced, and seemed so even to contemporary critics. Arnaldo Frateili's introduction to *Scrittrici e scribacchine* unexpectedly turned into a harshly critical review of the volume and of its author, whom he accused of confusing aesthetic and moral criteria in his judgment. But such confusion is in itself indicative of the difficult predicament in which women writers found themselves. The call for women to withdraw from the literary scene is a particular case of the more general attitude towards women working outside the home. In 1929 'Il doganiere' also appealed to the ostensibly ubiquitous 'tradizionale buon senso italiano' (traditional Italian common sense), and encouraged his fellow Fascists to extend women's exclusion from politics to other domains, 'soprattutto nell'arte e nelle lettere'[39] (in particular to literature and the arts). A woman writer was thus in danger of being perceived as the usurper of a man's prerogatives, as well as a betrayer of her most authentic mission. The portrayal of the mother in a woman writer's work, therefore, risked exposing the contradictions inherent in her role as an intellectual and her own attitude towards the regime.

Mothers at War

'Disse ad Abramo il Signore: / Levati, e togli il fanciullo per mano'[40] (God said to Abraham: Stand up, and take your child by the hand): thus begins Margherita Sarfatti's poem 'Il sacrificio' ('The Sacrifice'), inspired by the death of her son Roberto in the First World War. The writer's biblical imagery stresses the enormity of the sacrifice and the difficulty of comprehending the designs of a distant God. Roberto was but one of the six hundred thousand Italians (mostly young men from rural areas) who lost their lives on the battlefields of the First World War.[41] The link between the Italian notion of motherhood and the Catholic model was made even more poignant by the dramatic events of the war. Like the Virgin, who had lost Christ to redeem the world, mothers were asked to immolate their sons at the altar of a higher cause. One poem in Sarfatti's collection makes the Marian allusion particularly clear. The poet's cry over her dead son ('Figlio bianco e vermiglio' [Fair and rosy-cheeked son])[42] borrows directly from the lament of the Madonna, as imagined by the medieval poet Jacopone da Todi. The soldiers' mothers represented in novels, short stories, and poems of the early Fascist years are dumbfounded by pain. The narrator of Ada Negri's short story 'La madre' ('The Mother,' 1926) walks out of a church on the island of Capri to find herself in the midst of a Fascist celebration, in stark contrast to the peaceful atmosphere of the island.[43] Even more incongruous appears the figure of Caterina Trama, the mother of the first soldier from Capri to die in the war. Standing still in her old-fashioned black dress and oversized shoes, she passively accepts a large bouquet of white flowers and seems strangely unable to hear the war song about crossing the Piave River. She mechanically performs the actions that are required of her, showing no sign of emotional participation. Only after the ceremony do her feelings emerge, as she tries to place her flowers on the stone commemorating the soldiers who died in the war. Her only words ('U voglio mmettere ccà' [I want to put it there]), uttered in the local dialect, highlight her distance from the official, national ceremony that has just taken place. The stone is too high, and she needs help to complete her task:

> Il mazzo è là, finalmente, al suo posto, fra le corone: diritto come lo teneva, sul palco, la madre: col grande e puro giglio nel mezzo. Ella è contenta, adesso: respira.
> Ma non sa piú che fare delle sue mani vuote; e stringe, stringe le falangi dalle aspre nocche sul petto dove splendono le due medaglie di bronzo.[44]

> The bouquet is finally there, in its place, among the reeds: it stands straight, the same way the mother was holding it on stage, with the large and pure lily in the middle. She is happy now and breathes.
> But she doesn't know what to do with her empty hands; and she squeezes her fingers, with her rough knuckles on her chest, where two bronze medals shine.

The celebration of military sacrifice was an important component of Fascist ideology. Founded only one year after the end of the First World War, the party had exploited 'the popular myth of the "mutilated victory", the widespread feeling that Italy had been cheated out of its territorial rights by the Treaty of Versailles.'[45] The sacrifice in human lives paid by the country was a crucial justification for the nation's territorial expansion.[46] Negri's account, however, does not stress the sacrifice of the humble soldier from Capri (whose name is not even mentioned), or his mother's stoic resignation, but rather the irreconcilable divide between the rights of the individual and the demands of the regime. Caterina Trama, with her black dress, her sorrow, and her dialect, is totally foreign to the clamour and chants of the Fascist, national, and nationalistic ceremony. There was an obvious contradiction between the ideology of motherhood that Fascism had inherited and tried to foster and the regime's need for soldiers to use and sacrifice in battle. While Mussolini, on the verge of entering the Second World War, could boast about the spoils to be obtained by 'throwing a few thousand bodies on the negotiation table,'[47] mothers resisted giving up their sons to be used as disposable pawns in the game of international politics. The discrepancy was clearly stated (and resolved with upbeat optimism) in 1933 by Manlio Pompei, who reminded his readers of the precedent of the First World War:

> Vogliamo fare dei nostri figli dei combattenti? E sarebbe il trepido cuore della madre in contrasto con questo fine che è dello Stato? No: perché noi non educhiamo soldati di ventura per portare ruina e desolazione, ma soldati pronti a difendere la Patria, quella Patria che per i grigioverdi di quindici anni or sono, benaltrimenti ignari e spiritualmente incolti che non la gioventú d'oggi, si materializzò, e si comprese fatta zolla, petra e amore, nella casa e nel campo lasciati e nel volto della madre benedicente.[48]

> Do we intend to make fighters out of our children? And is a mother's trembling heart in contrast with the State's goal? No: because we are not raising mercenary soldiers to bring ruin and desolation, but soldiers ready to defend the Fatherland. Fifteen years ago, our soldiers dressed in grey and green, although much less aware and spiritually prepared than today's youth, realized that the Fatherland was represented by the stones, soil, and love in the house, in the field, and in the face of the blessing mothers they had left behind.

Women writers might have provided a less emphatic answer. The irreconcilability of motherhood with war is clear to the protagonist of 'Tuo figlio sta bene' ('Your Son Is Fine'), an intense short story from Negri's 1923 collection *Finestre alte* (*Tall Windows*):

> Mamma, nient'altro che mamma, si era rifiutata di spiegarsi le ragioni essenziali della guerra. Mostruoso le era sempre parso il fatto del combattere: sangue e sangue: assassini e assassinati: la pazzia rossa: suo figlio, il suo unico figlio, travolto in quella carneficina: nulla poteva fare per trattenerlo: nulla possono le madri per le loro creature.[49]

> A mother, nothing but a mother, she had always refused to explain to herself the important reasons for the war. Fighting had always seemed monstrous to her: blood and blood; the murderers and the murdered; the red madness. Her son, her only son, swept away in that massacre. There was

nothing she could do to hold him back. Mothers can do nothing for their creatures.

The anonymous character in Ada Negri's short story, being 'nothing but a mother,' experiences an instinctive, visceral opposition to everything that war, 'the red madness,' represents. Her silent reflection contains a germ of rebellion, albeit one confined to the consciousness of this particular character. In recent years, Sara Ruddick has explored the intrinsic contradiction between mothering and war in her influential *Maternal Thinking*. Although a mother, like any other individual, may be personally inclined to justify or favour a particular war, the practice of mothering involves ways of thinking and acting that sharply contrast with the logic of war. Maternal practice involves nurturing, listening, caring, and negotiating, and can thus provide, Ruddick maintains, a model for peace politics.[50] It is certainly not a coincidence that those who considered war the solution to Italy's problems saw mothers as their sworn enemies. In 'Manifeste de la femme futuriste' ('Manifesto of the futurist Woman,' 1912), Valentine de Saint-Point attacked women who shielded their sons from war, and reminded them in the last line that their duty was to produce heroes for the human race ('À l'humanité vous devez des héros. Donnez-les lui').[51] The impending catastrophe lent a sense of urgency to these pleas. In 1914, Giovanni Papini applauded the onset of the First World War, 'un caldo bagno di sangue nero dopo tanti umidicci e tiepidumi di latte materno' (a warm bath of black blood, after so much humid and lukewarm maternal milk), and invited his friends to love war 'con tutto il nostro cuore di maschi' (with all our male hearts).[52]

An adamant rebuttal not only to the military rhetoric surrounding the First World War, but also to the idea of war as a logical and natural manifestation of a country's identity can be found in *Mors tua...* (1926), Matilde Serao's last novel. That one of the most popular Italian women of her times should conclude her long career by making such a firm statement must have taken many readers by surprise. After all, this was the same writer who in *Parla una donna: Diario femminile di guerra* (*A Woman Speaks: A Feminine War Diary*), published in 1916, had indulged in representing the heroism of Italian soldiers and their families, urging mothers to abide by God's mysterious designs:

Siete voi vere cristiane [...]? Se tanto voi siete, [...] voi dovete dire, a voi stesse, voi *sapete già* che Iddio ha permesso, per sue late e misteriose ragioni

> questa guerra, voi sapete già che Egli volle tutto questo, e che tutta quanta questa tribolazione, è da Dio che viene su voi, su noi.⁵³

> Are you true Christians [...]? If you really are, [...] you must say to yourselves, you *already know* that God has permitted, for His hidden and mysterious reasons, this war. You already know that He wanted all this and that it is from God that all this sorrow falls upon you, upon us.

In a stunning reversal Serao, a few months before her death, published a novel that constitutes a powerful anti-war manifesto in the name of motherhood. In *Mors tua...*, the argument of a mysterious divine justification is adduced only to be rejected. This is how a prospective soldier challenges Don Giulio, the priest who had invoked God's will to explain the necessity of war:

> Questi Austriaci ci avranno la moglie e i figli come me, le creature loro, non è vero, don Giulio? [...] Allora, costoro sono il mio prossimo? E voi non predicate ogni giorno, alle donne e agli uomini, di amare il prossimo? Dite che Dio lo consiglia, lo vuole, lo comanda? E adesso che comanda, Dio, di ammazzarci, fra noi e il prossimo?⁵⁴

> These Austrians must have wives and children, their beloved ones, as I do. Isn't it true, Don Giulio? Aren't they my neighbour? And don't you preach every day, to men and women, that they should love their neighbour? Don't you say that this is what God suggests, wants, orders? And now, what does God command? That we kill each other, among neighbours?

This conversation introduces a first doubt in Don Giulio. After witnessing the carnage of war, he loses his faith altogether.

The novel follows the lives of several characters from the eve of the First World War to its aftermath. Dedicated to 'La madre ignota' (The Unknown Mother), it opens, significantly, with three mothers remembering the days when their children were born and worrying about the impending threat. The narration then follows the lives of their sons during the war, devoting particular attention to the transformation that takes place in one of them. Fausto was a vehement supporter of the war, but after his younger brother's death in battle, and after having witnessed the horrors of war himself, he returns to his mother to apologize for his past enthusiasm. He is ready to acknowledge that what he mistook for 'bellezza, sacrificio, eroismo' (beauty, sacrifice, and heroism) has turned out to be 'flagello, distruzione e putredine'[55] (wreckage, destruction, and putrefaction). Fausto's metamorphosis began the day he wrote a letter to a dead soldier's mother and found military rhetoric profoundly inadequate for the task. His evolution mirrors Serao's own transformation, from the proud nationalism of *Parla una donna* to the plea for peace of her last novel.

Each of the three mothers presented at the beginning of the novel loses a child as a result of the war. Carolina Leoni, whose daughter Loreta has disappeared in the city after her fiancé's death in battle, leaves to be a volunteer at a leper hospital; Marta Ardore spends her days in her dead son's bedroom; Antonia Scalese falls into insanity and obsessively talks to a brick in the floor from under which she believes she hears her son's voice. In Serao's novel, the experience of motherhood makes women strangers to the world of war. The 'madre ignota' to whom the book is dedicated stands in clear and polemical opposition to the 'milite ignoto' (unknown soldier), to whom Fascism dedicated an imposing monument in the centre of Rome. Such a powerful criticism of the war fell just short of being a direct attack on Mussolini, who had vehemently supported Italy's participation in the First World War and made military preparedness a national priority. In her biography of Matilde Serao, Anna Banti suggests that it was because of this novel that the Fascist government opposed the author's nomination for the Nobel Prize.[56] Although harshly critical of the novel's flaws, Banti applaudes Serao's courage:

> Sebbene letterariamente nullo, macchinoso, edulcorato e retorico, il romanzo *Mors tua* ha, bisogna riconoscerlo, il valore di una strenua testimonianza di fede in una umanità pacifica [...] Ne sono protagonisti giovani e madri distrutti, gente sacrificata senza un perché, e che tardi si accorge dell'errore in cui è caduta [...] Se fra i meriti dei candidati al Nobel conta soprattutto quello di contribuire alla pace fra i popoli, questo brutto romanzo di un valoroso scrittore avrebbe dovuto trovare maggiore indulgenza.[57]

> However void of literary merit, artificial, edulcorated, and rhetorical, *Mors tua* has, we must admit, the value of a compelling testimonial of the faith in a peaceful humanity [...] Its protagonists are destroyed youth and mothers, people sacrificed without a reason, who realize their mistake only too late [...] If the contribution to world peace is among the merits of a Nobel candidate, this bad novel by a noble writer should have found greater indulgence.

Besides undermining all militarist rhetoric, Serao's portrayal of women's attitude towards the war conveyed an image of motherhood totally foreign to that which the regime sought to create.

'Like War Is to Men'

Giving birth in Fascist Italy was still a dangerous undertaking for women, as complications and even death were far from uncommon. In spite of this, not only abortion but also contraception was outlawed in 1926.[58] Giuseppe De Libero, one of the country's most virulent opponents of birth control, considered it an unsuitable choice, even when a pregnancy could endanger a woman's life. He argued:

> Se il sacerdote ed il medico debbono rischiare la vita in tempo di epidemia, se l'agente di pubblica sicurezza ed il pompiere debbono far quasi getto della propria esistenza, in un tumulto, in un incendio, se tante volte il soldato deve andare incontro alla morte durante una lunga guerra, se costoro debbono essere eroi in un dato momento, in certe circostanze si deve essere eroi anche nel matrimonio.[59]

> If the priest and the doctor must risk their lives in an epidemic, if the policeman and the firefighter must all but throw their lives away in an uprising or a fire, if so many times soldiers must face death during a long war, if they all have to be heroes at a given time, in certain circumstances one must be a hero in marriage as well.

De Libero's position is of course not a complete novelty. Already in 1920 Gina Lombroso had argued that 'no mother has ever refused to face the perils of death and suffering in order to perpetuate the race, just as no man hesitates to give his life for the cause he believes in.'[60] This principle acquires a more specific meaning in the new context. The generic 'cause' mentioned by Gina Lombroso is replaced in De Libero's statement by a long list of dangerous activities that finds its rhetorical culmination in the image of the soldier at war. Gina Lombroso's vision of women ready to sacrifice themselves for the perpetuation of the 'race' sounds like a sinister omen when read in the context of a regime that would eventually include a supposed racial purity among its objectives. Mussolini himself synthesized this theory with one of his catchy slogans: 'La guerra sta all'uomo come la maternità alla donna' (War is to men what maternity is to women).[61] The analogy is based not only on the necessity for men and women to act in conformity with their supposed natures, but also on the inevitable dangers both activities entailed.

Literary works of these years abound with women dying during or soon after childbirth. Such is the destiny of Ilda, the protagonist of one of the poems in Ada Negri's collection *Vespertina* (1930), whose only regret is not being able to nurse and tend to her baby. Maria Luisa Fiumi, one of the most popular writers of her times, decided instead to extol sacrifice and represented motherhood as the only dignified condition for a woman, to be obtained at all costs. Teresa Ghiberti, the protagonist of *La moglie* (*The Wife*, 1933), endures a very difficult pregnancy that results in a miscarriage. Although she knows that her chances of surviving a second pregnancy are extremely slim, she tries and manages to get pregnant again. On the eve of the delivery, she confesses to her husband that she has made a vow: she has asked God to take her life for her son's.

> Ma vedi, mi sarei rassegnata a non aver figlioli. Sì; se ti fossi potuta rimanere accanto, se ... se avessi avuto ancora l'illusione di bastare alla tua felicità [...] Quando mi sono accorta che io non ero niente, per te: peggio che niente, una catena, un peso morto attaccato alla tua vita, allora ho detto: e io che ci sto a fare al mondo [...] Intendimi, allora ho fatto un voto: Dio si prenda questa mia vita inutile purché mi conceda di lasciarti un figlio [...] Ecco: un figlio sarà l'unica forza buona nella tua vita; sarà tutto quello che non ho potuto essere io.[62]

> You see, I would have resigned myself to being childless if I could have stayed next to you, if I had had the illusion that I was sufficient for your happiness [...] When I realized that I was nothing for you, or even less than nothing, a chain, a dead weight attached to your life, then I said: why am I in this world [...] Listen, I then made a vow: God may take this useless life of mine, provided that He allows me to leave you a child [...] Here: my son will be the only good force in your life; he will be everything I could not be.

No happy ending mitigates the absurdity of the offer: Teresa does indeed die, after giving her husband a son.[63]

These kinds of stories, in which women's devotion to their maternal mission reaches quasi-suicidal extremes, must have been particularly pleasing to the ideologues of the time. It is not surprising that Stanis Ruinas praised Fiumi as 'una delle nostre scrittrici piú quadrate e leggibili' (one of our most solid and readable writers) and that Mussolini himself selected her to take part in a cultural propaganda mission in Spain.[64]

Future as a Revised Version of the Past

Two of the short stories in Ada Negri's collection *Finestre alte* explore motherhood as a possibility for women to reshape the past and to correct its mistakes. The protagonist of 'Il suo diritto' ('Her Right') is heating a special iron to curl her hair when her daughter Lucetta gets too close to the stove and is horribly burned. Interpreting the accident as a punishment for her vanity, the woman devotes herself exclusively to her daughter, alienating her husband and son. Lucetta becomes a talented pianist and the lover of a famous cellist. When the man leaves, she is pregnant and dies during delivery. The protagonist takes the newborn girl, 'una nuova Lucetta' (a new Lucetta), who bears an uncanny resemblance to her mother before the accident that changed her life, and rejoins the rest of the family. A similar pattern underlies 'Ombra' ('Shadow'), where a woman who was born blind marries a man who has lost his sight after an accident. The couple, apprehensive about the possibility that their children will be blind, are overjoyed when their daughter is born in good health and able to see. In these stories, motherhood is represented as a force capable of providing a fresh start and becomes a means of turning back the clock, supposedly compensating the protagonists for their unjust destiny.

Annie Vivanti investigated the more perturbing side of this potential, while confirming her predilection for genealogies. Whereas her 1910 novel *I divoratori* had exposed the law that forced daughters to follow in their mothers' footsteps,[65] *Mea culpa!* (1927) focused on a secret (and implausible) link tying together three generations. The action takes place during the British colonization of Egypt. Astrid, the protagonist, is soon to be married to an English officer, but she grows increasingly critical of the colonialist mentality around her and develops a deep attraction to an Egyptian man, Saad Nassir. When she discovers that her fiancé is about to participate in a punitive attack on an Egyptian village, she runs away in order to warn Saad of the impending danger. The two escape to the desert, where they spend a few passionate days before Astrid decides to return home and resume her ordinary life. Soon after her wedding, the discovery that she is pregnant leads to a great deal of uncertainty about the identity of the child's father. When a reassuringly blond and fair-skinned daughter is born, Astrid is overwhelmingly relieved:

> Così nell'anima di Astrid la maternità irruppe, turbine soave, a cancellare ogni altra passione, ogni altro desiderio. Ella sentì che la bionda bambina concessale dalla Divina clemenza l'aveva purificata e redimita. Darling era per lei l'assoluzione e la salvezza. Darling era il perdono di Dio.[66]

> Maternity entered Astrid's soul like a sweet tornado, cancelling every other passion, every other desire. She felt that the little blond girl granted to her by Divine clemency had purified and redeemed her. For her, Darling was absolution and salvation. Darling was God's forgiveness.

As in *I divoratori*, motherhood becomes such an absorbing task that it destroys all of the mother's other concerns. It is only after Darling's marriage to an English officer that Astrid begins to perform some charitable work and is struck by the misery of Egyptian society. Her solidarity with the victims of colonialism, already apparent in her relationship with Saad Nassir, becomes deeper and more informed as she realizes that the poverty that devastates the country is the result of deliberate policies.[67]

When Darling dies in childbirth, the family's sorrow is doubled by a puzzling discovery, which only Astrid can interpret correctly:

> Non per un attimo dubitò della verità. Sangue orientale – arabo sangue! – scorreva nelle vene di questa creatura, affiorava alla delicata epidermide, splendeva nella tenebrosa pupilla. Il sangue oscuro tramandato da lei, attraverso le vene di sua figlia, rifluiva nella creatura novella. La natura capricciosa e inesorabile, col salto d'una generazione, riaffermava il suo imperio. Darling, così bianca e bionda, Darling dai dorati capelli, dalle lattee carni – era figlia di Saad Nassir![68]

> Not for a second did she doubt that she knew the truth. Oriental blood – Arab blood! – was flowing through the baby's veins, rising to the surface of her delicate skin, shining in her dark pupils. That dark blood, transmitted to her, through her daughter's blood, was flowing in the new creature. A relentless, capricious nature, after skipping a generation, was affirming its power. White and blond Darling, Darling with her golden locks, with her milky skin, was Saad Nassir's daughter!

The novel ends with Astrid's choice to reveal the truth. She takes the baby with her and rejoins Saad Nassir, who has apparently been waiting for her all along.

Vivanti's earlier plots had in some cases challenged logic and common sense, but she had never resorted to such an implausible scientific explanation. Despite the unlikelihood of such a conclusion, her readers did not desert her, and the novel quickly became a leading best-seller. Obvious flaws aside, Astrid's story allowed Vivanti to look at motherhood from a different perspective, one that very much complements Negri's. While Negri's short stories portray motherhood as a way to redress an unjust destiny, *Mea culpa!* alludes to a more perturbing link, one that leads daughters to bear the consequences of their mothers' actions. Darling becomes the unknowing vessel of a shameful secret that resurfaces when it is least expected. While resurrecting the past, motherhood also allows for the return of the repressed. At the same time, this new and vicarious motherhood gives Astrid a second chance. Her youthful instinctive rebellion – which had inspired her brief escape to the desert – has evolved and led to a mature choice that is ideological as well as sentimental.

Originally published in 1927, *Mea culpa!* would reach its ninth edition in 1937, selling a total of 100,000 copies by 1943,[69] when colonialism and the related fear of miscegenation had become common topics in the Italian cultural and political discourse. Fascist propaganda tried to establish a clear difference between the unjustified and destructive English colonialism and the allegedly civilizing mission Italy was accomplishing in Ethiopia, resurrecting Rome's imperial vocation. Vivanti's critique could therefore easily be perceived as directed at England more than at colonialism per se. The birth of Darling's 'Arab' son, however, must have impressed Fascist ideologues as a terrifying omen.

Barely a month after the conquest of Ethiopia, the jubilation over the reconstruction of the empire had already begun to give way to apprehension about the perceived threat of racial mixing. In his regular column in *Critica fascista*, 'Il doganiere' emphatically agreed with the opinions expressed in the newspaper *Il messaggero*, according to which 'gli incroci sono sempre deprecabili' (cross-breeding is always deplorable). On the same page, a letter to the editor expressed similar dismay at the possibility that Italian blood might be contaminated ('il nostro sangue non deve venire inquinato').[70] These feelings became increasingly widespread in 1938 when Italy, following in the footsteps of Nazi Germany, implemented its own racial laws. Once again, control over women's bodies was a crucial part of the battle for the 'defence of the race.'[71] In an article published in *Critica fascista* and significantly titled

'La funzione della donna nella politica razziale' ('The Function of Women in Racial Politics'), Adolfo Dolmetta stressed the possible dangers of women's choices and behaviour:

> La donna è la depositaria più preziosa dei caratteri ereditari della razza: in nessun caso pertanto le è consentito distruggere il tesoro di possibilità in essa latente [...] Non lo deve dissipare nell'impero, prediligendo uomini di colore. Questo fatto è un obbrobrio, una mostruosità, suscettibile di risolversi in una grave sciagura per l'avvenire della stirpe: l'antropologia insegna che il decadere di molti popoli non ebbe nel passato altra causa all'infuori di una indiscriminata fusione di razze.[72]

> Women are the most precious vessel of hereditary racial characteristics; under no circumstances should they destroy the potential treasure that is latent within them [...] They must not waste it in the empire, privileging men of colour. This is an abomination, a monstrosity, that can result in disgrace for the future of the race. Anthropology teaches us that the only reason for the decadence of a population in the past was an indiscriminate fusion of races.

The continued success of Vivanti's novel can be explained precisely on the basis of its irrational, almost metaphysical component. It exploited (and, in turn, contributed to) the fear that the consequences of an occasional contact with a different race could linger for decades, lurking in the secrecy of an individual's genes, before resurfacing when least expected. The epilogue of the novel, in which a defiant Astrid takes her dark-skinned grandchild to the desert, marks the triumph of hybridization.[73] This is not a surprising conclusion from an author who, in her most famous poem, had proclaimed the entire earth to be her country, drawing attention to her rich and multifaceted cultural heritage:

> [...] non ho paese; è mia tutta la terra!
> La patria mia qual è? Mamma è tedesca
> babbo italiano, io nacqui in Inghilterra.
> [...] sono battezzata protestante,
> di nome e di profilo sono ebrea.[74]

> I have no country; the entire earth is mine!
> What is my homeland? My mother is German
> my father Italian, I was born in England.

> [...] I was baptized Protestant,
> by name and by profile I am Jewish.

This poem, entitled 'Ego,' opened Vivanti's first collection of poetry, which was published in 1890. In the late 1930s, however, such a flaunting declaration of multiculturalism could only be considered a threat to a regime that had locked itself into a parochial defence of a supposed racial purity. Despite her popular success, Vivanti became increasingly isolated, an easy target of senseless persecution. After the humiliation of mandatory confinement in Arezzo in 1940, she returned to Torino, where she died soon after, in 1942. Racial laws forbade writers, journalists, and friends from publicly commemorating this 'woman of genius.'[75]

While the works examined thus far portray motherhood as a force capable of correcting an individual's history (Negri) or bringing the past back to life (Vivanti), Paola Drigo's *Maria Zef* (1936) represents motherhood as a form of servitude handed down from mother to daughter. The novel tells a disturbing and tragic story of isolation and abuse, set in the mountainous region of Friuli. Old and frail Catine travels from village to village with her daughters Mariute (or Mariutine, about fourteen years old) and Rosùte (Rosutine, about six). When she dies, the two girls return to their isolated shack with their uncle, Barbe Zef. Mariute's isolation becomes complete after Rosùte is taken to the hospital to be treated for an infection. The atmosphere becomes increasingly oppressive as a particularly harsh winter forces the uncle and his niece to spend entire days trapped within the house, a dark shed with minuscule windows. A sense of claustrophobia and impending tragedy pervades this part of the novel. One night, Barbe Zef gets drunk and rapes Mariute. After repeated attacks, the young woman fears that she is pregnant and remembers a mysterious lady she had visited with her mother years before. She manages with great difficulty to find the woman and discovers her mother's story. Also abused by Barbe Zef, Catine had undergone several abortions, finally succumbing to the venereal disease that Barbe Zef had transmitted to her and that now threatens Mariute herself. Upon her return to the cabin, Mariute realizes that a similar destiny presumably awaits her sister. As Barbe Zef has found a job in the city for Mariute, the little girl will be alone in the shed with the man (who is, presumably, her father). Mariute's love for Rosute gives her the strength to prevent this tragic fate. Like a modern Judith, she serves the uncle liquor until he is drunk and asleep. Then, in the dark, she rises, an axe in her hand.

Drigo provides a ghastly portrayal, and a demystifying critique, of the rural life that Fascism had set as a model for the entire country.[76] Oppression, darkness, and lack of communication (almost no words are exchanged between Barbe Zef and Mariute) dominate a significant portion of the novel. Indeed, human relationships seem to share the qualities of the landscape:

> È raro che la montagna offra un'immagine di serenità: piú spesso i suoi aspetti offrono una visione di violenza e di angoscia, come un pietrificato tormento, il dramma delle forme. Il suo silenzio ha il senso grandioso e disumano della solitudine di cui è figlio; la sua solitudine è così austera e senza moto, che spaura l'anima che l'interroga assai piú della mobile immensità del mare.[77]

> It is rare for the mountains to offer an image of serenity. More often they present a vision of violence and anguish, like a petrified torment, the drama of forms. The silence has the grandiose and inhuman quality of the solitude from which it derives. The solitude is so austere and motionless that it frightens the soul that questions it much more than does the ever-moving immensity of the ocean.[78]

The few 'images of serenity' offered to Mariute derive from a brief idyll with Pieri, a kind young man who is about to emigrate. More important, and decisive in a way that readers can appreciate only at the end of the story, is Mariute's encounter with her dead mother:

> Ed ora, ecco, senza chiamarla, la madre le veniva incontro: ella, come le era rimasta nella memoria inconsapevolmente dai giorni dell'infanzia: svelta e diritta, coi lucidi capelli neri, portando Rosúte piccina tra le braccia. Avanzava tra gli sterpi in silenzio, e la guardava. Brucavano le pecore la corta erba intorno ... Poi piú tardi ... quando? ... forse c'è un distacco di anni tra l'una e l'altra immagine, *ella* è seduta laggiú su quel tronco appena abbattuto che domani sarà scagliato al torrente: già coi capelli meno neri, già curva e triste ... Ha posato per terra la sporta col desinare di Barbe Zef che scenderà dal bosco a mezzodì. Attende. Poi ancora ... La mâri degli ultimi tempi, terrea, col fazzoletto legato sotto il mento come una vecchia ... Scende dalla montagna, attraversa la ceppaia colla gerla carica sulle spalle, si avvia lenta verso casa ... Come si trascinano stanchi i suoi poveri piedi; gonfi, sformati ... Un colpo di tosse ...[79]

> And now, behold, without having called her up, her mother was coming to meet her: *she*, as she had remained in memory unconsciously from the days of childhood: lithe and erect, with shining dark hair, carrying baby Rosùte in her arms. She was coming forward among the stumps in silence, and she was looking at Mariutine. The sheep were grazing on the short grass all around ... Then later ... when? ... Maybe there was a gap of years between the one and the other vision. *She* is seated over there on that trunk just recently felled that tomorrow will be given up to the rushing stream: already with her hair not so dark, already bent and sad ... She has placed on the ground the bag with the lunch for Barbe Zef, who will come down from the woods at midday. She is waiting. Then still more ... The *mâri* of the last days, pale and drawn, with the kerchief tied under her chin like an old woman ... She comes down from the mountain, crossing through the stand of stumps with the heavy bag on her shoulders, she goes slowly towards home ... as though she were dragging her poor tired feet, swollen and deformed ... A paroxysm of coughing ...[80]

Towards the end of the novel, it becomes clear that, apart from condensing Catine's life, these snapshots serve as a prefiguration of Mariute's own destiny. The 'tall and well built' girl met at the beginning of the novel has undergone dramatic changes: she already feels the first symptoms of the disease that had killed her mother and knows that she could soon be carrying Barbe Zef's child in her arms, ultimately succumbing to poverty and sickness like her mother. Rosùte would suffer the same fate.

The acknowledgment of the similarities between the lives of mother and daughter had marked the awakening of the introspective protagonist of Sibilla Aleramo's *Una donna*. In a crucial chapter of the 1906 novel, the woman discovers a diary entry in which her mother had expressed the intention to leave her husband, children, and loveless destiny. She had obviously lacked the courage to carry out her resolution and had slowly slipped into unhappiness, attempting to kill herself and ultimately losing all reason. The awareness of having followed in her mother's footsteps, together with the knowledge of what the future would be like if she continued to do so, gave the protagonist the courage to choose another path. In a similar fashion, Mariute, when she can finally interpret her mother's destiny as her own, decides to break the chain of humiliation and sorrow that is about to extend to her younger sister. Her decision does not imply a rejection of the mother as an individual. On the contrary, it is precisely through the acknowledgment of their similarities that the daughters understand their mothers' secret struggles and painful realizations. As in Aleramo's novel, changing the course of one's own destiny becomes a way to rewrite the mother's story with a different ending.

Such a departure from the familiar plots of obedience and resignation prepares the terrain for future, alternative developments. In this lies, however, a sharp difference between Aleramo's and Drigo's novels. While the educated and articulate protagonist of *Una donna* concludes her story with a hopeful glance at the future, Mariute's path ends with her rebellion, as she raises her arm in the darkness and delivers a fatal blow. 'Not a cry – only a gush of blood.'[81]

No Turning Back

By 1936, when Alba De Céspedes published her remarkable *Nessuno torna indietro* (*There Is No Turning Back*), the regime was beginning to acknowledge its defeat. Not only was the demographic goal far from being achieved, but the birth rate had in fact been steadily declining since Mussolini's rise to power: from 28.9 (for one thousand inhabitants) per year at the beginning of the 1920s, it had dropped to 25.1 a decade later, and even further, to 23.1, in the years 1935–7.[82] The decline was so pronounced, especially among working-class and rural families, as to lead modern historians such as Luisa Passerini and Chiara Saraceno to speak respectively of 'resistenza demografica' ('demographic resistance') and 'sciopero demografico' ('demographic strike').[83] Fascist critics also read this tendency as a form of opposition to the regime, to be deplored and erased as such. Feminism was accused once again of fostering selfish and individualistic ideals, whereas working women were blamed for their alleged weak maternal instinct.[84] In 1938, a survey of a thousand Roman women aged 16–18 revealed that only 10 per cent of them were interested in domestic chores, and very few in the traditional female occupation of knitting. All preferred spending time with people their own age (and some even with boys), rather than with children; they loved novels, dancing, and sports; they were inclined to giving orders, rather than obeying. Finally, 'Sono pochissime quelle che hanno dichiarato di desiderare molti figli, la famiglia numerosa essendo fonte di eccessive preoccupazioni, di incredibili fatiche: quindi un figlio o al massimo due'[85] (Very few expressed a desire to have many children, as a big family is the source of excessive worries and incredible fatigue; therefore [they all want] one child, or two at most).

De Céspedes must have struck a chord when, summoned by the authorities for the lack of Fascist ethos displayed by her characters, she declared that they resembled real women of her time.[86] The incredible success of her work attests to the public's desire for such a frank portrayal of contemporary women's attitudes and behaviour. At a time when most novels did not sell more than 2,000 copies, De Céspedes's novel sold 150,000 in five years, becoming one of the best-sellers of the *ventennio*.[87] Furthermore, the popularity of *Nessuno torna indietro* soon spread beyond Italy, as it was translated into several languages. Following their traditional mistrust of popular success, however, Italian literary critics have for decades neglected the novel,[88] in spite of its being one of the most engaging works of the Fascist years. One of the undeniable reasons for the interest in *Nessuno torna indietro* lies in its portrayal of a female community whose relationship with the opposite sex is rather restricted. This limitation turns out to be an unexpected privilege, as is stressed by one of the characters:

> Però è bello discorrere così, tra noi, tutte donne ... Se ci fosse un uomo, non oseremmo essere sincere, io non saprei esserlo nemmeno con mio padre; anzi, con lui meno che con altri. Le donne sono sincere soltanto tra loro. Non è vero? Quando papà esce di casa, la mamma e io usiamo un'altra voce ... Chissà perché, ma c'è sempre una certa ostilità verso l'uomo.[89]

> It is nice to be able to talk this way, among us women ... If a man were here, we would not dare be sincere. I could not be sincere even with my father; actually, with him less than with the others. Women are sincere only when they are among themselves. Isn't this true? When Father goes out, my mother and I use a different voice ... I do not know why, but there is always a certain hostility towards men.

Another reason for the novel's popularity is its poetic focus on the transition between adolescence and adulthood. For the young protagonists, life is, for a few months still, full of possibilities (a situation symbolized in the novel through the recurring metaphor of the bridge). A crucial turn will soon cause each of the women to lose sight of the others, making return impossible.

The Istituto Grimaldi, where the young women live, is a boarding house in the centre of Rome run by Catholic nuns. It provides suitable accommodation for female students pursuing a degree at the university. Education, however, is from the outset little more than a pretence for

Emanuela, who has come to Rome to be able to see her daughter Stefania once a week. Similarly, studying also loses its appeal for most of the other characters by the end of the novel. De Céspedes seems to be interested in portraying a variety of ways of being a woman and may be forgiven if her characters, locked into a single definition, may occasionally appear unidimensional (the dropout, the intellectual, the writer, etc.). What is remarkable, however, is how far they all are from the Fascist model of woman as mother. De Céspedes's criticism of the dominant ideology becomes particularly incisive in her portrayal of Emanuela. Through this character, the author sheds light on the contradictions inherent in the contemporary notion of motherhood, as well as on its consequences for young women.

When the action of the novel begins, Emanuela is already a single mother. Her fiancé, a pilot, died in a plane crash before she even found out she was pregnant. Even more than her marital status, however, De Céspedes's subtle analysis of Emanuela's psychology portrays the character as a total stranger in the culture of motherhood promoted by Fascism. In Emanuela, De Céspedes investigates with surprising candour the feelings of a young woman trapped in a situation she did not choose and was not prepared to face. Emanuela had decided to move from Florence to Rome in order to be able to see her five-year-old-daughter once a week, at the religious institution where the little girl lives. This decision, however, sharply contrasts with Emanuela's personality, her chameleonlike character:

> In Emanuela agiva una facoltà intuitiva rapida e sempre vigile: quella di rivelare e di illuminare di sé chi l'avvicinava, soltanto l'aspetto capace di suscitare una concordanza di simpatia. Così ognuno vedeva riflessa in lei la propria immagine come in uno specchio; e, sebbene lo specchio era di molte facce, scopriva soltanto quella che si animava di lui. E questo gioco di riflessi era una continua rivelazione anche per Emanuela che vedeva sorgere dal profondo di sé, e apparire alla superficie, sempre nuovi e fino allora ignorati aspetti della sua personalità.[90]

Emanuela possessed a fast and alert intuitive ability, that of revealing and highlighting only the aspect of her personality capable of eliciting the affection of those who approached her. Everybody saw their own faces reflected in Emanuela as if in a mirror; although the mirror had many faces, they discovered only the one activated by them. This game of reflections was a constant revelation even for Emanuela, who would see new and hitherto ignored aspects of her personality rise from the depth of herself and appear on the surface.

This characteristic also manifests itself as a peculiar ability to adapt to different phases of life. While other students at the Grimaldi mourn the imminent end of their communal life, Emanuela welcomes change with optimism and relief: 'A me la vita pare composta di tante brevi vite successive. In ognuna ricominciamo; e possiamo mostrarci ed essere completamente nuovi. Altrimenti finiremmo col venirci a noia, non vi sembra?'[91] (Life seems to me to be made up of many brief consecutive lives. In each of them we start all over again and can manifest ourselves and be completely new. Otherwise we would get bored with ourselves, don't you think?). The existence of her daughter is a significant obstacle toward the expression of her personality, as Stefania represents an event from the past that has unnaturally transgressed its boundaries to rule over Emanuela's present and threaten her future.

The idea of the individual as an unstable combination of different selves manifested on both a synchronic and a diachronic level had been powerfully elaborated by Pirandello. The playwright had shown an acute awareness of the tragedy that can occur when a random event in a man's life assumes an unintended defining importance and is taken to represent his essence and true self. Pirandello expressed this concept through the metaphor of the hook, which keeps an individual anchored to a point in the past, even though his personality has evolved in such a way as to make that event secondary or even irrelevant.[92] De Céspedes, however, applies Pirandello's observation to an event that was (and perhaps still is) considered of capital and defining importance in a woman's life – that of motherhood. Through memories and flashbacks, her character's past is pieced together. The reader thus learns that, despite her attachment to Stefano, pregnancy has made her desperate and resentful, as if a child would forever link her to her lover's death, more than to his life.

> No, era impossibile, Stefano era morto, non poteva tenerla legata a sé. Non doveva aver séguito la loro storia, altrimenti egli non se ne sarebbe andato, lasciandola così [...] Le repugnava l'idea di portare dentro di sé una creatura che accaparrava il suo sangue, che cresceva in lei a suo dispetto, padrona della sua vita già prima di nascere [...][93]
>
> No, it was impossible. Stefano was dead. He couldn't keep her attached to

him. Their story must not continue; otherwise he would not have left, leaving her like that [...] She was repelled by the idea of carrying inside her a creature who was taking her blood, growing in her in spite of her, already master of her life even before birth.

Emanuela has made remarkable sacrifices for her daughter: she refused to sever all ties with her or to give her up for adoption, as her family would have liked. In spite of or perhaps precisely for these reasons, she harbours a peculiar resentment towards Stefania, who connects her forever to a past she perceives as very distant – all the more so because she is soon to be married to Andrea, a young man who is unaware of the girl's very existence. This hidden ambivalence comes to the foreground when scarlet fever threatens Stefania's life and Emanuela is faced with a difficult choice: if she yields to her daughter's request and spends the night at her bedside, she will be expelled from the Grimaldi; if she goes back to the boarding house, she will leave Stefania alone on what could be the last night of her life. Unable to reconcile her different identities, Emanuela leaves Stefania to the care of the nuns, feeling guilty and ashamed. As soon as she steps out of the institute, however, her chameleonlike personality takes over again, and she becomes what she seems to any passer-by: a carefree young woman. It becomes clear that her ability to adjust to different situations is a strategy for survival in a world that does not allow her to develop her personality in all of its aspects. Taken by her new role, Emanuela contemplates with detachment – and even with relief – the possibility of Stefania's death:

> Se moriva, niente piú discorso ad Andrea. Avrebbe seguito il funerale, sola, con un velo in viso, e con l'ombra di quel padre ignoto che costruiva aeroplani [...] Tutto a posto, tutto regolare, come se Stefania non fosse mai nata. Del resto chi conosceva l'esistenza della bambina? Nessuno. Lei avrebbe potuto tornare indietro negli anni, leggera, leggera, in volo, fino al giorno in cui aveva incontrato Stefano sul Lungarno. Tutto era dipeso da pochi attimi: bastava che ella non avesse proseguito oltre il Ponte Vecchio, invogliata dalla stagione [...] 'Muore, è certo. E mi libera.'[94]

If Stefania died, there would be no need to tell Andrea about her. Emanuela, with a veil on her face, would attend the funeral alone, with the ghost of that unknown father who built airplanes. Everything would be fine, everything would be normal, as if Stefania had never been born. Who knew of her existence, anyway? Nobody. She would be able to go back in time, light, so light, as if flying, until the day when she had met Stefano on the Lungarno. Everything had depended on a few seconds. It would have been enough if she had not passed the Ponte Vecchio, drawn there by the season [...] 'She is dying, it is certain. And she will set me free').

This is a turning point. After a night riddled with guilt and nightmares, Emanuela runs to the institute to find that Stefania has survived and is on her way to recovery. She finds the strength to reveal the truth to her fiancé, Andrea, who then abandons her. Her friends at the Grimaldi are also dismayed to learn that she has concealed her daughter's existence from them for so long. After acknowledging her identity as a mother, however, Emanuela does not resort to the protection of the ONMI, the Fascist organization that could perhaps take care of her and her child. Escaping the stifling atmosphere of the Istituto Grimaldi, Emanuela takes on the challenge of inventing for herself a new notion of motherhood, one very much alien to the model promoted by the regime. The novel's lively final scene shows her and her daughter boarding a ship for a five-month cruise around the world. The ending is thus a new beginning, a liberation from the norms that imprisoned Emanuela and forced her to lead a divided existence. This open ending, this hopeful glance at the future, must have been particularly irritating to the authorities. The cinematographic adaptation would in fact replace it with a conventional happy ending, in which Andrea forgives Emanuela and the two 'presumably live happily ever after.'[95]

While it is not surprising that Fascist authorities would find the novel highly objectionable, its remarkable success suggests public appreciation for such a frank depiction of the female experience. Fascism had engaged in an anachronistic struggle to reduce women to their reproductive function. And yet modernity had infiltrated the country through movies, novels, and practices of everyday life. Fascism's own call for women's participation in public life through associations and rallies, although aimed at structuring and controlling their energy, had contributed to their interaction with the world outside their homes.[96] The introduction of female physical education in public schools had unintended consequences in terms of women's freedom and attitude towards their bodies – as stressed by the Catholic church's stern opposition to the new discipline.[97] While blaming young women for refusing a self-effacing role and for cherishing material goods such as the automobile, society preyed on and contributed to such attitudes. Indeed, even

Critica fascista in 1933–4 featured on its very cover automobile advertisements for cars aimed specifically at women. One of them portrays a young woman driving at full speed, her hair blowing in the wind. With a hand on the steering wheel, she waves an Italian flag with the other. The caption is a pun on the name of the car, Ardita, which means 'daring' and can therefore be interpreted as referring not only to the vehicle but also, and more appropriately, to the young woman behind the wheel: 'Ardita. Esce e conquista' (Ardita. Goes out and conquers). It is hard to imagine a more incongruous slogan for a Fascist woman.[98] Another advertisement features an elegantly dressed woman (miles away from the shabby prolific model proposed by the regime), seen from the back while she walks swiftly towards the driver's seat. The caption admiringly comments: 'Eleganza della signora!'[99] (A lady's elegance!). The women in these ads are powerful, at the wheel, and in control of their destiny. Times were indeed changing, and the self-effacing mother of six (or ten or fourteen) was rapidly fading from sight, on her way to becoming the exception, rather than the rule. For Italian mothers, as for the women at the Grimaldi boarding house, there would be no turning back.

chapter 3

Questioning Motherhood

Slow Changes

Among the various interpretations of Italian Fascism, two have enjoyed particular attention and popularity. The first, championed by Benedetto Croce, considered the dictatorship an accident, a moral disease that struck an otherwise healthy civil body. The second, proposed by Dennis Mack Smith, interpreted Fascism as the logical result of the development of post-unification Italian politics and society, the consequence of a historical process marked by inequalities and contradictions.[1] It is Mack Smith's theory, more than Croce's, that proves pertinent when applied to the history of Italian women. As Fascism carried notions of femininity and motherhood that largely pre-dated the dictatorship to their extreme conclusions, so did its fall have only a few immediate consequences for women's lives. The most significant change concerned electoral rights, which were finally achieved in the aftermath of the Second World War.[2] As Ginevra Conti Odorisio notes, however, this major accomplishment arrived at a time when the generation that had fought for it had already disappeared, while the one that reaped the benefits of the struggle was not in the best position to assess and profit from this extraordinary achievement. The nation that emerged from the catastrophe of the war was understandably eager to recover normalcy, heeding a *rappel à l'ordre* that in a patriarchal society could only be understood as a reaffirmation of traditional gender roles.[3]

It is symbolically significant that women partisans were prohibited from marching with men in the wake of the liberation, thus downplaying their contribution to the struggle for freedom and their entitlement to the rewards of victory.[4] The portrayal of the partisans in Italo

Calvino's 1947 novel *Il sentiero dei nidi di ragno* (*The Path to the Spiders' Nests*) is revealing in this context: male characters, despite their shortcomings, are fighting to 'costruire un'umanità senza piú rabbia, serena, in cui si possa non essere cattivi' (create a world that is serene, without resentment, a world in which no one has to be bad),[5] whereas Giglia, the only female presence in the detachment, causes havoc and distraction. The only other woman mentioned in the novel, Rina, betrays the group and causes the death of several partisans.

Another neo-realist masterpiece, Roberto Rossellini's film *Roma città aperta* (*Rome Open City*, 1945), displays a similar attitude. Rossellini chose to minimize the Fascists' role in the violence that shook Rome in the years 1943–4. As in Calvino's novel, collaborationism and betrayal are displaced onto the character of a woman, Marina, whose love for luxury and drug addiction (rather than political convictions) lead her to side with the invaders. Although for many years the status of *Roma città aperta* as the founding expression of neo-realism and the power of its haunting sequences (first and foremost, that of a pregnant woman, Pina, running to her death, in Anna Magnani's unforgettable performance) have prevented an in-depth discussion of its ideological ambiguity, recent criticism suggests that the time is finally ripe for a more balanced assessment.[6]

Even a character portrayed in far more sympathetic terms, such as Agnese in Renata Viganò's novel *L'Agnese va a morire* (*Agnese Goes to Die*, 1949), indirectly confirms the persistence of gender stereotypes. Her dignity and strength derive primarily from her self-effacing role as 'mamma Agnese,' who attends to the partisans and manages to recreate domestic warmth and routine under the most dire of circumstances.[7]

The ostracizing of female partisans, the firing of women from jobs they had held during the war, and the sharp increase in marriage and birth rates are clear signs of a society eager to return to normalcy after the social upheaval caused by the war.[8] These trends in post-war society help to explain why, electoral rights notwithstanding, little had changed for Italian women. Fascism had institutionalized many widespread attitudes and deeply rooted beliefs that managed to outlast the regime. The highly discriminatory laws introduced during the *ventennio* were abrogated slowly, one by one, sometimes only through bitter parliamentary battles. Only in 1963 were women admitted into all professions and granted equal pay, and it was not until 1971 that the ban on information on birth control (which dated back to 1926) was lifted.[9] The introduction of the new family code in 1975 was a milestone, because it assured greater equality between the sexes in marriage and in regard to children. It was not until 1981, however, that the laws concerning the 'delitto d'onore' (which considered murder a legitimate response to adultery) and the 'matrimonio riparatore' (which granted impunity to rapists who married their victims) were repealed. Finally, in 1996, ending a debate that had lasted seventeen years, the parliament managed to overcome its divisions and passed a law that changed the status of sexual violence. Formerly a crime against a generic 'morality,' which as such received rather lenient sanctions, rape came to be considered a crime against a person (i.e., a violent crime). 'Tarde non furon mai gratie divine' (divine favours are never late), as Machiavelli would have said.

Post-war Italy was also marked by a revamping of the cult of the Virgin Mary, in line with Pope Pius XII's emphasis on the 'Christian mother' as the 'true strength and pride of Italy.' The Catholic Church found a new ally in matters of family and morality in the Christian Democrats and called women to the forefront of the new battle against Communism, which they accused of undermining the integrity of the family unit.[10]

Indeed, literary works of the period from the end of the war to the social upheaval of the 1970s seem anchored to traditional notions of femininity and motherhood and hardly foresee the radical *remise en jeu* of the feminist movement. Nowhere is this more apparent than in Giuseppe Marotta's collection *Le madri* (*The Mothers*, 1952). The first two chapters juxtapose women, who had allegedly survived the war with minimal adjustments in their attitude and mentality, and mothers, who had experienced the life-changing event of motherhood.[11] Mothers belong, Marotta maintains, to a third sex, and their relationship to women is comparable to that of a butterfly to a caterpillar.[12] Following these introductory chapters, a collection of short stories depicts in all seriousness and with apparent admiration various forms of maternal devotion that border on the criminal (the mother who condemns a perfect stranger to death, rather than exposing her son to danger) and the grotesque (the mother who reverently polishes and kisses her son's shoes). Almost exclusively mothers of boys, and devoid of any feelings or instincts apart from those that tie them to their sons, the women in Marotta's book mirror the Catholic maternal icon to such a degree that, in the epilogue of one of the stories, the Virgin Mary appears in all her splendour: she comforts and shares the pain of a mother accused of having exaggerated her son's virtues.[13] Two years later, 'Tutte le mamme' ('All the Moms'), a catchy tune written by Gino Latilla and Giorgio Consolini, won the ever-popular song contest Festival of Sanremo.[14]

To find a wider range of mothers' attitudes towards their role and their children, one must turn to Natalia Ginzburg. Her characters, however, are often strangers to themselves, lost in the myriad of daily tasks that compose and consume their lives. The 'motivi imperscrutabili' (inscrutable motives) that cause a relationship to deteriorate in *Le voci della sera*[15] (*Voices of the Evening*, 1961) are no more mysterious than those that cause other characters to react in various, sometimes opposing, and always unpredictable ways to the challenges of life, including motherhood. The consequences of an unwanted pregnancy are described without comment by the protagonist of *La strada che va in città* (*The Road to the City*, 1942), who is forced to spend her days in a nearby village for fear that her neighbours might discover her condition.[16] Later, she shows little or no affection for her baby. Similarly, the protagonist of the short story 'La madre' ('The Mother,' 1948) displays utter indifference towards her children as she follows the tragic destiny that ultimately leads to her suicide. At the opposite end of the spectrum, we find the protagonist of *È stato così* (*This Is How It Happened*, 1947), whose life revolves around her little girl, to the point that her death results in the mother's loss of purpose, and perhaps in her madness.[17]

A deeper analysis of the implications of motherhood is conducted by Fausta Cialente in *Un inverno freddissimo* (*A Very Cold Winter*, 1966) through the character of Camilla, who struggles to balance her individuality, her 'insopprimibile senso del vivere'[18] (irrepressible feeling of living), and her responsibilities not only towards her own children, but also towards her sister's. What distinguishes Camilla from the other characters is the lucidity with which she analyses her condition in its specific cultural context, and reconciles its different components:

> In un paese disgraziato come l'Italia, a una donna della sua età e condizione altro non restava che il rischio dell'avventura [...] Le bruciava inoltre il senso d'incoerenza che realmente esisteva tra l'essere una donna desiderabile [...], e la sorte che le era toccata e continuava a pesare su di lei: tutte le responsabilità che doveva sobbarcarsi, da anni.[19]

> In a disgraceful country like Italy, the only escape left to a woman of her age and condition was a risky adventure [...] She was also struck by the real contradiction between her being a desirable woman [...] and the destiny that had been assigned to and still burdened her, all the responsibilities she had been forced to take upon herself, for years.

The struggle between the identities of woman and mother that marks the protagonists of so many novels is peacefully resolved by Camilla through a frank assessment of her needs, coupled with the awareness of the unreasonable burden society places on mothers. Her quiet rebellion is acknowledged, in the epilogue, through the perspective of Enzo, a character who had already appeared in the author's previous novel, *Ballata levantina* (*Levantine Ballad*, 1961): 'Camilla aveva detto cose amare e giuste per tutti quanti, anche per lui, e adesso gli piaceva di poterla immaginare, così diritta e giovane, in piedi in mezzo a un prato che verdeggiava a sorvegliare gli alberi in fiore, un poco rasserenata, finalmente – e nemmeno sola, forse'[20] (Camilla had said bitter and fair things about all of them, even about him. He enjoyed imagining her, upright and young, standing in the middle of a green meadow as she watched the trees in bloom, a little more serene, finally, and perhaps not alone).

Cialente's Camilla is arguably one of the most powerful female characters in the entire history of Italian literature. On the whole, though, the period between the end of the war and the rise of feminism was rather static, as the country tried to rebuild itself and sought strength and inspiration in traditional values. This is also the time in which a prodigious talent manifested itself. In the aftermath of the Second World War, Elsa Morante wrote the first of the four novels that would establish her as one of the greatest twentieth-century authors and a sublime interpreter of a mythical, primeval, and all-encompassing notion of motherhood.

The Tigress in the Snow

Elsa Morante's works are marked by a stringent fidelity to their own internal logic rather than to the influences of the environment in which they were written and published. In 1947, when the literary scene was dominated by neo-realism and Italian society was recovering from the shock of the dictatorship and the war, she published *Menzogna e sortilegio* (*House of Liars*), a monumental novel in which a woman tries to untangle the web of lies and illusions spun by three generations of her family. Hailed by Georg Lukacs as the 'greatest modern Italian novel,'[21] *Menzogna e sortilegio* seems nevertheless removed from the concerns of its time. Morante's own novel about the Second World War did not appear until 1974, in a completely different social and historical context, eliciting a chorus of passionate (and often negative) reactions. Interspersed between these two works, the lyrical and luminous *L'isola di Arturo* (*Arthur's Island*, 1957) and the bitter and disenchanted *Aracoeli* (1982) complete a cycle revolving around the themes of dream and deception, growth and disillusionment, in which the figure of the mother plays a pivotal role.

It is difficult to find an image of maternal abnegation comparable to that of Iduzza Ramundo in *La Storia: Romanzo*. In 1944, during the last months of the German occupation, Rome resembled, Morante writes, one of those impoverished Indian cities in which only the vultures have enough to feed themselves. Ida Ramundo, the female protagonist, engages in a desperate struggle to keep her son Useppe alive. The narrator comments:

> A lei stessa niente faceva gola, perfino la secrezione della saliva le si era prosciugata: tutti i suoi stimoli vitali si erano trasferiti su Useppe. Si racconta di una tigre che, in una solitudine gelata, si sostenne assieme ai propri nati leccando, per parte sua, la neve; e distribuendo ai piccoli dei brandelli di carne che lei stessa si strappava dal proprio corpo coi denti.[22]

> She did not crave anything for herself. Even her saliva had dried up. All her vital instincts had been transferred to Useppe. It is said that a tigress, in a frozen solitude, survived with her cubs by licking the snow to sustain herself; and she administered to her little ones pieces of flesh that she tore from her body with her teeth.

Sacrifice goes hand in hand with the protagonist's rise to an almost supernatural status. Animal metaphors had already been introduced to describe Ida, but their goal was merely to convey the character's humble and instinctive nature. Her eyes were said to have 'l'idiozia misteriosa degli animali' (the mysterious dumbness of animals), and her seizures were announced by a 'lamento di bestiola'[23] (the lament of a little animal). This time, however, the comparison elevates her to a majestic status: maternal love turns Ida into a tigress, self-regenerating in her sacrifice. The metaphor used to convey Ida's total devotion to Useppe also has strong religious undertones. Christian iconography has long seen the pelican, erroneously believed to feed its young with its own flesh and blood, as a symbol of Christ, who gives his body to redeem humanity. The image Morante adopts is therefore an important example of the religious symbolism that pervades the novel. Grace Zlobnicki Kalay, in her study *The Theme of Childhood in Elsa Morante*, points out the many similarities between the story of Ida and Useppe and that of Mary and Jesus: for instance, Ida's dream, in which she goes from one hospital to another and is systematically rejected.[24] In the image of the tigress in the snow, however, Iduzza seems to take on the attributes of Christ in addition to those of Mary. It is the mother and child – or, to be more precise, the mother and son[25] – couple that is central to Morante's narration. Indeed, the couple are so closely united that the attributes of the two members are conflated – Ida is not only Mary, but also Christ in one of his most powerful manifestations: Christ the Tiger.[26]

Of all the characters in Morante's works, Ida Ramundo is the one that comes closest to the definition of mothers given by the author in a 1984 interview: 'Adoro le madri, le vere madri [...] Ho un grande amore per la donna semplice. Non amo molto le femministe perché ritengo che la donna sia una creatura necessaria all'umanità, agli uomini'[27] (I adore mothers, real mothers [...] I feel great love for simple women. I don't love feminists because I believe women are necessary creatures to the human race, to men). Morante's love for 'real mothers' is proclaimed together with her aversion to the women's movement. In her concise remark, the author shows a deep understanding (and disapproval) of a fundamental premise of feminism: the notion that women, as individuals, have intrinsic dignity and value, apart from any function that they may or may not perform for society, and apart from their relationship to men.[28] It is this principle that Morante opposes when she claims that women are necessary 'to the human race, to men.' Ida Ramundo represents the most coherent expression of the ideal woman, inseparable as she is from her maternal function, to the point that her life loses all meaning when Useppe dies.

Yet, for all her power as a symbol not only of Mary but also of Christ, Ida does not manage to redeem the world or even simply to save Useppe. In spite of Morante's strong Catholic beliefs, God seems to have withdrawn completely from the world depicted in *La Storia*. It is certainly revealing that the first title chosen for the novel was *Senza i conforti della religione* (*Without the Solace of Religion*).[29] In this novel, all attempts to influence the course of history and to leave a positive mark on the world are futile. This constitutes a significant departure from the work of the greatest nineteenth-century Italian novelist, Alessandro Manzoni, whose 1827 *Promessi sposi* (*The Betrothed*) constitutes an obvious precedent for Morante's novel. Just as Manzoni had decided to describe the plight of 'genti meccaniche, e di piccol affare'[30] (working people of humble condition), Morante chose as her protagonists the outcasts, those who suffer the consequences of history, rather than those who decide its course. This ideological and moral stance is confirmed by the epigraphs that open *La Storia*: the biblical passage that refers to God's predilection for 'the little ones' ('Thou hast hidden these things from the wise and prudent, and hast revealed them to little ones,' Luke 10:21) and César Vallejo's noble paradox ('Por el analfabeto a quien escribo' [For the illiterate to whom I write]). The outlook and conclusions of Morante's novel, however, could not be more different from those of Manzoni's masterpiece. While Lucia, the female protagonist of the *Promessi sposi*, ends the novel by affirming her faith in a providential order, Morante's epic concludes on the same desperate note on which it began, underscoring the absence of redemption.

On an ideological level, a much more cogent parallel can be drawn not with Manzoni's novel but with a tragedy he wrote before his conversion to Catholicism. In *Adelchi*, the eponymous protagonist, on the verge of death, gives epigrammatic form to the same negativity ('loco a gentile, / ad innocente opra non v'è' [there is no room for kind, innocent deeds]), the same absence of a middle ground ('non resta che far torto, o patirlo' [we can only do wrong, or suffer it]), the same negation of the possibility of any constructive action in the world that is at the core of Morante's novel.[31]

But why is the world so hopeless; why is redemption impossible? The answer may lie in the importance given to mothers or, to be more precise, to the relevance assumed by the mother conceived as a figure indispensable 'to the human race, to men,' to use Morante's terms. In Morante's works, mothers are trapped in an irrational and instinctive role, as is indicated by the frequent animal metaphors used to describe them. Theirs is the world of animals and children.[32] They are trapped in a universe that is essentially prehistoric, and their influence stops with adulthood, when history begins. Logically, the legitimate inhabitants of the world should be men, but when we look for them in Morante's pages, we are bound to be disappointed. In particular, there is a striking shortage of fathers.[33] It would be easy to list the flaws of the fathers in Morante's works: from Nicola Monaco in *Menzogna e sortilegio* to Wilhem Gerace in *L'isola di Arturo* and Gunther in *La Storia*, Morante's fathers are absent, inadequate, indifferent, and irresponsible. The result of these shortcomings is nothing less than the impossibility of redemption in history.

A comparison with a very different text, Anna Maria Ortese's visionary novel *L'iguana* (1963), can prove fruitful in this context. The protagonist of the novel – or, at least, its nonreptilian protagonist – is Daddo, a Milanese count who sacrifices himself so that the iguana can gain (or regain) human form. His is a conscious decision preceded by the discovery that 'di sposi ve ne sono fin troppi, sulla terra, e di padri, per quanto ne so, nessuno'[34] (there are far too many husbands on earth, and no fathers, as far as I know). Daddo accepts (or perhaps creates for himself) the responsibility of being a father to the iguana, dies in an attempt to save her, and by doing so confers humanity upon her. Morante never shows us a character who becomes a father in such a full and redeeming sense, but her last novel can be read as the acknowledgment of a narrative impasse and the promise of future developments that her untimely death would make impossible.

According to this interpretation, each of Elsa Morante's major narrative works brought her closer to a crisis that she finally reached in *Aracoeli*. In this last novel, the search for the mother is revealed to be an inadequate solution. The protagonist is forty-three-year-old Manuele, who travels from Milan to El Almendral, the small Spanish village where his mother was born. His itinerary symbolizes a journey in time: what Manuele hopes to find at the end of the road is his mother, Aracoeli, the young woman who was the companion of the first, wonderful, mythical years of his life. Manuele is not the only character in Morante's works who enjoys such a blissful condition as a kid. The protagonist of *L'isola di Arturo* also lived an enchanted childhood before taking a metaphorical, as well as literal, boat to adulthood. In her last novel, Morante tried to reverse that passage. Instead of moving forward, Manuele goes backward, to a land that he knew only through his mother's allusions and to a forgotten language, the Spanish he used to speak in his conversations with Aracoeli but later erased from his memory. But it is as if, by taking this trip, Manuele has broken an unwritten taboo, perhaps the one to which the epigram of *L'isola di Arturo* alludes: 'Fuori del limbo non v'è Eliso' (Outside of limbo there's no Elysium). Every attempt to recover as an adult the enchanted world of childhood is destined to be futile or even dangerous. El Almendral, Aracoeli's village, though remote and difficult to reach, is far from uncontaminated: Manuele's last stop is a tavern, where a portrait of Francisco Franco hangs on the wall and a pile of pornographic magazines sits on a chair, in a synthetic depiction of history and adulthood as obscene profanations that is central to *La Storia*, the author's previous novel. At the same time, the resurfacing of Manuele's childhood memories only leads him to reconstruct the steps of Aracoeli's fall, of her grotesque metamorphosis from an inviolably chaste deity to an insatiably lustful witch, in a metaphysical shift that Manuele, the homodiegetic narrator, tries to attribute to an illness. As Cesare Garboli notes, in *Aracoeli* the 'glorious mother/son pattern' that had inspired the previous novels comes undone and is disintegrated and reduced to parody.'[35] Garboli's observation is particularly insightful in that it stresses how the debased Aracoeli presented at the end of the novel is the opposite not only of the one introduced at the beginning but also of the other mothers in Morante's work. This process of profanation finds its culmination in the conclusion of *Aracoeli*, when the adult protagonist reconstructs the final afternoon that he had spent with his mother as a six-year-old boy. They had gone to church, as they often did. This time, however, Aracoeli had not asked God for forgiveness and support. Rather, she behaved as if she wanted to challenge His authority. Sitting in the first row with her son, she did not kneel or participate in the service. The frightened boy heard distorted and meaningless refrains instead of the liturgy (such as 'ragno di Dio' instead of 'agnus Dei' ['spider of God' instead of 'lamb of God']), in an inversion typical of satanic rituals.

After Aracoeli's death, Manuele moved to Turin with his grandparents and could not visit Rome again until he was thirteen. His father, Eugenio, who had throughout the novel been depicted as desperately in love with Aracoeli and blind to her shortcomings, had moved to San Lorenzo, a working-class Roman neighbourhood near the cemetery, in order to be as close to her as possible. The final encounter between father and son concludes the novel and alludes to a possible solution. Manuele's childhood had been marked by total communion with his mother and by his father's distance. Eugenio had represented in his eyes the incarnation of two ideals, PATERNITY and VIRILITY, both written in all capital letters in the novel, from which he had felt hopelessly excluded. In his last visit, Manuele finds his father dirty, drunk, and alone in an airless apartment. After abandoning his position as a military officer, Eugenio is reduced to complete destitution. Father and son manage to exchange only a few awkward words. And yet the forty-three-year-old Manuele visiting El Almendral, looking back at himself as a thirteen-year-old boy crying in the streets of Rome after that meeting, finally understands, or at least interprets, those tears to have been shed because of love:

> Amore di chi? Di Aracoeli, lasciata indietro sola a decomporsi nell'orrido parco? No – impossibile. Per me, in quella stagione, Aracoeli era negazione – ripudio – vendetta – oblio. Niente amore di lei. NO. Di lei no. Amore di un altro, invece. E di chi?
> Di Eugenio Ottone Amedeo.

> Mai finora nel corso del tempo avevo amato costui. Ma durante la mia visita su all'interno 15 oggi, mentre mi rivoltavo di schifo alla sua presenza, io forse ne ero preso disperatamente d'amore. E se al salutarmi sulla soglia, invece di porgermi quella sua mano schifosa fredda e sudata, con quella stessa mano lui mi avesse carezzato la testa (una di quelle carezze istituzionali, da me sempre accolte in passato con una giusta frigida indifferenza) io forse gli avrei urlato: Ti amo![36]

Love of whom? Of Aracoeli, left behind, to decompose in the horrid park alone? No – impossible. For me, at that time, Aracoeli was denial – repudiation – vengeance – oblivion. Not love of her. NO. Not of her. Love of somebody else, rather. And of whom?
Of Eugenio Ottone Amedeo.
Never until now, in the course of time, had I loved him. But during my visit to apartment number 15 today, while I was repelled by his presence, I was perhaps desperately overcome with love for him. And if in saying goodbye to me at the door, instead of giving me that repulsive, cold, and sweaty hand, he had with that same hand caressed me (in one of his formal caresses, which I had always received in the past with the frigid indifference they deserved), I would perhaps have shouted to him: I love you!

This explanation, Manuele concludes, arrives too late. And perhaps it arrived too late for Morante herself, who tried to commit suicide a year after completing the novel (only five months after its publication), never fully recovered, and finally died in 1985. But in the discovery of the father, at the end of the journey, lay the possibility of breaking the enchanted spell that bound together the woman and her child, perhaps freeing them both. The discovery of the father brought with it the possibility of finding some intermediate ground between heaven and hell, and a space for redemption in history.

'Una Maternità Sociale': The Upheaval of the 1970s

While Elsa Morante, in her splendid isolation, developed her reflection on history, motherhood, evil, and redemption, Italian society was undergoing turbulent changes brought about by industrialization, internal migration, and political instability. Born in the wake of its American and European counterparts but soon acquiring its own distinctive voice, Italian feminism began to challenge traditional gender roles in society and within the family.[37] Often cited as the first Italian feminist manifesto,

Carla Lonzi's 1970 'Sputiamo su Hegel' ('Let's Spit on Hegel') contains, beyond the somewhat infelicitous title, a lucid critique of women's condition in society. Because of this manifesto, the Italian path to feminism is characterized from the outset by distinct attention to the concept of female difference. Lonzi skilfully disposes of the false alternative between equality and difference. Equality, in her words, is a legal principle, an elementary act of justice based on the 'common denominator' of every human being. Difference, on the other hand, is an existential principle that concerns the various ways of being human.[38] In this context, motherhood not only is not rejected, but instead becomes an essential female experience, almost a marker of women's difference:

> La maternità sia pure snaturata dal dissidio tra i sessi, dal mito impersonale della continuazione della specie e dalla dedizione coatta della vita della donna, è stata una nostra risorsa di pensieri e di sensazioni, la circostanza di una iniziazione particolare. Non siamo responsabili di aver generato l'umanità dalla nostra schiavitú: non è il figlio che ci ha fatto schiave, ma il padre.[39]

Maternity, however perverted by gender conflicts, by the impersonal myth of the continuation of the species, and by the sacrifice imposed upon women's lives, has been our resource of thoughts and feelings, the site of a particular form of initiation. We are not responsible for having generated humankind from our oppression; it is not the child who has enslaved us, but the father.

Lonzi's assessment and careful distinction between the private and institutionalized sides of motherhood constitute only one facet of the feminist debate on this issue. Soon after the publication of 'Sputiamo su Hegel,' in fact, motherhood began to be seen as an anxiety-producing, conflict-ridden, even dangerous experience for women.

The intensity and depth of the debate on the female condition proves difficult to reconstruct for those who, for ideological or chronological reasons, did not directly participate in it. Young – and not so young – women gathered in consciousness-raising groups, printed journals, and questioned deeply entrenched notions of self and gender, trying to find new ways of being a woman in twentieth-century Italy. Newsletters, often produced with minimal resources, advertised by word of mouth, and distributed by volunteers, appeared and disappeared with impressive frequency.[40] In this context, the first issue of *Quotidiano Donna* at the end of the 1970s constituted a momentous event: the name (*quotidiano* means 'daily') and the format (eight newspaper-size pages) were indicative of the publication's ambitious goals. From its first weekly issues, *Quotidiano Donna* was supposed to increase its frequency and become a daily, 'the first daily ever produced in the world by the feminist movement,' as two of its founders stated in an interview with Laura Lilli published in *La Repubblica* on 5 May 1978. The journal tended to identify the contributors only by their first names and did not feature editorials, which the founders feared would introduce, with their privileged position, an inappropriate discrimination among different points of view.[41] This decision exemplifies the opposition to hierarchy implicit in the editorial policies of many publications of the times. However laudable its ideological coherence, this position creates peculiar problems for the researcher who tries to reconstruct those creative and turbulent years. This aversion to authorship – rather pertinently identified with authority – makes it difficult in each case to determine exactly which point of view and whose position an article represents.

These challenges notwithstanding, the intensity of the debate surrounding motherhood is impossible to overestimate. The central role of this issue is apparent not only in *Quotidiano Donna* but also in many other publications of the time – including those that did not deal specifically with women's issues. The debate on motherhood is sometimes inserted in the context of a more general critique of the family, portrayed as the site of sexual repression, verbal and/or physical violence, and institutionalized hypocrisy. The new woman emerging from an arduous process of redefinition, socially engaged and responsible, feared motherhood as a force that could draw her back into the isolation and daily routines associated with the traditional family structure. Already in 1974, Eugenia Roccella denounced the role played by motherhood in the subjugation of women:

> Attraverso il mito sociale della maternità sono passate tutte le mistificazioni, i meccanismi di autogratificazione, che hanno permesso di tenere la donna in posizione subordinata [...] L'essere madre ha [...] voluto dire essere escluse dalla produzione, dal potere. La maternità come mito e come imposizione, come destino sociale della donna, ruolo al difuori del quale non vi è "realizzazione' e "felicità,' è il primo degli ostacoli alla liberazione femminile. Dobbiamo cominciare da qui.[42]

All the falsifications, all the mechanisms of self-gratification that have allowed women to be kept in a subordinate position have reached us through the social myth of motherhood [...] Being a mother [...] has meant being excluded from productivity and power. Motherhood as a myth and as an imposition, as women's social destiny, as the only role that confers 'fulfillment' and 'happiness' on us, is the first obstacle to women's liberation. We must start from here.

An essential element in a social structure that still assigned to women most of the responsibility for child-rearing, motherhood seemed incompatible with feminist awareness. In her novel *Donna in guerra* (*Woman at War*, 1975), Dacia Maraini describes a woman's slow and painful awakening. Her protagonist Vanna goes through a series of experiences that bring her to question traditional gender roles and her own marriage. When she realizes that her husband's desire to have a child was only a means for him to restore his fading supremacy,[43] she terminates her pregnancy and begins a new life, 'sola e [con] tutto da ricominciare' (alone, and [with] everything to begin again), as the last line of the novel states.[44] Similarly, Silvia, the protagonist of Carla Cerati's *Un matrimonio perfetto* (*A Perfect Marriage*, 1975), decides to end her marriage after realizing that 'una madre felice può ben essere una donna infelice, perché la maternità non è tutto, non può essere tutto'[45] (a happy mother can still be an unhappy woman because motherhood is not everything, and cannot be everything). It is a discovery that recalls, once again, the one made by the anonymous woman in Sibilla Aleramo's *Una donna* at the dawn of the twentieth century.

Indeed, while an unsigned article in *Quotidiano Donna* invited women to reconcile feminist militancy and motherhood,[46] many critics saw women's liberation and motherhood as essentially antithetical. Introducing a French collection of essays on feminism in 1979, Maria Antonietta Macciocchi declared the end of the women's movement. The decline, in her analysis, was brought about by a variety of elements, both internal and external to the movement, such as the attacks on feminist bookstores and radio stations[47] and women's own participation in terrorist groups. She saw motherhood as nothing more than one of these disasters, an insidious force capable of reducing women to their biological function:

Nous navigons déjà dans l'estuaire du Post-Féminisme, les voiles flasques [...] À l'horizon, sur la mer dévastée par la tempête, on aperçoit, comme la *baleine blanche*, le ventre d'une femme enceinte. Scandaleusement énorme, la partie cachée du fameux *iceberg* féministe. Son désire inconscient. Identification involontaire entre Sujet Féminin et Sexe reproducteur. La maternité, niée avec acharnement, est revenue en une vague de 'mongolfières' féministes.[48]

We are already navigating the Post-Feminist gulf, our sails unfurled [...] On the horizon, over the sea devastated by the storm, we see a pregnant woman, like a white whale. Outrageously enormous, the hidden part of the famous feminist iceberg. Its unconscious desire, its unwilling equation between Female Subject and Reproductive Sex. Motherhood, opposed with animosity, has come back in a wave of feminist hot air balloons.

Macciocchi's thesis and offensive choice of images (the whale, the hot-air ballon) could not go unnoticed or unanswered. In her rebuttal, Sandra Puccini finds Macciocchi guilty of neglecting a critical new element – that of choice:

L'elemento nuovo – espressione di un diverso e piú alto livello di coscienza sociale – è oggi quello rappresentato dall'essere la donna (o, meglio, alcuni strati sociali di donne), in grado di scegliere se fare o non fare figli.[49]

The new element – an expression of a different and higher level of social awareness – is represented by the fact that today women (or at least, women of some social groups) are capable of choosing whether or not to have children.

Puccini's clarification, however crucial, does not solve all of the problems. Even if women (or some socially privileged women) can choose whether or not to become mothers, to what extent can they choose the conditions of their motherhood? Or, as a contributor who identifies herself only as 'Albalisa' wonders a few years later in the magazine *Filodonna*: 'Può essere la maternità trasgressiva? E quale limite insidioso si cela nel credere di aver scelto di fare un/a figlio/a liberamente e consapevolmente?'[50] (Can motherhood be transgressive? And which insidious limit can be hidden in the belief of having freely and consciously chosen to have a child?).

The ambivalent feelings inspired by the desire to become a mother are analyzed in Lidia Ravera's *Bambino mio* (*Child of Mine*, 1979). The book is divided into two parts. The first, entitled 'Prima' ('Before'), deals with the split between the narrator's consciously chosen identity as a professional and politically committed woman and her desire to have a baby, which she struggles to confine to her moments of loneliness and weakness. The second, entitled 'Dopo' ('After'), is a series of snapshots that follow the baby's arrival. The decision to become a mother does not bring resolution to the narrator's competing desires. The fear of having surrendered to a traditional role permeates the book's final pages. Having chosen to have a child 'to get rid of a ghost' (ho voluto un figlio per liberarmi da un fantasma), the protagonist discovers that not only the desire to become a mother but also motherhood itself is ridden with 'anxiety' and 'contradiction.'[51] Despite the emphasis placed on friendship and community, the protagonist experiences motherhood as a challenging and isolating experience. She is alone to face her fears. It is certainly revealing that neither the child's father nor even the child himself is identified by his proper name.

Too Close, Too Far: Motherhood as a Dialogue with the Self

It is in this context that Oriana Fallaci wrote her most famous work, *Lettera a un bambino mai nato* (*Letter to a Child Never Born*). Published in 1975, at a time when abortion was still illegal[52] and when the debate on motherhood had yet to reach its most intense phase, this slim volume constitutes a deep meditation on the implications of becoming a mother. The text's extraordinary and immediate success attests to the fact that Fallaci had, indeed, hit a nerve. Starting from its explosive, controversial dedication ('A chi si pone il problema di dare la vita o negarla' [To those who face the dilemma of whether to give life or deny it]), the book situates itself squarely in the midst of the contemporary debate on abortion. And yet, a reading of *Lettera* as a pro-choice pamphlet is soon made problematic by its treatment of the fetus as a person and interlocutor. The very first lines ('Stanotte ho saputo che c'eri'[53] [Last night I found out that you existed]) firmly establish a precious relationship with the life that is just beginning. This treatment of the embryo as a full-fledged human being is more in line with Catholic doctrine than with the pro-choice position. This feature of *Lettera* proved somewhat disappointing to those who had hoped that Fallaci, the most famous Italian woman journalist of her times, would take a clear stance in support of abortion rights. In a 1975 interview with Nazareno Fabbretti, Fallaci addressed the contradiction at the core of her work, while declaring it inevitable: 'Sure, so as to use a foetus as an interlocutor, I've accepted, in a literary way, the Catholics' basic concept of the human person.'[54] Even if it is presented as a mere rhetorical device, this choice is laden with ideological consequences. The conferral of human status on the embryo brings the moral implications of the protagonist's struggle to the foreground.

The woman of *Lettera* is, in many ways, a product of the 1970s: she resists the intrusion of religious authorities into her life, she rejects traditional family structure, she enjoys a remarkable degree of sexual freedom, and she considers professional success to be a priority. Her life experiences have made her keenly aware of the failures of human nature. For a woman like her, motherhood, rather than being a defining moment or a gift, represents an extravagant risk, an anomalous choice.

I have already mentioned the controversial dedication of the book: 'A chi si pone il problema di dare la vita o negarla.' In a religious context, the implicit assertion of omnipotence is close to blasphemous: granting or denying life is God's prerogative, and any presumption to usurp that power constitutes an act of sinful hubris. Even an atheist may balk at such a confident profession of human control over life. And yet, with her bold dedication, Fallaci brings to light a central – though rarely acknowledged – aspect of the debate concerning motherhood: namely, that pregnancy and childbirth bring a woman as close to replicating God's generative powers as a human can possibly get.

In her re-examination of Greek thought, Adriana Cavarero sheds new light on the myth of Demeter, the goddess of fertility and agriculture, whose desperation and outrage at Hades's abduction of her daughter Kore make the earth sterile: 'Indeed, the central theme of the myth, apart from its agricultural interpretation, is the power of the mother, which is inscribed in all of nature as the power both to generate and not to generate [...] Thus the choice that belongs constitutively to maternal power carries within it, like all secrets, something truly dreadful: the possibility of nothingness, the annihilation of humankind, the desolation of the earth.'[55]

Women's potential, when redefined in these uncompromising terms, carries daunting implications.[56] Once women abandon their identity as vessels, once they stop considering themselves mechanisms central to the survival of the species, the organization of society, or even the order of the universe, motherhood becomes a solitary enterprise in need of justification. The features that so upset Fallaci's first critics are the same that make her book still so intriguing and challenging thirty years after its publication. Perhaps no other Italian writer has investigated in such detail pregnancy as an event that challenges a woman's notion of selfhood, while giving her a privileged perspective on the most crucial issues in a human life. At times, the protagonist bestows human qualities on her fetus and engages in a full dialogue with it; on other occasions, she acknowledges the fact that she is alone, and that her dialogue is in fact a monologue.[57] She struggles in a dialectic of self and other, trying to define a life so embedded in her own body that it is almost indistinguishable from it, and yet so mysterious and elusive that it can be studied only through clinical tests, followed in its development through pictures from magazines, and conceptualized through metaphors dealing with sidereal distances. This oscillation between proximity and distance culminates in the image of the dust that the protagonist collects from a tool used in an lunar mission but cannot keep:

> Me ne rimasi ferma a guardar la mia mano coperta di luna. Avevo la luna in mano e non sapevo dove appoggiarla, come conservarla [...] In albergo aprii il rubinetto dell'acqua, ci posai sotto la mano. Ne colò un liquido nero che presto scomparve in un vortice nero e sai che ti dico, bambino? Tu sei come la mia luna, la mia polvere di luna.[58]

> I stood there looking at my hand covered with the moon. I had the moon in my hand and I didn't know where to lay it down, how to keep it [...] In the hotel I turned on the tap and put my hand under it. A dark liquid drained away and soon disappeared in a dark whirlpool. You know what, kid? You are like my moon, my moon dust.

Through the protagonist's struggle, motherhood is defined as an experience that resists conceptualization, that demands at the same time a revisitation of an individual's personal history (the painful memories of the protagonist's life during and in the aftermath of the Second World War) and an attempt to transcend one's limited self. What the protagonist of *Lettera* tackles in her monologue fuelled by the invisible – and, in large part, imaginary – life hidden within her is nothing less than the meaning of life itself. Far from constituting a call for the legalization of abortion,[59] the book is a visceral, heartfelt meditation on the terrible responsibility of bringing a human being into the world and exposing him or her not only to the uncertainties of human existence but also, and tragically, to its only certainty. To give birth is indeed, as Sara Ruddick states, 'to create a life that cannot be kept safe, whose unfolding cannot be controlled, and whose eventual death is certain.'[60]

In this framework, it is crucial that the embryo take on the status of a person. This meditation on life driven by a recollection of past events needs an interlocutor, however fictional and silent, just as patients need the presence of psychoanalysts in order to give meaning to their narrative.[61] The book's final twist is tragic and ironic: the embryo is revealed to have never passed even the first stages of development. The woman who believed she was following its progress through documentaries and magazine clips has to confront reality and disillusionment. The lunar image returns, in order to stress the incommensurable distance between the earth and the universe, human life and eternity. After struggling in vain to preserve the moon dust, the protagonist suffers a new and harsher loss: 'Non voglio perder di nuovo la luna, vederla sparire in fondo a un lavabo. Ma è inutile. Con la stessa certezza che mi paralizzava la notte in cui seppi che esistevi, ora so che stai cessando di esistere' (I don't want to lose the moon again, to see it vanish again at the bottom of a washbasin. But it's useless. With the same certainty that paralysed me the night I found that you existed, I now know that your existence is ending.[62]

As John Gatt-Rutter has persuasively argued, the protagonist's surprise is mirrored by that of the readers, who realize they have been 'led into a double narrative trap, a self-deleting text, addressed to a discursively constructed interlocutor – the child – who is then abruptly dissolved in retrospect.'[63] And yet, the necessity of the addressee is confirmed by the fact that even the tragic discovery of its death does not mark its disappearance from the text. Even after the doctor's announcement of the miscarriage, the 'child' appears again in a dream, this time as an adult man, to take the stand in defence of his mother at the imaginary tribunal that has summoned her. In order to continue her journey of self-discovery, the woman of the story needs her 'child,' and struggles to keep reality at bay. The end of the novel marks her defeat, the acknowledgment of her loss and its consequences. Just as the discovery of a new presence ignited the meditation ('Stanotte ho saputo che c'eri'[64] [Last night I found out that you existed]), the revelation of the disappearance marks the end of discourse: 'Tu sei morto. Forse muoio anch'io. Ma non conta. Perché la vita non muore'[65] (You are dead. Maybe I'm dying, too. But it doesn't matter. Because life doesn't die).

Given that the protagonist had proudly proclaimed her independence from motherhood, it is paradoxical that the realization of her death as a potential mother coincides with, or even leads to, her death as an individual. This tragic irony would become even stronger in subsequent editions of the book, when Fallaci eliminated all doubts and rewrote the passage: 'Tu sei morto. Ora muoio anch'io' (You are dead. Now I am dying, too). However resisted and rejected, motherhood had indeed become a life-defining experience for the protagonist, whose power to generate malignantly turns into the curse of self-annihilation.[66]

The tenuous fiction on which the text was based thus reveals its inconsistency and gives way to silence. This stunning reversal is not the only one that readers are called to witness. While destroying the founding premises of the text, the development of *Lettera* provides a bitter annotation to its proud dedication. The claim that humans may be able to decide 'whether to give life or deny it' is exposed in its irresponsible arrogance. The woman's control over her child's destiny could be exercised only as a negation: she could decide to terminate her pregnancy, but she could not influence its continuation in a positive, constructive way. And while she agonized over her choice, something else – be it God, fate, or the laws of nature – had already decided for her.

chapter 4

Struggling with the Mother

Through the Daughters' Voices

It was perhaps inevitable that the search for a new meaning of motherhood would sooner or later lead to a confrontation with the women who had accepted it in ways that seemed passive and acritical. As Silvia Vegetti Finzi stated, 'Exploring maternity means first considering the figure of one's own mother [...], and opening up a comparison or a conflict that hinges on some failing, some lack of vital nutriment.'[1] Critics have noticed how the feminism of the 1970s was essentially a movement of daughters,[2] which chose as its antagonist the figure of the mother and everything she represented.[3] In the writings of the time, there is an intriguing confusion between the concrete, historical, and identifiable figure of one's own mother, and the mother as a symbolic figure. The confusion is indicative of the fact that no discussion of motherhood can develop independently from the subject's relationship with her own mother. At the same time, the modalities of that relationship depend largely on a set of expectations that transcend the mother as a real human being, taking into account her symbolic role and power as defined throughout the ages by cultural constructions such as mythology, religion, and psychoanalysis.

In her nuanced analysis, Marianne Hirsch describes four reasons for the feminist rejection of the mother: the perception of motherhood as an essentially patriarchal construction; the discomfort with the vulnerability and lack of control associated with maternity; a 'fear of the body' (for which Elizabeth V. Spellman coined the term 'somatophobia') that carried with it a certain distrust for activities – such as pregnancy, birth, nursing – that rooted women in their bodies; and, finally, ambivalence towards power and authority.[4] All these reasons contributed to the construction of the mother (both one's own mother and the maternal role she embodied) as an obstacle in the daughter's path towards emancipation. The void left by the erasure of the mother was to be filled by fellow feminists in an idealized sisterhood:

> Throughout the 1970s, the metaphor of sisterhood, of friendship or of surrogate motherhood has been the dominant model for female and feminist relationships. To say that "sisterhood is powerful,' however, is to isolate feminist discourse within one generation and to banish feminists who are mothers to the "mother-closet'. In the 1970s, the prototypical feminist voice was, to a large degree, the voice of the daughter attempting to separate from an overly connected or rejected mother, in order to bond with her sisters in a relationship of mutual nurturance and support among equals. With its possibilities of mutuality and its desire to avoid power, the paradigm of sisterhood has the advantage of freeing women from the biological function of giving birth, even while offering a specifically feminine relation model.[5]

Italian feminists found themselves struggling with similar concerns, as the debate surrounding Ingmar Bergman's 1978 *Autumn Sonata* clearly illustrates. 'Mother and daughter, what a terrible combination of feelings and confusion and destruction [...] It is as if the umbilical cord had never been cut': these words, uttered by a distressed daughter (played by Liv Ullman) to a mother (Ingrid Bergman) whom she accuses not only of being indifferent and neglectful, but also, significantly, of having hindered her own attempt to become a mother, struck a chord with Italian audiences. On 15 December 1978, the influential newspaper *La Repubblica* devoted its entire cultural section to the debate surrounding the movie. While Elisabetta Rasy reluctantly acknowledged the feminist movement's tendency to oppose the mother even more than the father, the anthropologist Ida Magli considered the rebellion against the mother a logical attempt, on the part of the daughters, to emancipate themselves from the biological function looming over their lives:

> Nella madre è tutto ciò che l'essere umano rifiuta, proprio perché è essere umano, e non classe zoologica: nella madre c'è il biologico, il fisico, il ripetititivo... la 'natura,' con quella presenza concreta, pesante, ottusa, che è il 'corpo.' [...] Ed è nella 'madre' che l'individualità della donna, la 'persona' si perde. La figlia, dunque, odia nella madre il proprio destino, il proprio futuro, la vita che rifiuta.[6]

> The mother is everything a human being refuses, precisely because it is a human being rather than a zoological species. The mother represents the biological, the physical, repetition, 'nature' with the concrete, heavy, and obtuse presence that is the 'body' [...] A woman's individuality, her being a 'person,' is lost in the 'mother.' The daughter thus hates the mother because she hates her own destiny, her own future, a life she doesn't want.

Magli describes, more than she criticizes, the psychological process at play in this rejection. Contempt for the mother is inextricably linked, in her words, to an aversion to the body (or 'somatophobia,' to use Spellman's terminology), seen as an obstacle to rather than a necessary component of our humanity.

Magli's analysis implicitly subscribes to a rigid binary split between public and private, mind and body. Far from being neutral or natural, this dichotomy is itself a product of patriarchal discourse. In her lucid *Man of Reason*, Genevieve Lloyd traces the development of this pattern in Western philosophy, from the Pythagoreans to Hegel, and concludes: 'What is valued – whether it be odd as against even numbers, "aggressive" as against 'nurturing' skills and capacities, or Reason as against emotion – has been readily identified with maleness. Within the context of this association of maleness with preferred traits, it is not just incidental to the feminine that female traits have been construed as inferior – or, more subtly, as "complementary" – to male norms of human excellence. Rationality has been conceived as transcendence of the feminine; and the "feminine" itself has been partly constituted by its occurrence within this structure.'[7]

As Lloyd acknowledges, there is no simple solution to this dilemma. Whether women decide to 'claim full participation in [Reason's] cultural manifestation' (104) or, on the contrary, extol the value of the traits traditionally associated with femininity (such as intuition and irrationality), they are still operating within a framework that sets rigid boundaries for their individuality.

A woman confronting these categories finds herself in a situation that could be defined as a 'double bind.' First introduced by Bateson, Jackson, Haley, and Weakland in their 1956 study on schizophrenia, the notion of 'double bind' carries momentous implications on the linguistic and sociological level and has been successfully applied to literary and cultural studies. In her analysis of Teresa de Avila's rhetorical strategies, Alison Weber stresses how 'the double bind is not a difficult choice but rather the illusion of choice within a relationship. The alternatives are illusory because they exist on different logical levels. For example, the command to "be independent" is paradoxical since spontaneous behaviour cannot be ordered; compliance with the order on one level violates it on another level. Such paradoxical injunctions are called *binds* not only because of the logical dilemmas they produce but also because they occur within an intensely important relationship that is essential to the subject's self-definition.'[8] Similarly, the injunction to be rational can be paradoxical if addressed to a woman in a framework that defines rationality as a prerogative of men and in opposition to the natural powers of the human body.[9] The underlying, tenuous fiction is destined to be shattered when a woman faces pregnancy, an event that exposes her body to events that escape rational control.

To heal the mind-body fracture was a monumental yet unavoidable task if motherhood were to be given more positive value. Feminists grew increasingly critical of the Western philosophical tradition and of psychoanalysis, which seemed to provide inadequate, if not misleading, tools. In her crucial *L'ordine simbolico della madre* (*The Symbolic Order of the Mother*, 1991), Luisa Muraro reconstructs the steps that brought her to the realization that Western philosophy had alienated her from the mother. In her analysis of Plato's influence, Muraro stresses the rivalry it established between philosophy and women's generative power:

> È un'operazione molto semplice, si confonde quasi con l'operazione della metafora, la piú comune delle figure: consiste nel trasferire alla produzione culturale (come la scienza, il diritto, la religione, ecc.) gli attributi della potenza e dell'opera della madre [...] riducendo lei a natura opaca e informe, sopra la quale il soggetto (conoscente, legislatore, credente, ecc.) deve innalzarsi per dominarla.[10]

> It is a very simple operation, which could almost be compared to a metaphor, the most common rhetorical device; it consists of transferring the qualities of the mother's power and work to cultural production (such as science, law, religion, etc.), while reducing her to opaque and shapeless matter, which the subject (the wise man, the legislator, the believer, etc.) must overcome, in order to dominate her).

Canonical psychoanalytical texts were also criticized for neglecting or misunderstanding the mother-daughter relationship. In particular, Freud's theory of female development, which entails the little girl's move from attachment to hatred of the mother, was denounced for having provided a fallacious, albeit extremely influential, paradigm.[11]

Through this critique, the rejection of mothers and motherhood could be better understood in its social and psychological determinants, but also denounced for the dangers it entailed. As Elaine Showalter noted, 'hating one's mother was for a woman only a metaphor for hating herself, and it was necessary for female literature to move beyond matrophobia, and to embark in a courageously sustained quest for the mother.'[12]

By the end of the 1970s, the dialogue could no longer be postponed. The need to communicate inspired many articles, such as this anonymous piece published in *Quotidiano Donna* on 27 January 1979:

> Due donne si fronteggiano, ma la parola è quasi sempre alla figlia, e la madre? In realtà il soggetto debole è lei, la famiglia, il ruolo che le è imposto la legano, la inchiodano, la liberazione della figlia passa sulla schiavizzazione della madre, i doveri della madre pesano, è piú difficile per lei ribellarsi, i carichi degli affetti la ingabbiano, la figlia sta fiorendo, lei sfiorendo, alla figlia si apre la società, alla madre si offre solo disinteresse, entrambe si snervano nello scontro, fino a quando? e se trasformassero il conflitto in solidarietà?[13]

> Two women face each other, but it is almost always the daughter who talks. What about the mother? In reality, she is the weak subject. Her family, and the role that is imposed upon her, limit her, nail her. The daughter's liberation takes place at the expense of the mother's enslavement. It is harder for the mother to rebel; the weight of her relations subjugates her. The daughter is blooming, the mother is withering. Society opens its doors to the daughter, while the mother is offered only indifference. They both grow frustrated in the struggle. Until when? What if they turned the conflict into solidarity?

This anonymous question and its implicit suggestion were not to go unanswered. Over and over again, novels of the last twenty years of the century stage the move from criticism to understanding, from estrangement to empathy. The progression can be partially attributed to a natural maturation, as the daughterly perspective gives way to a deeper understanding of the constraints all women face.

A revealing example can be extrapolated from two works that deal only marginally with motherhood. In her widely acclaimed *Casalinghitudine* (*Housewifery*, 1987), Clara Sereni created a new, hybrid genre, interspersing snapshots of her past with cooking recipes that had provided nourishment and comfort in those times, and are therefore able to res-

Struggling with the Mother   99

urrect the memories of crucial events in her life. The volume itself is organized like a cookbook, with chapters that follow a progression leading from the appetizers to the preserves. The most revealing passages about the protagonist's mother, Xenia, are in the chapter devoted to main courses ('Primi piatti'). The protagonist finds it difficult to reconcile her mother's public image[14] with her absence from the daughter's own private history. The mother's struggle against a terminal illness had, in fact, limited her influence within the family. Even the discovery of the mother's journal fails to bridge the distance between the two women:

> Anche mia madre ha il suo libro, una frase: 'In un momento in cui mi sentivo un po' meglio ho preso Clara sul letto, l'ho coccolata un poco, l'ho baciata. E lei subito ha chiesto: "Me lo farai anche domani?" Come è facile commuoversi e perdere tutte le forze ...' Mi risuona dentro un'eco vaghissima di tenerezza, non di piú. Nella memoria mia madre è sempre stata morta.[15]
>
> My mother also has her own book, with a sentence: 'In a moment when I felt a little better, I took Clara in bed, I cuddled and kissed her. And she immediately asked: "Are you going to do this tomorrow as well?" It is so easy to be moved and lose all strength ...' A very faint echo of tenderness reverberates inside me. That's all. In my memory, my mother has always been dead).

A few years later, in *Il gioco dei regni* (*The Game of the Kingdoms*, 1993), the author approached the same scene from a different perspective. The relationship between mother and daughter is this time only part of a larger framework that combines personal and collective history. This departure from the self-centred view of the previous novel is reflected by the omniscient narration. We are introduced to Xenia's struggle against her illness and follow her as she cautiously moves around the kitchen. With great effort she cuts little strips of bread, dips them in egg, and feeds her daughter Clara. The simple dinner is soon over:

> Clara si voltò verso sua madre, chiese:
> – Domani. Me lo farai anche domani?
> Xenia abbassò gli occhi, lucidi. Poi pian piano si alzò e andò verso il suo letto, piena di dolori.[16]
>
> Clara turned toward her mother and asked:

– Tomorrow. Are you going to do this tomorrow as well?
Xenia lowered her wet eyes. Then, very slowly, she got up and moved towards her bed, full of pain.

While in *Casalinghitudine* readers are forced to adopt the egocentric point of view of the daughter, who interprets her mother's illness as a betrayal, in *Il gioco dei regni* Clara's comment stands out for its unintentional cruelty, set in opposition to Xenia's silent heroism.

A better understanding of the mother's experience goes hand in hand with the acknowledgment of her inescapable influence on the daughter's development. In Carla Cerati's *La cattiva figlia* (*The Bad Daughter*, 1990), the protagonist is caught between her traditional, supportive daughterly role and her almost visceral aversion to her mother.[17] When the ageing woman moves in with her, the daughter finds herself locked in her room, so constrained by the mother's needs and desires that she develops psychosomatic disorders and finally decides to end the devastating cohabitation. Distance, however, does not allay the tension in the relationship. In order to fill the long Sunday afternoons she spends with her mother, Giulia resorts to interviewing her and recording their exchanges. The second part of the book is entirely devoted to this revisitation of the past. Giulia juxtaposes the events narrated by her mother with her own memory of them, or with other hitherto unknown or neglected episodes evoked by the old woman's tales. Most important, though, the recording sessions allow Giulia to see her mother for the first time as an autonomous individual who had already gone through momentous experiences before her daughter was born. Through her mother's reminiscence, Giulia perceives her own existence as an episode, however relevant, in someone else's life:

> Dopo un anno di febbre terzana era smagrita, stanchissima; quando si accorse di essere incinta per la terza volta sentí di non desiderare affatto un altro figlio, non cosí presto. Dato che il chinino si era dimostrato un efficace abortivo poteva utilizzarlo. Ma il farmaco non diede l'effetto sperato; ricorse allora ai pediluvi bollenti senapati, alle corse in bicicletta lungo strade sconnesse, provò a saltare dal tavolo a piè pari sul pavimento; ma questa volta il feto era ben attaccato e non intendeva lasciare la presa.
> Quel feto ero io, Giulia.[18]

After a year of malarial fever she was shrivelled and extremely tired; when she realized that she was pregnant for the third time, she felt no desire at all for another child, not so early. Since quinine had proven effective in inducing abortion, she used it. But the medicine did not work the way she had hoped; she therefore resorted to hot mustard foot baths, to bicycle rides on bumpy roads; she tried to jump from the table to the floor with her feet together; this time, however, the fetus was well attached and had no intention of giving up.

That fetus was me, Giulia.

The narrative mechanism in this passage is the same that operates at an intertextual level in Sereni's books – namely, a shift in perspective. In this particular case, the homodiegetic narrator disappears and leaves the stage to the mother, only to return in the last sentence. More precisely, we are surprised by the narrator's switch, from mere observer to agent, to follow Wayne Booth's distinction.[19] This change is accentuated by the self-defining power of the first-person pronoun and the proper name ('io, Giulia'), which, while revealing the protagonist's association with that threatened and stubborn fetus, also indicate her enormous distance from it. The revelation sheds light on the conflicting relationship between the two women, but it does not miraculously improve communication and dissipate misunderstandings. The eponymous 'bad daughter' is alternately attentive and neglectful, torn as she is between her sense of duty and her rebellion against a task that she perceives as unfairly imposed upon all women.[20] While her knowledge of her mother's life deepens, the emotional distance between the two women is never filled, as if avoiding psychological proximity could spare the protagonist the weakness embodied by her ageing, ailing mother.[21] It is only after her death, through the process of writing, that the protagonist finally acknowledges her mother's importance in her development:

> Soltanto oggi mi rendo conto di quanto posto abbia occupato questa donna, mia madre, malgrado io non glielo volessi concedere; e di come la sua figura si sia ingigantita nei ricordi che mi trascinano lontano, sempre piú lontano, come accade con certe onde anomale che si abbattono sulla spiaggia, solitarie e improvvise, quando all'orizzonte passa, sagoma quasi invisibile, una grande nave.[22]

> Only today do I realize how much space my mother occupied, in spite of the fact that I didn't want to concede it to her; and how her figure has been magnified in the memories that take me farther and farther away, as it happens with certain irregular, isolated, and sudden waves that crash on the

beach when the almost invisible silhouette of a big ship moves along the horizon.

The novels by Sereni and Cerati portray a meaningful shift in the daughters' comprehension, and therefore a momentous change in the representation of motherhood. The analysis of that relationship is indeed of paramount importance because it entails not only an understanding of the daughter's past but also, and crucially, the possibility of the future.[23] The relationship with the mother is, in fact, connected to the daughter's own attitude towards motherhood as a sociobiological role; it calls into question the daughter's conceptualization of her own generative powers, and her decision to become – or not to become – a mother. As a contributor identified only as 'D.V.' wrote in the magazine *Effe*: 'Finché non abbiamo esorcizzato la sua figura, che modella il nostro rapporto tra fisiologia e umanità, non sapremo davvero se e perché vogliamo diventare madri'[24] (As long as we have not exorcized her figure, which shapes our relationship between physiology and humanity, we cannot really know if and why we want to become mothers). Taking on the task of 'exorcizing' the mother's figure, several writers have recently examined the link between the figure of the mother and the daughter's attitude towards mothering.[25]

The Mother and the City

In Fabrizia Ramondino's *Althénopis* (1981), the mystery surrounding the figure of the mother merges with the mystery of the city of Naples. As readers learn in the first pages of the book, German soldiers during the Second World War were disappointed by the appearance of the city, which they found unworthy of the idyllic descriptions sketched by Mozart and Goethe. They had thus decided to change the city's original name, which means 'virgin's eye,' into 'althénopis,' which means 'old hag's eye.' In lyrical prose punctuated by informative notes, the homodiegetic narrator/protagonist recalls the events of her childhood in a family marked by the presence of strong women and in a brutal, yet enchanting, natural environment. This highly selective account is divided into three parts of different lengths. After the initial, long section dominated by the figure of the grandmother, a central, shorter portion evokes the different houses that the family is forced to inhabit because of financial constraints. It is only in the third and shortest section, however, that the work finds its focus and moves towards its conclusion, with an abrupt change in perspective. The second section ends with the narrator's decision to move to northern Italy, but the third, quite unexpectedly, features a homecoming. The homodiegetic mode that has filtered the events disappears, and Mother and Daughter (rigorously identified by capital letters) are left alone to face each other:

> La Madre sembrava impersonare la debolezza, le privazioni, la tremula esitazione e fragilità di un uccello in gabbia, che imita l'istinto rarefatto invece di uccidersi contro le sbarre. Ed era arrivata la Figlia, con la sua macchina biologica perfetta [...] Fu tagliato per la seconda volta il cordone ombelicale; bisognava imparare a respirare in modo diverso, e la Figlia si ammalò nel respiro. La Madre sino allora aveva portato la Figlia nel suo ventre, da allora la Figlia cominciò a portare la Madre sulle spalle.[26]

> The Mother seemed to embody weakness, deprivation, the trembling hesitation and fragility of a caged bird that imitates a rarefied instinct rather than killing itself against the bars. And the Daughter had arrived, with her perfect biological machine [...] The umbilical cord was cut for the second time. It was necessary to learn how to breathe differently, and the daughter became ill in her breathing. If until then the Mother had carried the Daughter in her womb, from then on the Daughter began to carry the Mother on her shoulders.

The image of the Daughter carrying the Mother is a powerful one, as it evokes that of Aeneas carrying Anchises on his shoulders during the flight from Troy (*Aeneid* II, 707–11). But one element is missing from the picture: while carrying Anchises on his shoulders, Aeneas is simultaneously holding his son Ascanius by the hand, in an image of patriarchal continuity that found its most powerful expression in Lorenzo Bernini's masterful sculpture. The parallel is therefore imperfect. The cycle will be broken if the Daughter, while carrying the Mother on her shoulders, does not fulfil her role in an uninterrupted sequence – if she does not become, like the woman who preceded her, both daughter *and* mother. But the never-described voyage to the north has produced a broken soul. In the most remote corner of the house, the Daughter stubbornly nourishes herself and fights against hallucinations that, as a new note to the text informs the reader, are described in psychiatry as preludes to schizophrenia. She finally emerges as a new, stronger woman. She is able to interpret the Mother's death as the demise of a tribal chief who withdraws once his task accomplished, concerned only with the survival of his group ('capi tribali, che, finito il loro compito, si ritirano per dar posto ad altri, perché la difesa della propria specie prevale su ogni altro istinto').[27] Just like a tribal chief who leaves an amulet, an oracle, or a sign to those around him (followers who are not always ready to receive it and interpret it), the Mother sends out a message, however weak and incertain. During her last days, she contemplates her own sex 'senza pudore, e con insistenza' (shamelessly and with insistence) and responds to those who try to stop her by repeating: 'Sono una bambina, sono una bambina' (I am a little girl, I am a little girl). This is the sign that the Daughter needed to find her direction in the world: 'Quel gesto, che per tanti anni era rimasto sepolto, venne ad adagiarsi su quel grembo, a reclamare i suoi diritti e a dichiararli, a separarsi dal vecchio corpo morente per entrare nell'anima di chi lo intese, togliere il divieto e fecondarla, affinché vedessero la luce altri nati di donna"[28] (That sign, which had been buried for so many years, came to rest on that womb, to claim and declare its rights, to separate from the old, dying body and enter the soul of the woman who understood it, to lift the prohibition and make it fruitful, so that others may come to the light, of woman born). This enigmatic message dissolves the spell and frees the daughter's generative powers. 'The mortal female body becomes the generator of the immortal continuum of life.'[29]

Although the epilogue of Ramondino's novel features a positive outcome, other works demonstrate how the enduring conflict with the mother can, on the contrary, lead the daughter to physical as well as emotional sterility. This is the condition exemplified by Delia, the protagonist and narrator of Elena Ferrante's *L'amore molesto* (*Harassing Love*, 1992), one of the most complex and stylistically refined novels that Italy has produced in recent times.[30] On Delia's birthday, her mother, Amalia, drowns in mysterious circumstances, prompting the daughter to return to her hometown (which is, in this case also, Naples). Rather than revealing the mystery of Amalia's death, Delia's investigation casts light on the intricate relationship between the two women or, more precisely, on the daughter's ambivalent feelings towards her mother. A complex puzzle is skilfully arranged before the reader's eyes: the mother's playful nature oppressed by a jealous and violent husband whose sentiments the narrator seems, uncannily, to share; her relationship of more than forty years with Caserta, an ambiguous character who is witness to and perhaps partly responsible for her death; the elaborate game of transpositions and psychological disguises through which Delia tried in her childhood to replicate Amalia's erotic encounters – either real or merely imagined – with Caserta, in a dangerous gamble that would eventually lead to her becoming a victim of child abuse. This descent into Delia's psyche coincides with a descent into the city of Naples, its interiors, its subway, and the old basement shop in which the violence took place forty years earlier. The movement downward begins when Delia, after taking the elevator to the top floor in her mother's building just as she did as a child, accepts the challenge and decides to face her mother and her past: 'Lo sapevo da sempre. C'era una linea che non riuscivo a varcare, quando pensavo ad Amalia. Forse ero lí per riuscire a varcarla. Me ne spaventai, premetti il pulsante con il numero tre e l'ascensore ebbe uno scossone rumoroso. Cigolando cominciai a scendere verso l'appartamento di mia madre'[31] (I had always known. There was a line that I could not cross when I thought of Amalia. Perhaps I was there to finally cross it. I was scared. I pressed the button with the number three on it, and the elevator moved with a noisy jolt. My creaking descent towards my mother's apartment had begun).

The first daughter of an attractive eighteen-year-old woman, Delia was so influenced by her father's obsessive jealousy that she adopted his stance. Even as an adult, defending her mother from her uncle's insinuations, Delia uneasily admits her ambiguous feelings: 'Forse non tolleravo che la parte piú segreta di me si servisse della sua solidarietà per avvalorare un'ipotesi coltivata altrettanto segretamente: che mia madre portasse inscritta nel corpo una colpevolezza naturale, indipendente dalla sua volontà e da ciò che realmente faceva, pronta ad apparire all'occorrenza in ogni gesto, in ogni sospiro'[32] (Perhaps I could not tolerate the fact that the most secret part of myself used [my father's] solidarity to give credit to a hypothesis that I harboured just as secretly: that my mother bore, inscribed in her body, a natural guilt, independent of her will and of what she actually did, ready to manifest itself in the right situation in every gesture, in every sigh).

This perception of the mother is paradoxically coupled with a visceral desire to identify with her, to become her or, more precisely, to be the version of Amalia constructed by her husband's obsessive jealousy.[33] This leads five-year-old Delia to replicate with little Antonio the erotic games that she imagines her mother plays with Caserta, Antonio's father. Delia is, at the same time, convinced that she is Amalia, and yet she is aware that her disguise is incomplete.[34] Abused by Antonio's grandfather, she runs home to tell her family, but in her confusion (and perhaps following an unconscious desire to punish her mother for the events), she attributes the acts that have just taken place between her and Antonio's grandfather to Amalia and Caserta. The terrible scene that follows, in which Amalia and Caserta are savagely beaten and even little Antonio risks his life, is the last glimpse of Delia's childhood available to the reader.

Perhaps the episode served as a warning for the little girl, alerting her to the dangers lurking in her games of imitation and transposition. Growing up, she tries to remove all traces of her connection with Amalia. In a moment of lucid introspection, she realizes that her decision not to become a mother herself is linked to her incapacity to deal with her relationship with Amalia, to find a middle ground between identification and rejection:

> Negli anni, per odio, per paura, avevo desiderato di perdere ogni radice in lei, fino alle piú profonde: i suoi gesti, le sue inflessioni di voce, il modo di prendere un bicchiere o bere da una tazza [...] e poi la lingua, la città, i ritmi del respiro. Tutto rifatto, per diventare io e staccarmi da lei.
>
> D'altro canto non avevo voluto o non ero riuscita a radicare in me nessuno. Tra qualche tempo avrei perso anche la possibilità di avere figli. Nessun essere umano si sarebbe staccato mai da me con l'angoscia con cui io mi ero staccata da mia madre [...] Sarei rimasta io fino alla fine, infelice, scontenta di quello che avevo trascinato furtivamente fuori dal corpo di Amalia.[35]

> Throughout the years, because of hatred and fear, I had wished to lose even my deepest connections with her: her expressions, the inflections of her voice, the way she held a glass or drank from a cup, [...] her language, her city, the rhythms of her breath. I did everything over in order to become myself and detach myself from her.
>
> On the other hand, I had not wanted or managed to root anybody in me. Soon I would lose even the possibility of having children. No human being would ever detach from me with the anxiety with which I had moved away from Amalia [...] I would be myself until the end, unhappy, dissatisfied with what I had furtively dragged outside Amalia's body.

The similarities between *L'amore molesto* and Fabrizia Ramondino's *Althénopis* are intriguing. The association between the mother and the city of Naples, with its dialect, its physicality, its vitality, and its desperation, is in both cases the informing principle of the narration. In *Althénopis*, however, the mother, on the verge of death, leaves a sign that releases the daughter's potential. As if embedded in a secret code, her message, though ambiguous to the reader, is interpreted effortlessly by the daughter as the sign that allows for the possibility of future human beings 'of woman born.' *L'amore molesto* does not offer a similarly clear-cut resolution, but rather moves towards the appropriation of the mother's heritage, the acknowledgment of a proximity that needs to be accepted. The last scene shows the protagonist by the shore, the site of both the family's summer vacations and her mother's death. At this point, she has already given a possible reconstruction of Amalia's last hours. After a copious dinner with Caserta and perhaps after drinking too much wine, Amalia had entered the water, wearing the refined lingerie she had bought as a present for Delia. Her playfulness, her desire to escape the possessive male glances that had ruled her all her life, led her to find refuge in the water's embrace. The image of the old woman wearing clothes intended for her daughter haunts the novel, together with Delia's identity photo, altered in a way that makes her resemble Amalia.[36] In a telling reversal, the epilogue shows Delia wearing her mother's blue dress,[37] intent on retouching her image:

> Il sole cominciò a scaldarmi. Mi frugai nella borsetta ed estrassi la mia carta d'identità. Fissai la foto a lungo, studiandomi di riconoscere Amalia in quella immagine. Era una foto recente, fatta apposta per rinnovare il documento scaduto. Con un pennarello, mentre il sole mi scottava il collo, disegnai intorno ai miei lineamenti la pettinatura di mia madre [...] Mi guardai, mi sorrisi. Quell'acconciatura antiquata, in uso negli anni Quaranta ma già rara alla fine degli anni Cinquanta, mi donava. Amalia c'era stata. Io ero Amalia.[38]

> The sun began to warm me. I looked in my bag and took out my identity card. I looked at the picture for a long time, trying to recognize Amalia in that image. It was a recent photo, taken specifically for the renewal of the document. With a marker, while the sun burned my neck, I drew around my own features my mother's hairdo [...] I looked at myself and smiled. That antiquated coiffure, popular in the '40s but already unusual at the end of the '50s, fit me well. Amalia had been there. I was Amalia.

The novel concludes on this ambiguous note, as it is impossible to determine whether Delia's identification with Amalia's picture symbolizes the acknowledgment of the mother's legacy, and therefore a positive resolution, or, on the contrary, the perpetuation of a disastrous confusion.[39]

The pattern described by Ferrante can be compared to that found in

Storia di Piera (*Piera's Story*, 1980), a transcript of the conversations between the actress Piera Degli Esposti and the writer Dacia Maraini. Piera Degli Esposti discusses the difficulty of keeping her identity separate from her mother's[40] and its link with her decision not to have children herself: 'Il fatto è che io ero la figlia di me stessa. Io ero la mia bambina. Non potevo partorire che me stessa'[41] (The problem is that I was the daughter of myself. I was my child. I could only give birth to myself). Once again, the daughter needs to find her position in a world ruled by her mother's presence. As Mazzoni states in her discussion of Irigaray, 'The relationship with the mother is indispensable for the daughter's symbolization of her, and abandonment is not, cannot be the antidote to fusion.'[42]

The city of Naples, which provides the link between Ramondino's and Ferrante's novels, also constitutes a possible solution to the mystery that surrounds the protagonist of Cristina Comencini's *Matrioška* (2002). Antonia, a famous sculptor threatened by obesity and a terminal illness, tells the story of her life to a biographer, Chiara, whose professional detachment is soon jeopardized by the parallels she recognizes between their lives:

> Le nostre vite cosí diverse, opposte per un certo verso, hanno questa congiunzione: il rifiuto materno. Il disgusto di sé ha tormentato Antonia per tutta la vita. Mi sembra un punto importante della sua personalità, ne parla spesso come di un peso, un fardello portato fin dall'infanzia [...] La sensazione di indegnità che mi tormentava da bambina è sparita con la nascita di Giovanni e lei racconta che quel disgusto l'abbandonava solo quando scolpiva. Devo annotare questa analogia, forse non servirà, ma devo ricordarmi di trascriverla.[43]

> Our very different, almost opposite, lives have this in common: our mothers' rejection. Self-contempt has tormented Antonia throughout her life. This seems to me an important part of her personality: she often speaks of it as if it were a weight, a burden that she has carried since infancy [...] The feeling of indignity that tormented me as a child disappeared only when Giovanni was born. She says that her self-contempt disappeared when she sculpted. I must write down this analogy. Perhaps it is useless, but I must remember to make a note of it.

Although 'perhaps' useless, the analogy between creativity and procreation carries with it the suspicion of mutual exclusion. Chiara had painfully abandoned all ambition of becoming a creative writer when her first son was born. Her activity as a biographer is safely presented as a 'job,' which as such does not imply the same degree of involvement as art. Yet she perceives her participation in Antonia's life as a betrayal, mysteriously linked to her son's sudden illness:

> La prima notte che è stato male, quando l'abbiamo portato in ospedale perché la febbre non scendeva, ho giurato, come sempre, che se non fosse stato niente di grave, non avrei scritto piú nella mia vita, avrei fatto solo la madre e la moglie, mi sarei cercata un mestiere senza nessuna pretesa. Ora che sta meglio, mi chiedo come posso essere cosí superstiziosa, nel ventunesimo secolo. Eppure in quei momenti, mi sembra matematico. Loro hanno bisogno di me, io penso ad altro, loro si ammalano. La verità è che scrivere di Antonia mi fa dimenticare tutto, e loro mi puniscono.[44]

> The night he got sick, when we took him to the hospital because his fever wouldn't go down, I swore as always that, if he didn't have anything serious, I would never in my life write again. I would be only a mother and a wife; I would look for a simple job. Now that he is better, I wonder how I can be so superstitious, in the twenty-first century. But in those moments, everything seems very logical to me. They need me; I think of something else; they get sick. The reality is that writing about Antonia makes me forget everything, and they punish me.

This passage reveals the consequences for a woman's psyche of the 'either/or' theory that defined creativity and procreation as mutually exclusive for women. The ancient prejudice – already implicit in the punishment that befell the successful woman author in Pirandello's *Suo marito*[45] – had found a powerful ally in psychoanalysis. More precisely, as Susan Suleiman states, 'psychoanalysis lent scientific prestige to a widespread cultural prejudice, reinforcing it and elevating it to the status of a "natural" law.'[46] Internalized by women, this law created the anxiety and guilt exemplified in Comencini's novel. While condemning her vows as 'superstition,' Chiara also acknowledges the inescapable influence that the notion of motherhood as woman's only mission has on her life.

The friendship between Chiara and Antonia parallels the one – intuitively perceived by Chiara but never explicitly confirmed in the text – between the sculptor and Chiara's mother, who lived in Naples during the same years and had perhaps met.[47] Chiara begins to suspect that the similarities she notices are more than a coincidence, and that Antonia may have chosen her as a biographer for a precise reason. This suspicion is neither dispelled nor confirmed at the end of the novel. As in *L'amore molesto*, a certain ambiguity remains, as if the mystery represented by the mother could not be solved completely. Much like to the Russian dolls from which the book takes its title, each woman contains her younger self, as well as her mother's past.

Daughter *and* Mother

'We are, none of us, "either" mothers or daughters; to our amazement, confusion, and greater complexity, we are both':[48] Adrienne Rich's statement epitomizes the web of desire, misunderstanding, and remorse so elegantly portrayed in Francesca Sanvitale's *Madre e figlia* (*Mother and Daughter*, 1980). Once again, rhetorical choices serve as powerful indicators of the complexity of the relationship.[49] The homodiegetic narrator who introduces the story reveals at the outset her failed attempt to replicate her mother's image: 'Succede che alcune volte, mentre cammino per la strada, vedo il suo passo, lo fermo con un impressionante tremito nelle vene: è lei. Fisso la vetrina di un negozio, blocco quelle gambe che camminano: non è lei, sono io che ripropongo ma ostacolo nella falsità la sua vera apparizione. Sono solo io'[50] (Sometimes, when I walk the streets, I see her stride, and I stop it with a sharp quiver in my veins: it's her. I stare at a shop window, and stop those walking legs. It's not her; it's I who recreate yet hinder with deception her true appearance. It's only me). Soon after, however, the narrator withdraws into omniscience, reporting the story of Marianna (the mother) and Sonia (the daughter who in turn becomes a mother) as if it did not coincide with her own. In one of the rare exceptions to this pattern, the narrator hints at her deteriorating physical condition, which makes her the reflection of the converging images of Sonia and Marianna:

> Stamani davanti allo specchio ho sputato il dentrifricio e ho osservato i miei denti. Ingialliscono, si sono allungati, sembrano staccati tra loro. Provo se tentennano, non sono fragili. Eppure le gengive si ritirano. Se chiudo la bocca, se sorrido, i denti tornano bianchi e compatti, possono ricordare la bocca di un'adolescente, cioè di Sonia. Però è un'illusione. I miei denti già vecchi sono uguali a quelli della signora Marianna del 1945.[51]

> This morning, in front of the mirror, I spat out the toothpaste and looked

at my teeth. They are getting yellow, longer, and seem to be separated from one another. I check if they move; they are not weak. And yet the gums are receding. If I close my mouth or smile, my teeth are still white and compact; they may recall the mouth of an adolescent – that is, Sonia. But it's an illusion. My already old teeth are the same as Signora Marianna's in 1945.

Though the narrator should logically share the personal pronoun with Sonia, time has shaped her to resemble Marianna. Identification with the mother runs, once again, through the body,[52] to the point that Sonia awaits the illness that has marked Marianna's life, certain that it will touch her own.[53] The two women are linked by elusive ties and relationships – epitomized by the narrator's ambiguous position – throughout a narration that dissolves the boundaries between true and imagined events, reality and dreams. The narrator opens the story with words of unconditional love for Marianna, but Sonia as a character is torn between affection and resentment because of the intricate connections she perceives between her destiny and that of her mother:

> Gli avvenimenti addensati e scoppiati, come un tifone senza precedenti e quasi grottesco nella sua forza, in una sola settimana proposero a Sonia analogie e richiami. Non era un caso stupefacente che la madre avesse avuto un tumore quando lei si era sposata e adesso che avrebbe dovuto iniziare una vita diversa il tumore tornasse? Non era il tempo pieno di circolarità e non era la madre stessa che la richiamava a sé con questo male? Non la stava defraudando, ancora una volta, di tutto per costringerla a vivere di lei? E contro il destino di essere senza alcuna ragione nel mondo, o contro sua madre, c'era qualche cosa da fare?[54]

The events that had thickened and burst in just a week, like an unprecedented typhoon almost grotesque in its force, suggested analogies and similarities to Sonia. Wasn't it a surprising coincidence that her mother was diagnosed with cancer when she got married, and that the cancer came back now, when she was about to start a new life? Wasn't time spinning in circles, wasn't her mother calling her back with this disease? Wasn't she depriving her, once again, of everything, forcing her to live off her mother? And could anything be done to counter her destiny of having no purpose in life, or to counter her mother?.

Resentment, in turn, generates remorse, which is the driving force of the novel. The feeling of not being able to care for her mother adequately is coupled with Sonia's equally painful realization – that she replicated with her son the patterns of her relationship with Marianna:

> Ma nella seconda metà della vita, quando diventò madre essa stessa, il buio notturno fu presto funestato anche dai rimorsi a proposito del bambino. Quale madre era stata mai ed era, proprio lei che dall'infanzia aveva ricavato tutto il dolore possibile, per procurare giorni tanto aridi a suo figlio, per punirlo, condizionarlo e piegarlo?[55]

> But in the second half of her life, when she became a mother herself, the darkness of the night began to be haunted by her remorse concerning her son as well. What kind of mother had she ever been, and was she still, to procure for her son such bitter days, to punish, mould, and bend him, in spite of having suffered so much herself during her childhood?

Dissatisfied with her behaviour towards her mother and towards her child, and aware of a connection between the two,[56] Sonia, through the narrator, offers the story as a final, healing tribute to the mother. Two visions frame the novel: In the first, the mother leaves an old palace to face 'una folla asserragliata al di là della strada, che l'aspetta con i bastoni alzati, le vanghe, i coltelli e che le vuole dimostrare dileggio e disprezzo'[57] (a crowd gathered on the other side of the street, waiting for her and raising their clubs, shovels, and knives, intent on showing mockery and contempt), while the narrator is ready to intervene in her defence. In the second, which concludes the novel, the narrator is travelling with her adolescent son to a foreign city, where she finds herself between a land devastated by war and 'lo spettacolo piú grandioso visto nella [sua] vita'[58] (the most grandiose spectacle ever seen in [her] life). A very old lady in a wheelchair, whom the narrator immediately identifies as the Queen, looks mysteriously into an abyss before her, which seems to give her peace and tranquillity. Two rows of young knights on white horses escort her and her group. When the meditation is over, they all turn to the stone wall:

> Ma ecco che in un attimo di mutazione davanti al mio sguardo la parete lavorata dal tempo si trasforma e la pietra diventa la facciata di un palazzo regale, e le caverne allineate finestre, e come in uno stupendo sogno d'amore per ciò che possono, insieme al tempo, fare gli uomini, s'intrecciano nodi scolpiti e la grandiosità della roccia diventa tutta umana: è il palazzo del regno dove, finita la meditazione e protetti dai cavalleggeri, i vecchi rientreranno.[59]

All of a sudden, a transformation takes place before my eyes. The wall, worn down by time, changes, the stone becomes the facade of a royal palace, and the caves turn into rows of windows. As in a marvellous dream of love for what humans can do together with time, sculpted knots are woven, and the grandiose rock becomes human. This is the palace of the kingdom where, having ended the meditation and under the protection of the knights, the old people will return.

It is a supreme effort, achieved only in a dream, to reconcile past and present, natural forces and human needs, the disasters brought by time and the healing power of the mind. The presence of the son, albeit mentioned only in passing, is crucial to the composition: like the young knights on white horses, only he can protect the narrator's identity as daughter *and* mother, at a loving yet safe distance from both Sonia and Marianna, a person in her own right.

chapter 5

Mothers without Children

From Flesh to Phantom

> Vedi:
> questo è il mio bambino
> finto.
>
> Gli ho fatto il vestitino
> all'uncinetto
> con la lana bianca.
>
> Dice anche 'mamma' –
> sí –
> se lo rovesci sopra il dorso.
>
> Dammelo qui in braccio
> per un pochino:
> ecco,
> hai sentito
> come ha detto
>
> 'mamma'?
>
> Questo è il mio bambino –
> vedi –
> il mio bambino
> finto.[1]

Look: this is my fake baby. I knitted him a little dress in white wool. He even says 'mamma' – yes he does – if I turn him over. Let me hold him a little bit: listen, did you hear how he said 'mamma'? This is my baby – you see – this fake baby of mine.

An expression of Antonia Pozzi's visceral and frustrated desire for motherhood, this poem dates back to 1933 and serves as a reminder of literature's ability to escape the neat boundaries critics create for it. At a time when motherhood was the object of intense ideological propaganda, Pozzi, in complete isolation, sketched a child that existed only in her imagination. In retrospect, knowing the brief span and tragic outcome of Pozzi's life,[2] it is tempting to read these lines as a premonition. The poem in which Pozzi, at age twenty-one, describes her imaginary baby *becomes* her child, her link with the future and her hope for transcendence. Her creation of an ersatz child foreshadows the phenomenon that would take place at the end of the twentieth century, when various historical, social, and cultural factors combined in separating the biological from the psychological aspects of mothering.

Whereas in the 1930s Pozzi had expressed her longings with her trademark lightness and grace, Susanna Tamaro, writing near the end of the twentieth century, explored the darker side of a frustrated desire for motherhood in 'Sotto la neve' ('Under the Snow'), a short story in her collection *Per voce sola* (*For Solo Voice*, 1994). The story is organized in three long letters that the protagonist, Emanuela, writes to the son she was forced to abandon at birth, although it is not clear at the beginning whether he will ever receive them. In the letters, the woman revisits the events of her adolescence: her encounter with an American soldier in the aftermath of the Second World War; her pregnancy; the soldier's betrayal and departure; and finally the birth of a baby boy who was promptly taken away from her in order to preserve social appearances and avoid the complications and scandal an illegitimate child would have entailed. From that day forward, the woman explains, she was reduced to an empty container similar to the skin snakes shed in spring, which reflects with perturbing precision the living body that has slid away. The narrator's choice of images is telling. In introducing Vegetti Finzi's work, Cinzia Zanardi describes the contradiction observed in clinical practice between an adolescent's awareness of her reproductive powers and the constraints of socialized motherhood: 'As woman becomes mother, both idealized and imprisoned in a role of biological and social reproduction, she loses her identity, she loses contact with her body. Her womb becomes in her fantasy an empty space.'[3]

Emanuela's 'empty space' is soon inhabited again. Her mind gives her the illusion of having overcome the trauma of losing her child, but her body reenacts the stages of maternity and separation. Every year, the calendar of conception, pregnancy, and delivery repeats itself, but every year the sequence bears no fruit. 'Stagione dopo stagione, per venticinque anni, una parte di me ancora viva ha compiuto questo rito'[4] (Year after year, for twenty-five years, a part of me that was still alive performed this ritual). Much to the protagonist's surprise, even menopause does not alter her body's pattern. She finally consults a doctor, only to find out that her body has been harbouring a cancer. Tamaro's story is remarkable in that it stretches to the extreme the analogy between pregnancy and disease,[5] while developing at the same time the theme of the child's absence and of his inadequate and perverse replacements. Woman's ability to give life, turned from power to curse by social conventions, haunts the protagonist. For years, her body mimics the stages of pregnancy while bearing no fruit, and ultimately delivering a malignant offspring.

The Symbolic Order of the Mother

The years 1981–2004 saw the consequences of the steady, and seemingly unstoppable, decline of the birth rate. While hardly limited to Italy, this trend reached unique proportions in the peninsula. In the first months of 1981, the Italian population stopped increasing, which fuelled aversion to feminism – accused of distracting women from their true mission – and caused much anxiety about the future of Italian society.[6] Despite some initiatives adopted in support of families (such as the extension of parental benefits to fathers), the trend has, until very recently, continued, and in 1998 the birth rate sank to a stunning 1.19 children per woman, one of the lowest in the world.[7] The decline has been so steady for so long that Italy is currently the country with the oldest population in the world, and only a wave of immigration (an unprecedented phenomenon for a country of emigrants) has prevented the situation from becoming catastrophic.[8]

Sociologists have cited various factors to explain this phenomenon. Italian youth seem to show a pronounced tendency towards delaying the choices that would lead to adulthood and to the assumption of parental responsibilities (chief among them, leaving their families of origin).[9]

'Un figlio è essere come non si era prima'[10] (A child means that you are no longer what you used to be), concludes the protagonist of Valeria Viganò's *Il piroscafo olandese* (*The Dutch Steamer*, 1999), at the end of her reflection on the scarce appeal of motherhood. Marina Piazza stresses how the main characteristic of people born in the 1960s is the

> moratoria, cioè la posticipazione di massa dei *marker events*, le pietre miliari dell'età adulta: l'andarsene di casa, l'indipendenza economica attraverso il lavoro, la formazione di nuove coppie, il fare figli. Tanto piú sono usciti in fretta dall'infanzia e dalla pubertà, tanto piú diventa lunghissima la fase di un'adolescenza prolungata. Cosicché si potrebbe anche supporre che il termine "adolescenza' non designi piú un'età, ma una categoria dello spirito, un modo di essere trasversale a tutte le età, un'anima da *puer* all'interno del *senex*.[11]

> the 'moratorium,' i.e. the postponement, on a mass scale, of the marker events, the milestones of adulthood: leaving one's family home, gaining economic independence through one's work, forming a couple, having children. The more quickly they leave infancy and puberty, the longer they live in a protracted adolescence. One could even say that the word "adolescence' no longer designates a particular age, but rather a spiritual condition, a way of being that can be experienced at any age, a child's soul inside an old person.

This tendency to extend childhood beyond its chronological boundaries, together with the availability of birth control, the discrimination against mothers in the workplace,[12] and an intricate combination of shifting priorities and financial constraints that has made professional satisfaction both an ambition and an obligation for women, made childbearing a somewhat rare enterprise in late twentieth-century Italy.

No longer their destiny, motherhood had even ceased to be a life experience for many Italians. And yet the relation to the mother continued to be a defining factor in women's existence. In 1983, the Libreria delle Donne in Milan[13] issued a document that acknowledged the difficulties women still faced in society and their often neglected 'voglia di vincere' (desire to succeed). In this framework, the ideal of sisterhood, with its resulting equality, gave way to a more realistic assessment of the differences among women and an analysis of their implications:

> Generally we do not admit of difference and disparity in our groups, in the

name of an egalitarianism inherited from the youth movement. But this refusal is also and perhaps fundamentally a reaction to the obliteration of the mother in our society [...] We have come to understand that we can engage with disparities between women in our political practice and that this is precious. To recognize that someone like us has 'something extra' breaks the rule of male society [...] At the same time it liberates us, intimidated or inferiorized as we are in relation with men, from a reactive need to feel on a par with our own kind at least. Women were also brought into the world by a mother. In order to struggle against patriarchal society we must give real strength within our relationships to that ancient relationship in which there could be, fused together, love and esteem for another woman. Every woman had, in her mother, her first love and her first model.[14]

This document can be interpreted as the outcome of a decade of reflection on the maternal role in Italian feminist thought. No longer perceived as a danger that could annihilate a women's potential, nor viewed as the biological factor that had historically made women accomplices in the patriarchal order, motherhood was instead recognized in this document as a source of inspiration. Furthermore, it was defined as a model for female relationships not only in the separate world of women, but in the society at large. This shift is the result of three distinct yet connected factors: first, the move from the daughterly perspective that had marked feminism in the 1970s to a wider acceptance of female realities; second, the critical analysis of philosophical, mythological, religious, and psychoanalytical theories that had linked motherhood with biology, nature, and submission; and finally, an understanding of mothering as symbol and potential, rather than as physical reality.

The importance of the document lies not only in its assessment of the situation but also in its articulation of a strategy for overcoming women's shared difficulties in society. The mother-daughter relationship, with its inevitable disparity but also the emotional strength it entails, was the inspiring force behind the notion of 'affidamento' (entrustment), a system of fostering and mentorship that could be defined as 'the establishing of a relationship of mediation between women of different powers, positions, and skills, which would help those who are younger, less established, and less informed to negotiate the world beyond the separate world of women.'[15] Although far from being universally endorsed, the notion of entrustment has proven central to later discussions.[16] It represents at the same time a point of arrival and of departure. While exemplifying the new notion of motherhood and of mother-daughter relationships elaborated in feminist thought, it inspired further theoretical investigation in those domains.

A World of Mothers

In subsequent years, considerable attention was devoted to the symbolic value of motherhood, effectively separating its implications at the level of authority, power, nurturing, and emotion from its biological component. Luisa Muraro drew attention to the 'well-known and wonderful phenomenon' that allows the replacement of the biological mother with another individual, without necessarily changing the mother-child relationship:

> In questo fatto si potrebbe vedere l'irrilevanza dell'elemento naturale e la rilevanza esclusiva della struttura [...] Io vi leggo la predisposizione simbolica della madre la quale, come dire, si lascia sostituire da altri senza danno o senza grave danno per l'opera di creazione del mondo che ella compie insieme alla sua creatura.[17]

> This fact could be interpreted as a sign of the irrelevance of the natural element and the unique importance of structure [...] I take it to represent the symbolic tendency of the mother to be replaced by others without damage or without significant damage to the world she creates together with her child.

In psychoanalysis, Vegetti Finzi has opened a new field of enquiry, separating women's potential to generate and the interactive attitude that this entails from procreation and mothering, which are to a large extent socially constructed.[18] Women's predisposition towards bringing humans to life finds its powerful emblem in the 'child of the night,' as Vegetti Finzi calls the imaginary child produced in the fantasy of preadolescent girls.

Introducing her book on 'non-procreative motherhood,' Elaine Hansen speaks of the linguistic challenge posited by 'the bewildering fragmentation of a time in which one child may have a genetic mother, a gestational mother, and a custodial mother, each of whom is a different person.' She proceeds to identify 'a number of novels and stories that center on the "mother without child", a rubric that includes nontraditional mothers and "bad" mothers, including lesbians and slave mothers; women who have abortions and miscarriages; women who refuse to bear children, or whose children are stolen from them; and mothers who are [...] sometimes criminals, murderers, prisoners, suicides, time travelers, tricksters, or ghosts.'[19]

An adapted rubric of 'the childless mother' more aptly describes the specificity of the Italian cultural landscape. Mothers without children, in an Italian context, are not, as Hansen describes, mothers who have lost their offspring, but rather women who establish nurturing relationships with children to whom they are not biologically related. In this framework, motherhood becomes an attitude, a state of mind, a practice, or, as Sara Ruddick states, 'a political act.' Ruddick also makes a distinction between 'birthing labor, which is women's prerogative and finds its culminating moment and defining hope [in] the act of giving birth,' and motherhood, which is always adoptive, can be chosen by men and women (at least in theory), and entails a commitment 'to protecting, nurturing, and training particular children.'[20] To be sure, the idea of 'adoptive motherhood' as a province of both sexes seems at best, at least in Italian society, wishful thinking. Yet, the idea that 'all mothers are adoptive' holds great potential for the twenty-first century, when the links between the biological and the social have become both weaker and more complex. The notion of 'affidamento' developed by the women at the Libreria delle Donne di Milano can be interpreted precisely as an 'elective mother-daughter relationship,'[21] a 'social contract.'[22] Contemporary Italian fiction offers meaningful examples of this tendency towards a wider – one could even say a more generous – notion of motherhood. The last section of Valeria Viganò's *Prove di vite separate* (*Attempts at Separate Lives*, 1992) explores the attachment of the protagonist, Mabel, to a seven-year-old girl she has met by chance. During a summer afternoon, the two are surprised by a rainstorm:

> Nel ronzio dell'apparecchio, nel profumo di biancheria, nella voce della bambina che giocava da sola, Mabel si era sentita mancare. Per uno scriteriato attimo aveva immaginato che Matilde potesse essere una figlia. Nell'intimità e nei vapori del bagno, e ora che era calata la sera, avrebbe magari desiderato prepararle un pasto caldo e metterla a letto. Se Matilde glielo avesse chiesto le avrebbe anche narrato una storia. Ne aveva centinaia che si erano accumulate inespresse.[23]

> With the buzzing of the hair dryer, the smell of the laundry, the voice of the little girl playing alone, Mabel felt her strength abandon her. She had

imagined, for a senseless moment, that Matilde could be her daughter. In the intimacy and the steam from the bath, and now that the sun had set, she would perhaps have liked to prepare a hot meal for her and put her to bed. If Matilde asked her, she could also tell her a story. She had accumulated hundreds without ever telling them.

A similar pattern is present in Dacia Maraini's *Dolce per sé* (*Sweet in Itself*, 1997), an epistolary novel organized around the letters that for seven years a middle-aged woman writes to a little girl – correspondence that accompanies the addressee from childhood to adolescence. To extrapolate the tendencies of times that are so close to us is notoriously difficult. Nevertheless, it seems that there is a significant trend emerging, one which inverts the paradigm prevalent in the early nineteenth century. While in those times, the biological experience of motherhood could exist without the sentimental implications we have become accustomed to associating with the figure of the mother, late twentieth-century novels describe relationships that replicate the emotional ties of a maternal connection, but that are established by and between individuals who are not necessarily linked biologically.

This new notion of motherhood, no longer an event but rather a disposition of the self, was, paradoxically, anticipated by the writer who most vehemently opposed feminism and working women. In her pamphlet *Le idee di una donna* (1903), Neera repeated over and over again that motherhood was to be women's only mission. Apart from mocking women who harboured other ambitions, she tried to ignore the socio-economic factors that made marriage and motherhood impossible for many. Only in her last chapter did she acknowledge the fact that some women may never become mothers, in spite of their heartfelt desires. Turning to them, she envisioned for a moment the possibility of separating motherhood from its biological component:

> Siate madri. Se il vostro fianco non ha partorito fra i dolori il figlio delle vostre viscere, concepite moralmente. Siate con uno slancio di magnifico altruismo la madre di un orfano [...] La donna che sa educare, che plasma una intelligenza, che sviluppa un'anima, è madre [...]; occupa quindi la prima dignità femminile.[24]

> Be mothers. If your body did not deliver with pain the child of your womb, conceive morally. Become, with a leap of magnificent altruism, a mother to an orphan [...] The woman who educates, who shapes an intelligence and

develops a soul, is a mother [...]; she is worthy of the highest degree of female dignity.

Albeit confusedly, Neera hinted at a possibility that can be fully explored at the beginning of the third millennium, when birth control, reproductive technologies, and the growing practice of adoption stretch the meaning of motherhood to an extent unthinkable a century ago. The anxiety caused by this challenge to deeply rooted notions of lineage and parenting is undeniable, and perhaps unavoidable.[25] New conceptions come to light. They shape the ways in which every human being reckons with a figure indispensable to his or her arrival into this world, and the ways in which women interpret their role, power, and responsibility. Motherhood as nurturing and caring, as principle and practice, adapts and evolves through the history of humanity, and gives hopes and continuity to its development.

Notes

Introduction

1 Monnier 23.
2 *Recent Demographic Developments in Europe* 27.
3 See Colebrook 124.
4 Pale earthly representations of immortal deities, Gabriele D'Annunzio's female characters exemplify this tendency to reduce motherhood to its mythical component. See Nardi.
5 Pascoli 1269–70. I quote from Pascoli's Italian translation of the original Latin. For a more extreme and macabre portrayal of the mother as an individual oblivious to her fears and pain but oversensitive to her son's, see José Echegaray's poem 'Severed Heart' (qtd. in Bernard 4).
6 Here and elsewhere, translations are mine unless otherwise noted.
7 Nardi 79.
8 This problem is not specific to Italian culture. Introducing a collection of essays on Anglo-American narrations of motherhood, Brenda Daly and Maureen T. Reddy observe how 'even in women's accounts of motherhood, maternal perspectives are strangely absent. We most often hear daughters' voices in both literary and theoretical texts about mothers, mothering, and motherhood, even in those written by feminists who are mothers' (1).
9 Benjamin 78.
10 Benjamin 23.
11 Giorgio, 'Writing' 3.
12 Wellek, 'The Fall of Literary History' 75.
13 Bravo, 'La nuova Italia' 141.
14 Fattorini 281.
15 Bravo, 'La nuova Italia' 152.

16 Negri, *Maternità* 22.
17 Macciocchi 62–3.
18 Meldini 168.
19 Pickering-Iazzi, 'Introduction,' *Unspeakable Women* 7.
20 Giocondi 7–23.
21 See Pickering-Iazzi, 'Introduction,' *Unspeakable Women* 9.
22 Scattigno 283–8.
23 Ramondino 264.
24 Valeria Viganò poetically describes 'quel momento magico, sei mesi, un anno, per i piú fortunati anche cinque, nel quale i figli avanzano e i genitori retrocedono sui nastri paralleli delle esistenze e da pari a pari finalmente si incontrano e si intendono davvero, profondamente, gli uni di fronte agli altri, uguale la statura e la considerazione reciproca' (*Prove* 116). (that magical moment that lasts six months, a year, even five years for those who are really lucky, in which children progress while parents regress on the parallel conveyor belts of life. They finally meet as equals, before one another, at the same height and with mutual respect, and finally they truly and deeply understand each other). It is precisely this 'magical moment' that the characters of this group of novels miss.
25 See Giorgio, 'Writing the Mother-Daughter' 34–9.
26 Caldwell 103.
27 See in particular Cavarero, 'Dire la nascita'; Muraro, 'The Narrow Door.'
28 See Hansen 38.
29 Morante 643. For a more in-depth analysis of this passage, see chapter 3.

Chapter 1

1 Invernizio 177.
2 Bravo, 'La nuova Italia' 141.
3 Badinter 42. This new view of motherhood as a dynamic, evolving concept – rather than an immutable principle – can be linked to the similar revision of the notion of childhood proposed by Philippe Ariès in his momentous *L'enfant et la vie familiale sous l'ancien régime*.
4 Marcellini 480.
5 Marchesini 39. De Mauro (36) points out that in 1861 the overall literacy rate of the young kingdom of Italy was an astounding 22 per cent, and stresses the difficulties in implementing the Casati law (40–5).
6 See Manacorda 19.
7 This lack of professional choice is apparent to Didina, the protagonist of Ada Negri's *Stella mattutina* (*Morning Star*, 1921): 'Vuole studiar da maestra,

unicamente perché non intende logorarsi in un opificio come la madre, o divenir serva di signori in gioventú e portinaia in vecchiezza, come la nonna' (23–4) (She wants to study to become a teacher, only because she has no intention of wearing herself out in a factory like her mother, or of becoming a servant in her youth and a concierge in her old age, like her grandmother).
8 See Giorgio Bini.
9 Of humble origins, Italia Donati showed talent and determination in pursuing a teaching career. Her misfortunes began when she was sent to teach in a small Tuscan village. Alone in a hostile environment, ostracized by the community that accused her of being the mayor's mistress and of having had an abortion, Italia committed suicide in 1886, at age twenty-three. She left a letter asking that an autopsy be performed on her body to prove her innocence. Her story was reconstructed by Elena Gianini Belotti in *Prima della quiete* (*Before the Rest*).
10 Baccini 427.
11 Research on women writers, of course, has boomed in the last twenty years. Another useful anthology devoted to the nineteenth century was published by Santoro in 1987. See also the volumes by Amoia and Wood on the twentieth century, as well as Marotti, Russell, and Panizza and Wood on women writers throughout the history of Italian literature.
12 For the discussion on Neera, I am indebted to Antonia Arslan's pivotal essays, particularly to those collected in *Dame, galline e regine.*
13 According to De Giorgio, until the First World War the median age at which Italian women married was between twenty-five and twenty-six, but this figure includes widows who remarried.
14 Neera, *L'indomani* 14.
15 'Nella famiglia ottocentesca padri e madri non svolgono attività comuni, i loro compiti son divisi da una netta separazione dei ruoli e delle sfere di relazione. In questa struttura di rapporti famigliari a "ruoli segregati" che resiste ben oltre il XIX secolo, figli e figlie si muovono nel cerchio chiuso di valori e abitudini delle rispettive mascolinità e femminilità in miniatura' (De Giorgio 48) (In nineteenth-century families fathers and mothers do not have common activities. Their respective duties are divided by a clear separation of roles and spheres of relations. In this structure of family relationships marked by 'segregated roles' that endures far beyond the nineteenth century, sons and daughters move in the close circles of values and habits belonging to the respective masculinity and femininity in miniature). For the persistence of this model in Fascist Italy see Vené 73–5.
16 Neera, *L'indomani* 133. For an interpretation of this and other passages

describing women discoving they are pregnant, see Mazzoni, 'Pregnant Bodies,' and Mazzoni, *Maternal Impressions* 60–111.
17 Paolo Mantegazza had expressed the same notion in his popular *Fisiologia dell'amore* (*Physiology of Love*, 1873): 'L'uomo e la donna possono amarsi con la stessa forza, ma non si ameranno mai nella stessa maniera, dacché all'altare della loro passione portano una natura profondamente diversa, anche all'infuori della diversa missione genetica che spetta a ciascuno' (207) (A man and a woman can love each other with the same intensity, but not in the same way, as each brings a profoundly different nature to the altar of their passion, even without considering their different genetic mission). Later in the treatise, the author returns to the same concept, revealing the prescriptive, rather than descriptive, nature of his proposition: 'Ogni pensiero, ogni parola, ogni gesto d'uomo e di donna che ami riceve l'impronta del sesso; e quando i caratteri sono invertiti, ne nasce lo sconcio piú ributtante, e noi ci troviamo dinanzi una caricatura, un mostro, od anche ad un delitto' (216) (Every thought, every word, every gesture of a man or a woman in love brings the imprint of their sex; when these characteristics are inverted, the most revolting monstrosity is born, and we encounter a caricature, a monster, or even a crime).
18 Neera, *L'indomani* 144.
19 Arslan, *Dame, galline e regine* 131.
20 Arslan, *Dame, galline e regine* 134. See also Nardi 90–1.
21 Prosperi 376–7.
22 Prosperi 378.
23 Maternity as the answer to a woman's reluctance and uneasiness regarding marriage, however, will be a long-lasting narrative solution. It can be found in one of the last short stories written by Anna Banti, 'Una ragazza antica' ('An Ancient Girl,' 1984). Its protagonist, Rosa B., realizes that through motherhood she will finally learn to love her husband:

> Fu allora che addentrandosi in pensieri così difficili corse con la mente a un sentimento universalmente accettato come sacro, quello della maternità. Su questa naturale conseguenza del matrimonio non s'era mai fermata, ma ora l'ipotesi di un suo bambino la sconvolse: capì che per lui la parola giusta sarebbe stata soltanto amore. Amando suo figlio avrebbe imparato ad amare suo marito, lo sposo amico. (30)

> It was at this point that, as she became absorbed in such difficult considerations, she thought of a sentiment universally accepted as sacred – that of maternity. She had never pondered this natural consequence of

matrimony, but now she was shaken by the idea of having a child of her own. She realized that for him the only right word could be love. By loving him, she could learn how to love her husband, her husband friend.

24 Neera, *Le idee di una donna* 47.
25 Aleramo, *La donna e il femminismo* (*Women and Feminism*) 63.
26 'Certo che se i soli beni materiali sono l'essenza della nostra felicità, tutti essendo uguali, tutti dovremmo ugualmente parteciparne; e così siccome l'azione governativa sarebbe la causa del benessere e della sciagura sociale, tutti indistintamente dovremmo aver parte nel pubblico reggimento; allora mi associerei [...] invocando come un diritto inalienabile alle donne, come a tutti, un'azione direttissima sulla pubblica cosa. Ma il principio d'onde questi partono è poi vero?' (qtd. in Pieroni Bortolotti, *Socialismo e questione femminile* [*Socialism and the Female Issue*] 33) (Obviously, if material goods were the essence of our happiness, we all should share them, because we are all equals; similarly, because government actions cause social well-being and disgrace, we should all be part of them; in that case, I could agree [...] and invoke as a woman's inalienable right, indeed, as anyone's inalienable right, a most direct intervention in public affairs. But is this starting premise valid, after all?)
27 On the relationship between these two movements see Pieroni Bortolotti, *Socialismo e questione femminile*.
28 Neera, *Le idee* 68.
29 Lombroso and Ferrero 129. Paolo Mantegazza, in *Fisiologia della donna* (1893), will endorse this position. See Mazzoni, 'Impressive Cravings' 141.
30 Lombroso and Ferrero 79.
31 This tendency to keep different aspects of life rigorously separated seems to have been a mental habit of this author. Arslan notes that the letters Neera wrote to her family do not usually provide much information about her literary career: 'Poiché Neera distingueva con precisione e decisione la vita di famiglia dalla sua attività pubblica, [le sue lettere] di solito non recano notizie utili sul piano della letteratura' (Arslan, *L'archivio inedito* [*Unpublished Archive*] 217) (As Neera used to separate with precision and decisiveness her family life from public activity, [her letters] usually do not provide useful information about literature).
32 Neglected for decades after her death, and often mentioned more for her sentimental involvement with the poet and Nobel laureate Giosuè Carducci than for her own literary accomplishments, Vivanti has been rediscovered by critics in the last decade, as attested in particular by the recent publication of her letters to Carducci (*Addio Caro Orco*), of some of her short stories (*Racco-*

nti americani), and of a new edition of her first novel, *Marion, artista di caffè-concerto*.
33 The novel's characters bump into each other in distant corners of the world with disconcerting facility – and producing unintended comic effects. Reduced to poverty in New York City, Aldo, the male protagonist, sees by chance a rich woman he had once met in Monte Carlo. After Aldo's mysterious disappearance, it will be the female protagonist's turn to recognize, again by chance, the German nanny of her childhood, who will provide much-needed lodging.
34 Vivanti, *I divoratori* 115.
35 Vivanti, *I divoratori* 481–2.
36 Beauvoir 2: 190.
37 Vivanti left a tender portrayal of her daughter's childhood and talent in 'La storia di Vivien' in the collection *Zingaresca* (1918).
38 Lucienne Kroha points out that 'women writers never treated the subject of women writers' (26) and attributes their reticence to caution and self-censorship.
39 It is worth noting that this does not seem at first to create uneasiness in any of the protagonists. As we have seen, however, this arrangement does belong to a previous stage in the history of motherhood. It would thus be possible to read the novel as an example of the conflict between two notions of motherhood in which the old, nineteenth-century model is proven to be inadequate and even dangerous.
40 It is certainly revealing that the first English translation of the novel (by Martha King and Mary Ann Frese Witt) appeared only in 2000.
41 Pirandello, *L'umorismo* 146–7 (*On Humor* 125).
42 Dombroski 99.
43 The criticism of Silvia's novel *La casa dei nani* could easily have been directed at one of Pirandello's own works (especially to *Il fu Mattia Pascal*): 'Buon romanzo, sì ... forse; affermazione di un ingegno non comune senza dubbio; ma non poi quel capolavoro d'umorismo che s'era voluto proclamare' (Pirandello, *Tutti i romanzi* 1, 613) (a good novel, all right... perhaps; the revelation of an uncommon talent, undoubtedly; but not that masterpiece of humour that some claimed). Later in the novel, another critic comments:

> Perché il grande della sua arte è ... non saprei ... in alcuni guizzi, eh? non vi pare? subitanei, improvvisi ... in certi bruschi arresti che vi scuotono e vi stonano. Noi siamo abituati a un solo tono, ecco; a quelli che ci dicono: la vita è questa, questa e questa; ad altri che ci dicono:

è quest'altra, quest'altra e quest'altra, è vero? La Roncella vi dipinge un lato, anch'essa; ma poi d'un tratto si volta e vi presenta l'altro lato, subito. Ecco, questo mi pare!' (704)

Because what is great in her art is ... I don't know ... certain sudden, abrupt quivers ... don't you think? Certain sudden halts that shock you and throw you out of tune. We are used to only one tone, we are used to those who say: life is this, and that, and then also that; or to those who say: no, it's this other thing, and this, and that. Roncella also depicts one side, but then all of a sudden turns around and shows you the other side. This is it, I think!

44 Kroha 147.
45 On the 'either/or' theory see Suleiman 359–60. On the persistence of this theory see the discussion on Cristina Comencini's *Matrioška* (2002) in chapter 4.
46 Gina Lombroso 12.
47 Gina Lombroso 12–13.
48 Qtd. in Angelone 64.
49 'I try to distinguish between two meanings of motherhood, one superimposed on the other: the potential relationship of any woman to her powers of reproduction and to children; and the institution, which aims at ensuring that potential – and all women – shall remain under male control ... [The institution] has alienated women from our bodies by incarcerating us in them. At certain points in history, and in certain cultures, the idea of women-as-mothers has worked to endow all women with respect, even with awe, and to give women some say in the life of a people or a clan. But for most of what we know as the "mainstream" of recorded history, motherhood as institution has ghettoized and degraded female potentialities' (Rich 13).
50 Aleramo, *La donna e il femminismo* (*Woman and Feminism*) 186.
51 Aleramo, *Una donna* 193–4.
52 Chodorow 7.
53 Chodorow 203.
54 'I diritti della maternità (a proposito d'un romanzo)' ('Motherhood Rights [About a Novel]'), *Avanti!*, January 15, 1907, qtd. in Angelone 63 and Conti and Morino 34. The same assessment, in a different light, is expressed by a modern critic, Maria Antonietta Macciocchi: 'Una donna spezza la catena della schiavitù. È la rivolta. La rivolta emancipatrice contro l'umiliazione della donna sull'altare della maternità' (qtd. in Kroha 125) (A woman breaks the chain of slavery. It is the revolution. The revolution of emancipation, against the humiliation of women at the altar of motherhood).

55 Giacosa 167.
56 Qtd. in Angelone 63.
57 See Buttafuoco 158.
58 The letters to which I refer in this discussion were first published by Annarita Buttafuoco in 1986. Both Buttafuoco (1988) and Zancan (*Il doppio itinerario*, 1998) have inserted extensive passages of this correspondence in their subsequent analyses.
59 Qtd. in Zancan, *Il doppio itinerario* 186.
60 See Aleramo's heart-wrenching note about her meeting with her adult son in Conti and Morino 254.
61 Aleramo, *Andando e stando* (*Going and Staying*) 116.
62 See in particular Bassanese 141–5.
63 'Finalmente, finalmente era solo col suo bambino; nessuno piú poteva toglierglielo, nessuno piú poteva mettersi fra loro. E sul suo infinito accoramento sentiva calare un tenue velo di pace, e quasi di gioia – simile alla vaporosità di quella misteriosa notte autunnale, – perché l'anima sua si trovava finalmente sola, purificata dal dolore, sola e libera da ogni umana passione, davanti al Signore grande e misericordioso' (Deledda, *Romanzi e novelle* 166–7) (Finally, finally he was alone with his child; nobody could take him away from him, nobody could come between the two of them. And he felt that over his infinite sorrow lay a delicate veil of peace, and almost of happiness – similar to the vapours of that mysterious autumn night – because his soul was finally alone, purged of pain, alone and free of all human passion, in front of a great and compassionate God).
64 Deledda, *Romanzi e novelle* 564.
65 Girard 18.
66 Girard 64.
67 Piano 26.
68 Deledda, *Romanzi e novelle* 605.
69 Deledda, *Romanzi e novelle* 690.
70 Qtd. in Neiger 7.
71 De Giorgio 38.
72 Vivanti, *Vae Victis!* 233.
73 Vivanti, *Vae Victis!* 345.
74 *L'invasore* opened in Milan in the summer of 1915 and was favourably received by the public and the critics. For some of the contemporary reviews, see Urbancic 121–3.
75 Vivanti, *Vae Victis!* 346.
76 Vivanti, *Vae Victis!* 196.
77 Vivanti, *Vae Victis!* 221.

78 Vivanti, *Vae Victis!* 222. The dramatic situation described by Vivanti strikes a chord with the contemporary reader who may still remember Pope John Paul II's condemnation of the Bosnian women who, pregnant as a result of wartime rapes, opted for abortion.
79 Vivanti, *Vae Victis!* 205.
80 See Mazzoni, 'Pregnant Bodies' 232.
81 Saint-Point 18.
82 DuPlessis 179. Vivanti's novel presents intriguing similarities with Pirandello's short story 'Ignare' ('Unaware,' 1912), which also features a collective female protagonist: three nuns whose pregnancies are the consequence of violence. *Novelle per un anno* 268–81.
83 Deledda, *Romanzi e novelle* 743.
84 In contemporary spoken Italian, the word *aborto* is commonly used to indicate an abortion, whereas *aborto spontaneo* refers to a miscarriage.
85 Deledda, *Cosima* 56.
86 The theme of the rejection of motherhood is analyzed by Amoia in her volume *No Mothers We!*
87 Marchesa Colombi reveals a peculiar social awareness when she stresses the distance between her characters and her public in *In risaia* (*In the Rice Fields*, 1878), inviting her readers to bridge that gap and to make an effort to understand the life of rice-field workers. See, for instance, the following passage:

> E Nanna si faceva ogni dì più sospettosa e cattiva. Odiava la cognata, odiava Gaudenzio, odiava tutte le persone giovani e belle e felici. Aveva torto. Ma loro mie signore, che mi leggono sedute nel loro salotto accanto ad uno sposo che le adora, loro in cui l'educazione ha raffinato il senso morale, mi dicano, colla mano sulla coscienza, possono giurare che non avrebbero fatto altrettanto alla prova di quelle piccole torture d'ogni momento? (138)

> Nanna became increasingly mean and suspicious every day. She hated her sister-in-law, she hated Gaudenzio, she hated all the young, beautiful, happy people. She was wrong. But you, my dear ladies, who are reading these lines while sitting in your living room, next to a husband who adores you, you, whose moral sentiment has been refined through education, can you be sure that you would not have done the same, if submitted to those little continuous tortures?

88 De Giorgio 39.
89 This was particularly true for the textile sector. In 1890 the silk industry, for

instance, employed 120,386 women, 36,586 children, and only 15,384 men (Camilla Ravera 30).
90 Qtd. in Pieroni Bortolotti, *Alle origini* 224.
91 Alla povera bimba mancava il latte, giacché alla madre scarseggiava il pane. Ella deperì rapidamente, e invano Nedda tentò spremere fra i labbruzzi affamati il sangue del suo seno. Una sera d'inverno, sul tramonto, mentre la neve fioccava sul tetto, e il vento scuoteva l'uscio mal chiuso, la povera bambina, tutta fredda, livida, colle manine contratte, fissò gli occhi vitrei su quelli ardenti della madre, diede un guizzo, e non si mosse più. (Verga, 'Nedda' 29)

The poor girl did not get enough milk because her mother did not have enough bread. She deteriorated rapidly, and Nedda tried in vain to squeeze between her little hungry lips the blood of her breast. One winter evening, at sunset, while the snow was falling on the roof and the wind was shaking the barely closed door, the poor cold and pale girl, her little hands clenched, fixed her bleak eyes on her mother's burning eyes, shivered, and moved no more.
92 Negri, *Maternità* 22.
93 Negri, *Maternità* 37.
94 Negri, *Maternità* 58.
95 After describing *Maternità* as something between sociology and religion, Croce comments: 'Ma, si sa, ogni tentativo di fare dell'arte una missione uccide l'arte. La poesia è fine e non mezzo: abbassata a mezzo, si disfà, e scorre via di tra le dita come sabbia fine. Giacché tutto può entrare nell'opera poetica, e niente può esservi messo di proposito' (352) (But we know that all attempts to make a mission out of art end by killing art itself. Poetry is an end, not a means; when you degrade it to a means, it falls apart and slips through your fingers like fine sand. Everything can be part of art, but nothing can be forced into it on purpose).
96 See Pickering-Iazzi, 'Introduction,' *Unspeakable Women* 7.

Chapter 2

1 Mussolini, *Discorsi del 1925* 59–64.
2 See De Grazia 37–8.
3 This reversal prompted journalist Wanda Gorjux to report with glee, and unintended humour, that thanks to Fascism voting rights had ceased to be of primary concern not only for women, but for Italians in general ('Il voto non ha più ragione di essere scopo della vita neppure per gli uomini' [qtd. in Meldini 225]).

4 Mussolini, *Discorsi del 1927* 78. For an analysis of this speech, see Spackman 143–55.
5 See De Grazia 62–5.
6 See De Grazia 70. For more pronatalist policies, see Caldwell, 'Reproducers' 117–19.
7 Macciocchi, *La donna 'nera'* 62–3. For a comparison between these policies and those implemented in Nazi Germany, see 66–8. Mariolina Graziosi stresses the continuity between these laws and the backlash against women's employment that marked Italian society in the aftermath of the First World War.
8 Qtd. in Meldini 81.
9 'On June 5, 1940, the dictatorship suspended all quotas on women's work, and women began to be hired to substitute for some of the 1.63 million men called to arms' (De Grazia 282).
10 For an overview of the relationship between Fascism and literature, see Pertile.
11 Frateili 359–60.
12 Qtd. in *Critica fascista* 11, no. 19 (1 October 1933): 371.
13 See, for instance, his comment in *Critica fascista* 11, no. 21 (1 November 1933):

> I letterati sono in ritardo sul rinnovato ritmo della vita italiana, abbarbicati ancora alla piccola, misera vicenda particolare che scambiano per l'essenza stessa della vita. Questo è il punto fondamentale, la ragione prima della distanza che separa ancora le lettere d'oggi dal tempo nostro. Il giorno in cui gli scrittori, abbandonando l'empireo artificiale in cui vivono, si decideranno a vivere questa difficile e bellissima vita d'oggi, allora anche per le lettere e per l'arte sorgerà un tempo nuovo.

> Writers are late in embracing the renewed rhythm of Italian life, clinging as they do to the petty, miserable individual events they mistake for the essence of life. This is the fundamental point, the primary reason for the distance that still separates today's literature from our era. The day writers decide to abandon their artificial heaven for today's difficult and wonderful life, a new time will begin for literature and the arts.

'Il doganiere' is commonly identified as Gherardo Casini, editor of *Il lavoro fascista* and co-editor of *Critica fascista*. See, for instance, Breschi and Longo 421 and Offen 486, n. 19.
14 Manzini, 'The Pomegranate' 74–5.
15 The image of a pregnant woman conversing with her unborn baby is a recur-

rent feature in Manzini's work. See 'Ritratto di bambina' ('Portrait of a Girl') 99, and the following passage from 'A White Cloud,' a 1939 short story in which Manzini presents the relationship between a pregnant woman and her unborn child: 'My baby girl! I feel her in my blood as it rises inside me. My blood recognizes her, has felt her for years in its fitful pulse, knowing it could be calmed only if its beating were united with hers' (79).

16 Pirandello, *Maschere nude* 3: 82.
17 Airoldi Namer 149.
18 Pirandello introduced considerable changes to the plot he had already summarized in his 1911 novel *Suo marito* (see chapter 1). In particular, nature's rebellion in the novel followed La Spera's murder of her son, while in the play it becomes explicitly directed against the men who want to separate her from the child. For a detailed comparison between the two plots see Airoldi Namer 150–2 and Daniela Bini 65–7.
19 See Tomasello 63.
20 See Aguirre D'Amico 215–18. For possible criticism of Fascist ideology and practices hidden in *La nuova colonia* see Daniela Bini 75–6.
21 'L'eccessiva cura della propria eleganza, se avvantaggia di ben poco le probabilità matrimoniali, è invece il più forte degli ostacoli opposti a la fecondità [...] La bellezza femminile favorisce notevolmente il matrimonio e ostacola, in misura assai minore, la funzione riproduttiva' (qtd. in Meldini 190) (Excessive care of one's elegance raises the chances of matrimony, but is the strongest obstacle to fecundity [...] Female beauty facilitates marriage and hinders, to a lesser degree, reproductive functions). On the relationship between fashion and reproduction, see Caldwell, 'Reproducers' 113.
22 See De Grazia 71. In light of the close association between the figure of the mother and that of the Virgin Mary discussed in chapter 1, it is certainly meaningful that the date designated as Mother's Day was 24 December, Christmas Eve.
23 See Guida 42.
24 'Only nine women have been identified as veterans of the movement's first gathering at Piazza San Sepolcro in Milan on March 23, 1919, and female followers did not exceed several hundred until close to fascism's March on Rome on October 28, 1922. Nor did the so-called fascists of the first hour make any special gestures to reach out to a female constituency, except such as were in keeping with the movement's opportunistic tergiversations' (De Grazia 30).
25 Casartelli Cabrini 206. In their analysis of the changes undergone by the *Almanacco* during the Fascist years, Marisa Saracinelli and Nilde Totti discuss the ambiguities and contradictions of Casartelli Cabrini's articles, but also

stress the 'generoso sussulto di fierezza' (90) (generous proud reaction) that inspired her last piece, her 'canto del cigno' (92) (swan's song).
26 Saracinelli and Totti (83) consider Casartelli Cabrini's departure and her replacement with Lombardo as clear indications of the new direction taken by the *Almanacco*.
27 Lombardo 295.
28 On the Fasci femminili, see De Grazia 246–50 and Caldwell, 'Reproducers' 130–3.
29 Compare Re 77–8.
30 De Grazia 9.
31 De Grazia 12. Addis Saba stresses the difficulties of reconstructing women's responses to the dictatorship in 'La donna "muliebre"' 1–5.
32 Pickering-Iazzi, *Unspeakable Women* 102.
33 Ruinas 32.
34 Ruinas 41.
35 Ruinas 168.
36 Ruinas 139.
37 Ruinas 195.
38 Ruinas 157.
39 *Critica fascista* 7, no. 19 (1 October, 1929): 378.
40 Sarfatti 146. On Margherita Sarfatti's complex personality see Cannistraro and Sullivan, *Il Duce's Other Woman*, and Urso, *Margherita Sarfatti*.
41 Procacci 487.
42 Sarfatti 165. I followed Hughes for the translation of Jacopone da Todi's lines (280).
43 'Ma sono io davvero in Capri? ... Fascisti, nazionalisti, cerimonie ufficiali, in Capri?' (Am I really in Capri? ... How can Fascists, nationalists, official ceremonies be in Capri?) (Negri, 'La madre' 28).
44 Negri, 'La madre' 33.
45 Pertile 164.
46 See, for instance, the 'discorso della mobilitazione,' in which Mussolini stated his intention to pursue his colonial goals in Africa, in spite of international opposition: 'Dopo la Vittoria comune, alla quale l'Italia aveva dato il contributo supremo di 670.000 morti, 400.000 mutilati, e un milione di feriti, attorno al tavolo della pace esosa non toccarono all'Italia che scarse briciole del ricco bottino coloniale' (Mussolini, *Scritti* 218) (After the common victory, to which Italy made the supreme contribution of 670,000 dead, 400,000 maimed, and a million wounded, at the table of the greedy peace Italy received but the crumbs of the rich colonial spoils).
47 See Salvatorelli and Mira 1038.

48 Pompei 165.
49 Negri, 'Tuo figlio' 277.
50 Ruddick 220–1.
51 Saint-Point 10 and 15.
52 Papini 329 and 331.
53 Serao, *Parla una donna* 3.
54 Serao, *Mors tua...* 44. See also 147 and 279.
55 Serao, *Mors tua...* 326.
56 Banti, *Matilde Serao* 248.
57 Banti, *Matilde Serao* 285–6.
58 The laws against abortion and birth control were confirmed in the new Penal Code, approved on 19 October 1930, which proscribed both as 'crimes against the integrity and health of the race' (De Grazia 55).
59 Qtd. in Meldini 97.
60 Gina Lombroso 12.
61 Mussolini, *Scritti* 98.
62 Fiumi 189–90.
63 One may wonder if a daughter would have been worth such a sacrifice.
64 Ruinas 152–3.
65 See chapter I.
66 Vivanti, *Mea culpa!* 225.
67 See in particular 287, where a missionary explains to Astrid how the land that once produced cereal and rice is now cultivated only for cotton. 'Capirà [...] l'Inghilterra trae dal cotone immensi benefizi' (You must understand [...] England reaps immense profits from cotton).
68 Vivanti, *Mea culpa!* 310–11.
69 Giocondi 18.
70 *Critica fascista* 14, no. 15 (1 June 1936): 232.
71 *La difesa della razza* was indeed the title of the lurid magazine directed by Telesio Interlandi and charged with the mission of spreading racist and antisemitic propaganda. Its first issue came out on 6 August 1938.
72 Dolmetta, 'La funzione' 218.
73 The link between *Mea culpa!* and Vivanti's previous novel *Vae Victis!* (see chapter 1) is stressed by Graziella Parati, who states: 'Vivanti is particularly interested in exploring inter-racial relationships and their offspring and creates narrative plots in which women are confronted with their role as "hybridizers," as those who can destroy established separations between races' ('Maculate Conceptions' 327).
74 Qtd. in Pancrazi 19.
75 See Pancrazi 88.

76 'Drigo's representation [...] engages with and undermines the idealized images of country living constructed by the regime as part of a major ruralization campaign' (Pickering-Iazzi, *Politics of the Visible* 154). Publicized by Mussolini's bare-chested appearances as a field worker, this exaltation of a presumed rural essence of the Italian people was vociferously upheld by the 'Strapaese' movement and its magazine, *Il selvaggio*, published from 1924 to 1943. See Luti 156–70.
77 Drigo 68.
78 Drigo, *Maria Zef*, trans. Steinberg Kirschenbaum 60.
79 Drigo 52–3.
80 Drigo, *Maria Zef*, trans. Steinberg Kirschenbaum 44.
81 Drigo, *Maria Zef*, trans. Steinberg Kirschenbaum 182.
82 Livi-Bacci 62.
83 Qtd. in Addis Saba, 'La donna "muliebre"' 50.
84 See for instance Amedeo Ratta's article 'Donne e lavoro' ('Women and Work') published in *L'assalto* (14 August 1937) and summarized in *Critica fascista* 15, no. 21 (1 September 1937): 368. For the link between working women, emancipation, and the decline in fertility, see Dolmetta, 'Donna e lavoro femminile' ('Women and Female Work').
85 Qtd. in Meldini 264.
86 See Gallucci and Nerenberg 22.
87 See Giocondi 10 and 17.
88 Starting in the 1980s, De Céspedes has received considerable critical attention in North America. For an overview of this scholarship see Benedetti, 'La ricezione.' The new surge in the interest for this author in Italy is linked chiefly to the exhibit and conference organized by Marina Zancan in 2001 and to the two volumes edited by the same critic in 2001 and 2005.
89 De Céspedes 102.
90 De Céspedes 134.
91 De Céspedes 298.
92 'Il gancio' ('The Hook') is, significantly, the title of the 1902 short story in which Pirandello first explored this theme. The short story would be republished in 1910 in a revised version and with the new title of 'Il dovere del medico' ('The Doctor's Duty'). In 1913, it became one of the first plays by Pirandello to be brought to the stage. On Pirandello's influence in the representation of Emanuela, see Gallucci 207 and Benedetti, 'Pure battono' 209–12.
93 De Céspedes 96. Emanuela's feelings echo those of Nedda, the eponymous protagonist of the short story by Verga examined in chapter 1. After her lover's death, she feels inside her 'qualcosa che quel morto le lasciava

come un triste ricordo' (28) (something the dead man left her, like a sad memory).
94 De Céspedes 238.
95 Reich 142.
96 See De Grazia 147, Addis Saba ('La donna "muliebre"' 5) and Pickering-Iazzi ('Introduction,' *Mothers of Invention* xvii).
97 See Isidori Frasca.
98 This ad appeared for the first time on the back cover of *Critica fascista* 11, no. 9 (1 May 1933).
99 *Critica fascista* 12, no. 14 (15 July 1934), back cover.

Chapter 3

1 See de Felice, especially 14–30.
2 Women were granted the right to vote on 1 February 1945.
3 See Conti Odorisio 172.
4 'To legitimate itself as a force capable of ruling Italian society, the left discouraged women in uniform from participating in the celebratory parades' (De Grazia 287). See also Addis Saba, *Partigiane* xv, 157–60.
5 Calvino, *Romanzi e racconti* 106 (and *Path* 140).
6 For a stimulating discussion of the movie, see Forgacs (in particular 63–71).
7 See, for example, Renata Viganò 91–2, 112, and 129. Compare Zaczek 83 (note 3). Anna Bravo highlights the contradiction between the partisans' need of female participation and their mistrust of women ('Simboli del materno' 110–11).
8 See Mafai 262–6.
9 See Cutrufelli. For a chronology of some legal changes in the status of women see Birnbaum 89–90.
10 Cutrufelli 141. On this renewed devotion to the Virgin Mary see Scaraffia.
11 Marotta's treatment of this theme uncannily recalls one of Mussolini's slogans that proclaimed that maternity is to women what war is to men (see chapter 2).
12 Marotta 5.
13 Marotta 127.
14 'Son tutte belle le mamme del mondo / quando un bambino si stringono al cuor. / Son le bellezze di un bene profondo / fatto di sogni, rinunce ed amor. / È tanto bello quel volto di donna / che veglia un bimbo e riposo non ha; / sembra l'immagine d'una Madonna, / sembra l'immagine della bontà.' (All the moms in the world are beautiful when they hold their child to their heart. These are the beauties of deep fondness made of dreams,

sacrifice, and love. It's so beautiful, the face of a woman who watches a baby and doesn't rest. She is the image of the Madonna, she is the image of good).
15 Ginzburg 315.
16 Ginzburg 53.
17 On *È stato cosí* and its relationship with Alba de Céspedes's *Dalla parte di lei*, see Carletti.
18 Cialente 54.
19 Cialente 54 and 186.
20 Cialente 280.
21 See Bardini 213.
22 Morante 2: 643.
23 Morante 2: 287.
24 See Kalay 85–7.
25 The mother-son dyad is undoubtedly privileged in the universe created by the author. *Menzogna e sortilegio* explores two facets of that bond: the delightful complicity that allows Alessandra to relive childhood with her son Francesco and the pathological devotion that leads Concetta to ignore the reality of her son's death. This visceral dedication is in stark contrast with the indifference and even hostility that mothers in the novel feel for their daughters, as exemplified in the relationship between Concetta and Augusta and between Anna and Elisa. Love between mother and son constitutes also, and obviously, the very core of *L'isola di Arturo*.
26 Compare T.S. Eliot's *Gerontion*: 'The word within a word, unable to speak a word, / Swaddled with darkness. In the juvescence of the year / came Christ the tiger' (29). The hypothesis that Eliot's poem might have influenced Morante's image is supported by a closer look at the landscape surrounding Morante's tigress: 'una solitudine gelata' [a frozen solitude], reminiscent of T.S. Eliot's *The Waste Land.* Morante, however, may also have been familiar with medieval bestiaries that described the maternal instincts of the tiger. It was believed that a female tiger, when looking at a mirror on the ground, would mistake its own reflection for one of her cubs and feel an irresistible urge to nurse it. See, for instance, the description of the tigress in the Aberdeen *Bestiary* (ca. 1200) at http://www.abdn.ac.uk/bestiary/translat/8r.hti.
27 Qtd. in Kalay 46.
28 This is how this principle is formulated in the 1970 'Manifesto di Rivolta Femminile': 'La donna non va definita in rapporto all'uomo. Su questa coscienza si fondano tanto la nostra lotta quanto la nostra libertà' (Lonzi 11) (Woman must not be defined in relation to man. This awareness is the basis of our struggle and our freedom).
29 See Cecchi and Garboli lxxxii.

30 Manzoni, *I promessi sposi* 6.
31 Manzoni, *Adelchi* v, 352–4.
32 See, for instance, the games Alessandra plays with her son Francesco in *Menzogna e sortilegio* (Morante 1: 444–5) and the description of Ida's daily commute and routine as a teacher: 'Per tutta la strada, il cuore le sbatteva di spavento, fra la folla estranea dei tram, che la schiacciava e la spingeva, in una lotta dove lei sempre cedeva e restava indietro. Ma all'entrare in classe, già súbito quel puzzo speciale di bambini sporchi [...] la racconsolava con la sua dolcezza fraterna, inerme, e riparata dalle violenze adulte' (Morante 2: 298) (All along the road, her heart beat with fear. She was among the strangers in the tram, who pushed and shoved her, in a struggle where she always had to surrender and be left behind. But as soon as she entered her classroom, that special smell of dirty children [...] consoled her with its fraternal and defenseless sweetness, sheltered from the violence of the adults).
33 See Rosa 256.
34 Ortese 81.
35 '[*Aracoeli*] è un romanzo morantiano rotto, sconvolto, frantumato, e in fondo, deriso; i pezzi di vetro che lo compongono riflettono i rottami di un antico universo; e il vecchio schema glorioso (madre/figlio; Nunziata/Arturo; Ida/Useppe) viene lapidato e dato in pasto ai cani perché ne facciano strazio. La parodia è un autodafé; un'esibizione oscena; il gesto con cui si straccia ciò che abbiamo amato di piú' (Garboli 174) ([*Aracoeli*] is a broken, upset, fragmented, and, deep down, mocked Morantean novel. Its glass pieces reflect the remains of an ancient universe, and the old glorious pattern (mother/son; Nunziata/Arturo; Ida/Useppe) is lapidated and thrown to the dogs. The parody is a confession, an obscene exhibition, the act with which one destroys what one has loved the most).
36 Morante 1: 1453.
37 On Italian feminism and its specificity, see among others Conti Odorisio, Bono and Kemp, Rutter, and Parati and West.
38 Lonzi 20.
39 Lonzi 40.
40 In Rome, a new library is being assembled in an attempt to collect and preserve documents and publications of that time. 'Archivia' is hosted in what used to be a wing of the Roman female penitentiary, brought to fame by Renato Castellani's 1958 movie *Nella città l'inferno* (*Hell in the City*, starring Anna Magnani and Giulietta Masina). During my visits in the summers of 2003 and 2004, the documents were being catalogued. I would like to thank Maria Paola Fiorensoli, whose competence and kindness brought important material to my attention. Information about 'Archivia' is now available at

http://www.uniurb.it/giornalismo/lavori2004/cuccato/Archivia.htm. For a list and a description of Italian feminist publications, see Bono and Kemp 408–18.
41 The interview was significantly titled '"Quotidiano Donna", un giornale tutto fatto dalle lettrici' ('"Quotidiano Donna," a Newspaper Entirely Written by Women Readers'). The first issue of *Quotidiano Donna* (which would not live up to its name and become a daily) appeared on Saturday, 6 May 1978. As far as the opposition to authorship is concerned, it is easy to object that the physical limitations of a newspaper make equality impossible. In the case of *Quotidiano Donna*, one could even argue that the negation of authorship amplifies the significance of a particular person's analysis or opinions. Articles that are not signed – or signed with a pseudonym – acquire particular significance for the simple fact of being in a prominent position, such as on the front page, thus acquiring a representative, universal value that the identification of a specific author could, if anything, limit.
42 Roccella 7.
43 'Giacinto mi spia. Aspetta il segnale di un cambiamento. Con il figlio lui pensa che tornerò la donna dolce, remissiva, disponibile, arresa di prima' (Maraini 261) (Giacinto is spying on me. He is waiting for the sign of a change. He thinks that, with a child, I will go back to being the sweet, submissive, compliant, subordinate woman that I used to be).
44 Maraini 269. The novel is useful from a sociological point of view, as it offers a glimpse of the uneasiness of women's condition and an assessment of the limiting role motherhood was perceived to play in a woman's life.
45 Cerati 279.
46 '"Trovarci tutte insieme per noi ha significato e significa vivere insieme la maternità e anche i figli come libera scelta della nostra vita" (Joining all together for us meant and means experiencing together maternity and parenting as free choices of our lives). "Insieme alla pancia mi è cresciuta la voglia di una "maternità sociale"' ('The Desire of a "Social Motherhood" Has Grown Together with My Belly']. *Quotidiano Donna*, 8 March 1979: 4–5.
47 The 9 January 1979 attack was particularly cowardly and brutal: a neo-Fascist group (the NAR, Nuclei Armati Rivoluzionari) entered the headquarters of Radio Città Futura and shot five women of the collettivo delle casalinghe (Housewives Collective), ages thirty-five to fifty-eight.
48 Macciocchi, 'Le post-féminisme' i–iii.
49 Puccini 9.
50 Albalisa 11.
51 'La maternità è sotto il segno dell'ansia. La maternità è sotto il segno della contraddizione' (Lidia Ravera 103).

52 Law 194, which legalized abortion, was approved in 1978.
53 Fallaci 7.
54 Qtd. in Gatt-Rutter 66.
55 Cavarero, *In Spite of Plato* 59 and 63. For another modern interpretation of the myth that lays the foundation for Cavarero's, see Irigaray, *Sexes and Genealogies* 131 ff.
56 See also Ruddick 36: 'The complexity of maternal power is poignantly expressed in a woman's biological ability to give birth and, therefore, her ability to refuse to do so.'
57 'Umanità! Ma sei un essere umano, tu? [...] Ciò che vedo in te non sei te: sono io! Ti ho attribuito una coscienza, ho dialogato con te, ma la tua coscienza era la mia coscienza e il nostro dialogo era un monologo: il mio! Basta con questa commedia, con questo delirio' (Fallaci 62) (Humanity! Are you a human being, you? [...] What I see in you isn't you: it's myself! I attributed to you a consciousness, I carried on a dialogue with you, but your consciousness was my consciousness, and our dialogue a monologue: my monologue! Enough of this comedy, this delirium).
58 Fallaci 73–4.
59 The only comment on the ongoing debate is oblique and implicit: upon hearing the news of the protagonist's pregnancy, several other characters (such as her partner and her doctor) suggest that she have an abortion, in spite of the illegality of the procedure. This lends support to an argument often used by pro-choice advocates, namely that abortion, albeit illegal, was always an option for women, and that only financial and social status made it more or less traumatic and/or dangerous.
60 Ruddick 72. As Mazzoni states: 'I am laboring so hard to bring my child into the world, yet this child is condemned to die: whether in days or in years, it *will* happen' (*Maternal Impressions* 157).
61 For different uses of the psychoanalyst-patient simile see Minghelli 150 and Gallop 324.
62 Fallaci 74.
63 Gatt-Rutter 62.
64 Fallaci 7.
65 Fallaci 101.
66 I would like to thank Beth Wilkie (Georgetown College '03) for bringing to my attention the discrepancies among the different editions, and for her insight on the epilogue.

Chapter 4

1 Vegetti Finzi 116. For Laura Grasso, 'maternità significa, di fondo, identifi-

cazione con la propria madre; maternità è ricerca di comunicazione con la madre, con una donna con la quale si è avuto un rapporto difficile, oppure con una donna che ha rappresentato l'unico modello di femminilità possibile, con la quale ci si è quindi identificate fino in fondo' (117) (maternity means, after all, identification with one's own mother; maternity is the search for communication with the mother, a woman with whom one has had a difficult relationship, or a woman who has represented the only possible model of femininity, with whom one has identified completely).

2 In 1980, Tudy Giordanelli still noticed that 'rispetto [...] al rapporto madre-figlia si può dire che il movimento delle donne sia stato, almeno finora, un "movimento delle figlie"' (*Maria, Medea e le altre* 136) (as far as the mother-daughter relationship is concerned, we can say that the women's movement has been, so far, a 'daughters' movement').

3 'Se nei confronti dei padri la presa di distanza era stata ambigua, ambivalente, la contrapposizione più forte avvenne nei confronti delle madri e dell'immagine del femminile che esse rappresentavano [...] La madre era tutto ciò che non si voleva diventare nella vita' (Scattigno 283) (Whereas the distancing from fathers had been ambiguous and ambivalent, the strongest conflict was with mothers and the female image they represented [...] The mother was everything one didn't want to become in life).

4 Hirsch 165–6. Compare Daly and Reddy 3, and Giorgio, 'The Passion for the Mother' 120–1.

5 Hirsch 164.

6 Magli's article has been republished in *Maria, Medea e le altre* 119–20.

7 Lloyd 104.

8 Weber 45.

9 'Reason, at least as Western philosophers had imagined Him, was infected by – and contributed to – the pervasive disrespect for women's minds and lives [...] For a woman to love Reason was to risk both self-contempt and a self-alienating misogyny' (Ruddick 4).

10 Muraro, *L'ordine simbolico* 10.

11 The theory put forth in *Three Essays on the Theory of Sexuality* (1905) had already attracted criticism in psychoanalytical circles (by Karen Horney and Melanie Klein, among others). However, it was mainly Luce Irigaray who drew attention to the ways in which the Freudian system worked to exclude the possibility of a positive relationship among women (and in particular between mother and daughter). See Irigaray, 'Ce Sexe' 35–64. Irigaray's influence on Italian feminism cannot be overestimated: see Bono and Kemp 12–13. For an overview of feminist criticism of Freud, see Mitchell 305–56.

12 Qtd. in Hirsch 125.

13 'Mamma è poco.' *Quotidiano donna.* 1 January 1979: 4–5.
14 'Secondo una tradizione consolidata e suffragata mia madre era una santa, un'eroina, una martire' (Sereni, *Casalinghitudine* 49) (According to an established and documented tradition, my mother was a saint, a heroine, a martyr).
15 Sereni, *Casalinghitudine* 49.
16 Sereni, *Il gioco* 402.
17 For a comparison of this novel and Francesca Sanvitale's *Madre e figlia*, see Gavioli.
18 Cerati, *La cattiva figlia* 144–5.
19 Booth 154.
20 See Cerati, *La cattiva figlia* 105.
21 See, for instance, the protagonist's reaction after bathing her mother: 'Che crudeltà doversi specchiare nel proprio futuro! Sí, perché in quel corpo ormai deformato dall'artrosi e dagli anni potevo ricostruire la nostra somiglianza, sapere senza possibili illusioni come sarei diventata' (Cerati, *La cattiva figlia* 106) (What a cruelty, having to confront one's own future! I understood how that body deformed by arthritis and by ageing resembled my own and realized, without any illusions, what would become of me).
22 Cerati, *La cattiva figlia* 263.
23 'When women today refuse to identify with motherhood, they are correct in wanting to reject the burden of that status; however, along with throwing off the restrictions of the past, they may be wiping out the possibilities of the future' (Vegetti Finzi 164).
24 *Maria, Medea e le altre* 68.
25 Given the scope of this volume, the mother-daughter relationship is discussed only insofar as it entails repercussions for the daughter's decision to become, in turn, a mother, and for her relationship with her children. For a more extensive treatment of the mother-daughter link, see Giorgio, 'The Passion for the Mother.'
26 Ramondino 234.
27 Ramondino 263.
28 Ramondino 264.
29 Giorgio, 'The Passion for the Mother' 128.
30 *L'amore molesto* was brought to the screen in 1995 by Mario Martone, in one of the most intelligent collaborations between literature and film in the history of Italian cinema.
31 Ferrante 25–6.
32 Ferrante 55–6.
33 For a frightening example of Amalia's husband's jealousy, see 65: 'Una volta

si convinse che un uomo nella ressa l'aveva toccata. La schiaffeggiò sotto gli occhi di tutti, sotto i nostri occhi. Io restai dolorosamente meravigliata. Ero certa che avrebbe ucciso l'uomo e non capivo perché, invece, avesse preso a schiaffi lei [...] Forse per punirla di aver subíto sulla stoffa del vestito, sulla pelle, il calore del corpo di quell'altro' (Once he became convinced that a man in a crowd had touched her. He slapped her under everybody's eyes, under our eyes. I was painfully surprised. I was sure he would kill the man and didn't understand why he had slapped her instead [...] Perhaps in order to punish her for having felt the warmth of the other man's body on her dress, her skin).

34 'Ero sicuramente Amalia, quando un giorno trovai la pasticceria vuota e quella porticina aperta [...] Ero, all'imperfetto [...] Ero identica a lei e tuttavia soffrivo per l'incompiutezza di quell'identità' (Ferrante 166) (I was certainly Amalia the day when I found the bakery empty and the little door open [...] I was, in the imperfect [...] I was identical to her and yet I was suffering for the incompleteness of that identity).

35 Ferrante 78. However irrational and rarely acknowledged, the separation anxiety described by Ferrante may constitute a deep reason for the daughter's resentment. It figures prominently in Isabella Santacroce's 2006 novel *Zoo*: 'Lei, figura insostituibile, madre e mostro, violenta presenza, mancanza continua. Forse per colpa di quell'abbandono che è il parto in cui esci dalla sua carne, ti espelle. Forse per questo strappo che non hai chiesto ti mancherà sempre' (39) (She, irreplaceable figure, mother and monster, violent presence, continual longing. Perhaps the fault lies in that abandonment, in the birth that makes you leave her flesh. She expels you. Perhaps, because of that laceration that you didn't ask for, you'll miss her forever').

36 See Ferrante 73.
37 'Sentii quell'abito vecchio come la narrazione estrema che mia madre mi aveva lasciato, e che ora con tutti gli artifici necessari mi calzava a pennello' (Ferrante 171) (I sensed that the old dress was the last tale my mother had left me, which now, with all the necessary adjustments, fit me perfectly).
38 Ferrante 178.
39 For a different interpretation see Giorgio, 'The Passion for the Mother' 131.
40 Degli Esposti and Maraini 21.
41 Degli Esposti and Maraini 64.
42 Mazzoni, *Maternal Impressions* 51.
43 Comencini 111.
44 Comencini 189.
45 For a discussion of *Suo marito*, see chapter 1.
46 Suleiman 360.

146 Notes to pages 109–16

47 See Comencini 116.
48 Rich 253.
49 Compare Giorgio, 'The Passion for the Mother' 135–6.
50 Sanvitale 4.
51 Sanvitale 86.
52 Compare Marotti, 'Ethnic Matriarchy' 183.
53 'Il suo corpo sopravvisse a questa esperienza come uno stampo che doveva in futuro ricevere un contenuto: il dolore fisico che la madre aveva provato e lei no. Per questo, negli anni che seguirono alla morte di lei, si guardava la lingua allo specchio per vedere se era paralizzata e le sembrava di sì. Avvertiva con preoccupazione e sollievo le trafitte ai seni e i noduli perché annunciavano la sorte uguale alla madre e che il suo corpo vuoto aspettava' (Sanvitale 210) (Her body survived that experience like a mould that would someday be filled: the physical pain that her mother, unlike her, had felt. For this reason, in the years that followed her mother's death, she looked at her tongue in the mirror to see if it was paralyzed, and she had the impression that it was. She felt with concern and relief the pangs in her breasts and the lumps because they foretold a destiny equal to her mother's, a destiny that her empty body was waiting for).
54 Sanvitale 199.
55 Sanvitale 154.
56 The narration gives ample space to Sonia's frustrated attempt to become a mother, in the form of a gruesomely described clandestine abortion (148–52) and a late-term miscarriage that inspires an intense and disturbing dream (147). Paradoxically, the only pregnancy that is not mentioned is also the only successful one.
57 Sanvitale 3.
58 Sanvitale 229.
59 Sanvitale 230.

Chapter 5

1 Pozzi 24. I have modified Lawrence Venuti's translation.
2 Born on 13 February 1912, Antonia Pozzi died on 3 December 1938, after a suicide attempt. See Venuti xi.
3 Zanardi viii.
4 Tamaro 113.
5 This analogy was implicit in several works. See for instance Verga ('Nedda' 28), Vivanti (*Vae Victis!* 222), and De Céspedes 96.
6 See Borla 5.

7 *Recent Demographic Developments in Europe* 27.
8 Indeed, immigration is largely responsible for the reversal of the trend that took place in 2004: for the first time since 1991, Italy witnessed more births than deaths, with a consequent increase in its population. A history of Italian motherhood in the twenty-first century will have to take into account ethnicity and pluralism. For the latest demographic data, see http://www.istat.it/salastampa/comunicati/in_calendario/bildem /20050627_00/. For an analysis of the data, see the article eloquently entitled 'In Italia siamo di piú. Grazie agli stranieri' ('There Are More of Us in Italy: Thanks to the Foreigners') in *Il corriere della sera*, 28 June 2005 (http://www.corriere.it/Primo_Piano/Cronache/2005/06_Giugno/27/istat.shtml).
9 See Barbagli 13.
10 Valeria Viganò, *Il piroscafo olandese* 43.
11 Piazza 16.
12 See Valentini, in particular 117 ff.
13 On the importance and the activities of the Libreria delle Donne, see Bono and Kemp 109–10.
14 I quote from the translation in Bono and Kemp 121–2.
15 Caldwell, 'Italian Feminism' 103.
16 For a critical discussion of the theory and practice of entrustment, see Parati and West (59) and Mazzoni, *Maternal Impressions* 55.
17 Muraro 55.
18 See Vegetti Finzi 1.
19 Hansen 10. Compare Giorgio, 'Writing the Mother-Daugher Relationship' 33–4.
20 Ruddick 51.
21 Parati and West 19.
22 Lazzaro-Weis 34.
23 Valeria Viganò, *Prove* 120.
24 Neera, *Le Idee* 145.
25 This uneasiness was probably the inspirational force that led millions of Italians to desert the polls on 12 and 13 June 2005, effectively keeping in force the most restrictive law on reproductive technology in the Western world.

Works Cited

The Aberdeen Bestiary. University of Aberdeen. http://www.abdn.ac.uk/bestiary/index.hti
Addis Saba, Marina, ed. *La corporazione delle donne: Ricerche e studi sui modelli femminili nel ventennio fascista*. Florence: Vallecchi, 1988.
– 'La donna "muliebre."' In *La corporazione delle donne* 1–71.
– *Partigiane: Tutte le donne della resistenza*. Milan: Mursia, 1998.
Aguirre D'Amico, Maria Luisa. *Album Pirandello*. Milan: Mondadori, 1992.
Airoldi Namer, Fulvia. 'Pirandello's Myth Plays.' In Julie Dashwood, ed., *Luigi Pirandello: The Theatre of Paradox*. Lewiston, Queenston, Lampeter: Edwin Mellen, 1996. 148–72.
Albalisa. [Untitled.] *Filodonna*. 5 November 1982: 11–12.
Aleramo, Sibilla. *Andando e stando*. Ed. Rita Guerricchio. Milan: Feltrinelli, 1997.
– *La donna e il femminismo: Scritti 1897–1910*. Ed. Bruna Conti. Rome: Editori Riuniti, 1978.
– *Una donna*. Milan: Feltrinelli, 1992 [1906].
Amoia, Alba della Fazia. *No Mothers We! Italian Women Writers and Their Revolt against Maternity*. Lanham, New York, and Oxford: UP of America, 2000.
– *20th-century Italian Women Writers: The Feminine Experience*. Carbondale: Southern Illinois UP, 1996.
Angelone, Matilde. *In difesa della donna: La condizione femminile in* Una donna *di Sibilla Aleramo: Fortuna del romanzo nel mondo anglosassone*. Naples: Conte, 1990.
Ariès, Philippe. *L'enfant et la vie familiale sous l'ancien régime*. Paris: Plon, 1960.
Arslan, Antonia. 'L'archivio inedito della corrispondenza di Neera (Anna Radius Zuccari).' In *La correspondance: édition, fonctions, signification*. Actes du Colloque franco-italien. Aix-en-Provence, 5–6 October 1983. Aix-en-Provence: Université de Provence, 1983. 217–23.

- *Dame, galline e regine: La scrittura femminile italiana fra '800 e '900.* Milan: Guerini, 1998.
Baccini, Ida. 'La maestra, l'educatrice.' In *La donna italiana descritta da scrittrici italiane in una serie di conferenze tenute all'esposizione Beatrice in Firenze.* Florence: Crivelli, 1890. 418–28.
Badinter, Elisabeth. *L'amour en plus: Histoire de l'amour maternel (XVIIe–XXe siècle).* Paris: Flammarion, 1980.
Banti, Anna. *Matilde Serao.* Turin: UTET, 1965.
- 'Una ragazza antica.' *Paragone* 412 (June 1984): 22–30.
Barbagli, Marzio, et al. *Fare famiglia in Italia: Un secolo di cambiamenti.* Bologna: Il Mulino, 2003.
Bardini, Marco. *Morante Elsa, Italiana: Di professione poeta.* Pisa: Nistri-Listri, 1999.
Bassanese, Fiora A. 'Sibilla Aleramo: Writing a Personal Myth.' In Pickering-Iazzi, *Mothers of Invention* 137–65.
Bateson, Gregory, et al. 'Toward a Theory of Schizophrenia.' *Behavioral Science* 1 (1956): 251–64.
Beauvoir, Simone de. *Le deuxième sexe.* 2 vols. Paris: Gallimard, 1949.
Bebel, August. *La donna e il socialismo.* Brescia: Vivi, 1945.
Benedetti, Laura. '"Pure battono alla porta": Spiriti e personaggi nel *Fu Mattia Pascal* e oltre.' In Pietro Frassica, ed., *Magia di un romanzo*: Il Fu Mattia Pascal *prima e dopo.*' Novara: Interlinea, 2005. 203–14.
- 'La ricezione dell'opera nella critica angloamericana.' In Zancan, *Alba de Céspedes,* 2005, 408–14.
Benedetti, Laura. et al., eds. *Gendered Contexts: New Perspectives in Italian Cultural Studies.* New York: Peter Lang, 1996.
Benjamin, Jessica. *The Bonds of Love: Psychoanalysis, Feminism, and the Problem of Domination.* New York: Pantheon, 1988.
Bernard, Jessie. *The Future of Motherhood.* New York: Dial, 1974.
Bini, Daniela. *Pirandello and His Muse. The Plays for Marta Abba.* Gainesville, FL: UP of Florida, 1998.
Bini, Giorgio. 'La maestra nella letteratura: Uno specchio della realtà.' In Soldani, 331–62.
Birnbaum, Lucia Chiavola. *Liberazione della donna: Feminism in Italy.* Middletown, CT: Wesleyan UP, 1986.
Bono, Paola, and Sandra Kemp, eds. *Italian Feminist Thought: A Reader.* Cambridge, MA, and Oxford, UK: Basil Blackwell 1991.
Booth, Wayne C. *The Rhetoric of Fiction.* Chicago: U of Chicago P, 1961.
Borio, Maria di. *Una moglie.* Milan: Cogliati, 1909.
Borla, Laura. 'La peste bianca non è un dramma.' *Quotidiano donna.* 27 February 1981: 5.

Bravo, Anna, ed. *Donne e uomini nelle guerre mondiali*. Rome-Bari: Laterza, 1991.
- 'La nuova Italia: Madri fra oppressione ed emancipazione.' In D'Amelia 138–83.
- 'Simboli del materno.' In *Donne e uomini* 96–134.
Breschi, Danilo, and Gisella Longo. *Camillo Pellizzi: La ricerca delle élites tra politica e sociologia (1896–1979)*. Soveria Mannelli (CZ): Rubbettino, 2004.
Brosio, Valentino. *Tre ritratti segreti: Annie Vivanti, Filippo De Pisis, Alex Ceslas Rzewuski O.P.* Turin: Fògola, 1983.
Buttafuoco, Annarita. 'Vite esemplari: Donne nuove di primo Novecento.' In Annarita Buttafuoco and Marina Zancan, eds., *Svelamento. Sibilla Aleramo: una biografia intellettuale*, Milan: Feltrinelli, 1988. 139–63.
Caldwell, Leslie. 'Italian Feminism: Some Considerations.' In Zygmunt G. Baranski and Shirley W. Vinall, eds., *Women and Italy: Essays on Gender, Culture, and History*. New York: St. Martin's, 1991. 95–116.
- 'Reproducers of the Nation: Women and the Family in Fascist Policy.' In Forgacs, *Rethinking Italian Fascism* 110–41.
Calvino, Italo. *The Path to the Spiders' Nests*. Rev. ed. Trans. Archibald Colquhoun. Rev. Martin McLaughlin. London: Ecco, 1998.
- *Romanzi e racconti*. Vol. 1. Milan: Mondadori, 1991.
Cannistraro, Philip V., and Brian R. Sullivan. *Il Duce's Other Woman*. New York: Morrow, 1993.
Carducci, Giosuè, and Annie Vivanti. *Addio Caro Orco: Lettere e ricordi (1880–1906)*. Ed. Anna Folli. Milan: Feltrinelli, 2004.
Carletti, Sandra. ''Gli ho sparato negli occhi': Gender Conflict and Homicide in Alba de Céspedes's *Dalla parte di lei* and Natalia Ginzburg's *È stato così*.' In Benedetti et al. 153–64.
Casartelli Cabrini, Laura. 'Rassegna del movimento femminile.' In *Almanacco della donna italiana 1925*. Florence: Bemporad, 1926. 205–47.
Cavarero, Adriana. 'Dire la nascita.' In Paolo Azzolini et al., eds., *Diotima. Mettere al mondo il mondo: Oggetto e oggettività alla luce della differenza sessuale*, Milan: La Tartaruga, 1990. 93–121.
- *In Spite of Plato: A Feminist Rewriting of Ancient Philosophy*. Trans. Serena Anderlini-D'Onofrio and Áine O'Healy. New York: Routledge, 1995.
Cecchi, Carlo, and Cesare Garboli. 'Cronologia.' In Morante, Vol. 1, xix–xciv.
Cerati, Carla. *La cattiva figlia*. Piacenza: Frassinelli, 1990.
- *Un matrimonio perfetto*. Venice: Marsilio, 1975.
Chodorow, Nancy. *The Reproduction of Mothering: Psychoanalysis and the Sociology of Gender*. Berkeley: U of California P, 1978.
Cialente, Fausta. *Ballata levantina*. Milan: Feltrinelli, 1961.
- *Un inverno freddissimo*. Milan: Feltrinelli, 1966.

Colebrook, Claire. *New Literary Histories: New Historicism and Contemporary Criticism.* Manchester, UK, and New York: Manchester UP, 1997.
Colombi, Marchesa (Maria Antonietta Torriani). *In risaia. Racconto di Natale.* Milan: Lombardi, 1992.
Comencini, Cristina. *Matrioska.* Milan: Feltrinelli, 2002.
Conti, Bruna, and Alba Morino, eds. *Sibilla Aleramo e il suo tempo: Vita raccontata e illustrata.* Milan: Feltrinelli, 1981.
Conti Odorisio, Ginevra. *Storia dell'idea femminista in Italia.* Turin: ERI, 1980.
Croce, Benedetto. *La letteratura della nuova Italia.* 6 vols. Bari: Laterza, 1940.
Cutrufelli, Maria Rosa, et al. *Il Novecento delle italiane: Una storia ancora da raccontare.* Rome: Riuniti, 2001.
Daly, Brenda O., and Maureen T. Reddy. 'Introduction.' In *Narrating Mothers: Theorizing Maternal Subjectivities,* 1–18. Knoxville: U of Tennessee P, 1991.
D'Amelia, Marina, ed. *Storia della maternità.* Turin: Einaudi, 1997.
D'Annunzio, Gabriele. *Il libro delle vergini.* Milan: Mondadori, 1980.
De Céspedes, Alba. *Nessuno torna indietro.* Milan: Mondadori, 1938.
De Giorgio, Michela. *Le Italiane dall'Unità a oggi: Modelli culturali e comportamenti sociali.* Rome-Bari: Laterza, 1992.
Degli Esposti, Piera, and Dacia Maraini. *Storia di Piera.* Milan: Bompiani, 1980.
De Grazia, Victoria. *How Fascism Ruled Women. Italy, 1922–1945.* Berkeley, Los Angeles, Oxford: University of California Press, 1992.
Deledda, Grazia. *Cosima.* Trans. Martha King. New York: Italica Press, 1988.
– *Romanzi e novelle.* Ed. Natalino Sapegno. Milan: Mondadori, 1971.
– *Romanzi sardi.* Milan: Mondadori, 1981.
De Mauro, Tullio. *Storia linguistica dell'Italia unita.* Bari: Laterza, 1995.
Dolmetta, Adolfo. 'La funzione della donna nella politica razziale.' *Critica fascista* 17, no. 14 (15 May 1939): 218–20.
– 'Donna e lavoro femminile.' *Critica fascista* 17, no. 17 (1 July 1939): 269–70.
Dombroski, Robert S. *Le totalità dell'artificio: Ideologia e forma nel romanzo di Pirandello.* Padua: Liviana, 1978.
Drigo, Paola. *Maria Zef.* Milan: Garzanti, 1982 [1939].
– *Maria Zef.* Trans. Blossom Steinberg Kirschenbaum. Lincoln and London: U of Nebraska P, 1989.
DuPlessis, Rachel Blau. *Writing beyond the Ending: Narrative Strategies of Twentieth-Century Women Writers.* Bloomington: Indiana UP, 1985.
Eliot, T.S. *Collected Poems: 1909–1962.* New York: Harcourt Brace Jovanovich, 1991.
Fallaci, Oriana. *Lettera a un bambino mai nato.* Milan: Rizzoli, 1975.
Fattorini, Emma. 'A Voyage to the Madonna.' In Lucetta Scaraffia and Gabriella Zarri, eds., *Women and Faith. Catholic Religious Life in Italy from Late Antiquity to the Present.* Cambridge, MA, and London, UK: Harvard UP, 1999. 281–93.

Felice, Renzo de. *Interpretations of Fascism*. Cambridge, MA, and London, UK: Harvard UP, 1977.
Ferrante, Elena. *L'amore molesto*. Rome: e/o, 1992.
I figli della guerra. Venice: Istituto Veneto di Arti Grafiche Venezia, 1919. http://digital.library.wisc.edu/1711.dl/History.AgliAmici
Fiumi, Maria Luisa. *La moglie*. Florence: Bemporad, 1933.
Forgacs, David, ed. *Rethinking Italian Fascism: Capitalism, Populism, and Culture*. London: Lawrence and Wishart, 1986.
– *Rome Open City (Roma città aperta)*. London: British Film Institute, 2000.
Frateili, Arnaldo. 'Rassegna letteraria.' *Critica fascista* 5, no. 18 (15 July 1927): 359–60.
Frenquellucci, Chiara. '*Una donna* e *Suo marito*: Sibilla Aleramo nei meccanismi di Luigi Pirandello.' *Italian Culture* 15 (1997): 147–62.
Gallop, Jane. 'Reading the Mother Tongue: Psychoanalytic Feminist Criticism.' *Critical Inquiry* 2 (1987): 314–29.
Gallucci, Carole C. 'Alba De Céspedes's *There's No Turning Back*: Challenging the New Woman's Future.' In Pickering-Iazzi, *Mothers of Invention*. 200–19.
Gallucci, Carole C., and Ellen Nerenberg, eds. *Writing Beyond Fascism: Cultural Resistance in the Life and Works of Alba de Céspedes*. London: Associated University Presses, 2000.
Garboli, Cesare. *Falbalas: Immagini del Novecento*. Milan: Garzanti, 1990.
Gatt-Rutter, John. *Oriana Fallaci: The Rhetoric of Freedom*. Oxford, Washington, DC: Berg, 1996.
Gavioli, Davida. 'In Search of the Mother's Lost Voice.' In Benedetti et al. 201–11.
Giacosa, Giuseppe. *Tristi amori*. Milan: Costa & Nolan, 1999.
Gianini Belotti, Elena. *Prima della quiete: Storia di Italia Donati*. Milan: Rizzoli, 2003.
Ginzburg, Natalia. *Cinque romanzi brevi*. Turin: Einaudi, 1964.
Giocondi, Michele. *Lettori in camicia nera: narrativa di successo nell'Italia fascista*. Florence: D'Anna, 1978.
Giorgio, Adalgisa. 'Mothers and Daughters in Western Europe: Mapping the Territory.' In Giorgio, *Writing Mothers and Daughters* 1–9.
– 'The Passion for the Mother: Conflicts and Idealisation in Contemporary Italian Narrative.' In Giorgio, *Writing Mothers and Daughters* 119–54.
– 'Writing the Mother-Daughter Relationship: Psychoanalysis, Culture, and Literary Criticism.' In Giorgio, *Writing Mothers and Daughters* 11–45.
– ed., *Writing Mothers and Daughters. Renegotiating the Mother in Western European Narratives*. New York and Oxford: Berghahn, 2002.
Girard, René. *La violence et le sacré*. Paris: Grasset, 1972.

Gramsci, Antonio. *Quaderni dal carcere*. Turin: Einaudi, 1975.
Grasso, Laura. *Madre amore donna: Per un'analisi del rapporto madre-figlia*. Rimini-Florence: Guaraldi, 1977.
Graziosi, Mariolina. 'Gender Struggle and the Social Manipulation and Ideological Use of Gender Identity in the Interwar Years.' In Pickering-Iazzi, *Mothers of Invention* 26–51.
Guida, Patrizia. *Letteratura femminile del Ventennio fascista*. Lecce: Pensa MultiMedia, 2000.
Hansen, Elaine Tuttle. *Mother without Child*. Berkeley, Los Angeles, London: U of California P, 1997.
Hirsch, Marianne. *The Mother/Daughter Plot: Narrative, Psychoanalysis, Feminism*. Bloomington and Indianapolis: Indiana UP, 1989.
Invernizio, Carolina. *Il bacio di una morta*. Milan: Bietti, 1974 [1886].
Irigaray, Luce. *Ce sexe qui n'en est pas un*. Paris: Minuit, 1977.
– *Sexes and Genealogies*. Trans. Gillian C. Gill. New York: Columbia UP, 1993.
Isidori Frasca, Rosella. 'L'educazione fisica e sportiva, e la "preparazione materna."' In Addis Saba, *La corporazione delle donne* 273–304.
Jacopone da Todi. *Lauds*. Trans. Serge and Elizabeth Hughes. New York, Ramsey, Toronto: Paulist, 1982.
Kalay, Grace Zlobnicki. *The Theme of Childhood in Elsa Morante*. U of Missouri: Romance Monographs, 1996.
Kroha, Lucienne. *The Woman Writer in Late-Nineteenth-Century Italy: Gender and Formation of Literary Identity*. Lewiston, Queenston, Lampeter: Edwin Mellen, 1992.
Lazzaro-Weis, Carol. 'The Concept of Difference in Italian Feminist Thought: Mothers, Daughters, Heretics.' In Parati and West, *Italian Feminist Theory and Practice* 31–49.
Lilli, Laura. '"Quotidiano Donna", un giornale tutto fatto dalle lettrici.' *La Repubblica*. 5 May 1978.
Livi-Bacci, Massimo. *A History of Italian Fertility during the Last Two Centuries*. Princeton: Princeton UP, 1977.
Lloyd, Genevieve. *Man of Reason: 'Male' and 'Female' in Western Philosophy*. Minneapolis: U of Minnesota P, 1993 [1984].
Lombardo, Ester. 'Rassegna del movimento femminile italiano.' In *Almanacco della donna Italiana 1928*. Florence: Bemporad, 1929. 299.
Lombroso, Cesare, and Guglielmo Ferrero. *La delinquente, la prostituta e la donna normale*. Milan: Bocca, 1923 [1893].
Lombroso, Gina. *The Soul of Woman. Reflections on Life*. New York: Dutton 1923.
Lonzi, Carla. *Sputiamo su Hegel: La donna clitoridea e la donna vaginale*. Milan: Scritti di Rivolta Femminile, 1974.

Luti, Giorgio. *La letteratura nel ventennio fascista: Cronache letterarie tra le due guerre, 1920–1940.* Florence: La Nuova Italia, 1972.
Macciocchi, Maria Antonietta. *La donna 'nera': 'Consenso' femminile e fascismo.* Milan: Feltrinelli, 1976.
– 'Le post-féminisme.' In Jacqueline Aubenas-Bastie, ed., *Les femmes et leurs maîtres.* Paris: Christian Bourgois, 1978. i–xxii.
Mafai, Miriam. *Pane nero. Donne e vita quotidiana nella seconda guerra mondiale.* Milan: Mondadori, 1987.
Magli, Ida. 'Quando si odia lo specchio.' *La Repubblica.* 15 December 1978. Reprinted in *Maria, Medea e le altre,* 119.
Manacorda, Mario Alighiero. 'Istruzione ed emancipazione della donna nel Risorgimento. Riletture e considerazioni.' In Soldani 1–33.
Mantegazza, Paolo. *Fisiologia della donna.* Milan: Treves, 1893.
– *Fisiologia dell'amore.* Florence: Bemporad, 1906 [1873].
Manzini, Gianna. 'The Pomegranate.' In Pickering-Iazzi, *Unspeakable Women* 74–8.
– 'Ritratto di bambina.' In *Venti racconti.* Verona: Mondadori, 1941. 95–9.
– 'A White Cloud.' In Pickering-Iazzi, *Unspeakable Women* 79–81.
Manzoni, Alessandro. *Adelchi.* Ed. Alberto Giordano. Milan: B.U.R., 1976.
– *I promessi sposi.* Vol. 1. Ed. Salvatore Silvano Nigro. Milan: Mondadori, 2002.
Maraini, Dacia. *Donna in guerra.* Turin: Einaudi, 1975.
Marcellini, Marcello. 'Un'analisi psicologico-storica del sentimento materno.' *Attualità in psicologia* 4 (1996): 479–92.
Marchesini, Daniele. 'L'analfabetismo femminile nell'Italia dell'Ottocento: Caratteristiche e dinamiche.' In Soldani 37–55.
Maria, Medea e le altre: Il materno nelle parole delle donne: Rassegna stampa. Cosenza: Lerici, 1982.
Marotta, Giuseppe. *Le madri.* Milan: Bompiani, 1952.
Marotti, Maria Ornella, ed. 'Ethnic Matriarchy: Fabrizia Ramondino's Neapolitan World.' In *Italian Women Writers* 173–85.
– *Italian Women Writers from the Renaissance to the Present: Revising the Canon.* University Park: Pennsylvania State UP, 1996.
Mazzoni, Cristina. 'Impressive Cravings, Impressionable Bodies: Pregnancy and Desire from Cesare Lombroso to Ada Negri.' *Annali d'Italianistica* 15 (1997): 137–57.
– *Maternal Impressions: Pregnancy and Childbirth in Literature and Theory.* Ithaca, NY: Cornell UP, 2002.
– 'Pregnant Bodies of Knowledge: Italian Narratives of Fetal Movement (1880's–1920's).' *Rivista di Studi Italiani* 1 (June 1999): 223–41.
Meldini, Piero. *Sposa e madre esemplare: Ideologia e politica della donna e della famiglia durante il fascismo.* Rimini-Florence: Guaraldi, 1975.

Minghelli, Giuliana. 'Leading the Pedagogue by Hand: Women and Education in Italo Svevo's Narrative.' In Benedetti et al., 143–52.
Mitchell, Juliet. *Psychoanalysis and Feminism.* New York: Pantheon, 1974.
Monnier, Alain. 'La situazione demografica dell'Europa.' In Antonio Golini et al., *Famiglia, figli e società in Europa. Crisi della natalità e politiche per la popolazione.* Turin: Edizioni della Fondazione Giovanni Agnelli, 1991. 21–68.
Morandini, Giuliana. *La voce che è in lei: Antologia della narrativa femminile italiana tra '800 e '900.* Milan: Bompiani, 1997 [1980].
Morante, Elsa. *Opere.* 2 vols. Ed. Carlo Cecchi and Cesare Garboli. Milan: Mondadori, 1988–90.
Muraro, Luisa. 'The Narrow Door.' In Benedetti et al., *Gendered Contexts* 7–17.
– *L'ordine simbolico della madre.* Rome: Editori Riuniti, 1991.
Mussolini, Benito. *Discorsi del 1925.* Milan: Alpes, 1926.
– *Discorsi del 1927.* Milan: Alpes, 1928.
– *Scritti politici.* Ed. Enzo Santarelli. Milan: Feltrinelli, 1979.
Nardi, Isabella. 'Le "cattive madri": Note sul tema della maternità nei romanzi dannunziani e oltre.' In Neiger 79–97.
Neera (Anna Radius Zuccari). *'Le idee di una donna' e 'Confessioni letterarie.'* Florence: Vallecchi, 1977.
– *L'indomani.* Palermo: Sellerio, 1981 [1890].
Negri, Ada. 'La madre.' In *Le strade* 27–33. Milan: Mondadori, 1926.
– *Maternità.* Milan: Fratelli Treves, 1920.
– *Stella mattutina.* Milan: La vita felice, 1995.
– 'Tuo figlio sta bene.' In *Finestre alte* 271–82. Rome-Milan: Mondadori, 1923.
Neiger, Ada, ed. *Maternità trasgressiva e letteratura.* Naples: Liguori, 1993.
Offen, Karen. *European Feminisms 1700–1950.* Stanford, CA: Stanford UP, 2000.
Ortese, Anna Maria. *L'Iguana.* Milan: Adelphi, 1986.
Pancrazi, Pietro. *Un amoroso incontro della fine Ottocento. Lettere e ricordi di G. Carducci e A. Vivanti.* Florence: Le Monnier, 1951.
Panizza, Letizia, and Sharon Wood, eds. *A History of Women's Writing in Italy.* Cambridge, UK, and New York: Cambridge UP, 2000.
Papini, Giovanni. 'Amiamo la guerra.' *Lacerba* 2, no. 20 (1914): 274–5. In Gianni Scalia, ed., *La cultura italiana del "900 attraverso le riviste.* Turin: Einaudi, 1961. Vol. 4, 329–31.
Parati, Graziella. 'Maculate Conceptions: Annie Vivanti's Textual Reproductions.' *Romance Languages Annual* 7 (1995): 327–32.
Parati, Graziella, and Rebecca West. 'Introduction.' In *Italian Feminist Theory and Practice.*
– *Italian Feminist Theory and Practice.* Madison, NJ: Fairleigh Dickinson UP, 2002.
Pascoli, Giovanni. *Opere.* Vol. 2. Ed. Maurizio Perugi. Milan-Naples: Ricciardi, 1981.

Pertile, Lino. 'Fascism and Literature.' In Forgacs, *Rethinking Italian Fascism* 162–84.
Piano, Maria Giovanna. *Onora la madre: Autorità femminile nella narrativa di Grazia Deledda.* Turin: Rosenberg & Sellier, 1998.
Piazza, Marina. *Le trentenni: Fra maternità e lavoro, alla ricerca di una nuova identità.* Milan: Mondadori, 2003.
Pickering-Iazzi, Robin. 'Introduction.' In *Mothers of Invention* ix–xxxii.
– 'Introduction.' In *Unspeakable Women* 1–22.
–, ed. *Mothers of Invention. Women, Italian Fascism, and Culture.* Minneapolis: U of Minnesota P, 1995.
– *Politics of the Visible: Writing Women, Culture, and Fascism.* Minneapolis and London: U of Minnesota P, 1997.
–, ed. and trans. *Unspeakable Women: Selected Short Stories Written by Italian Women during Fascism.* New York: Feminist Press, 1993.
Pieroni Bortolotti, Franca. *Alle origini del movimento femminile in Italia: 1848–1892.* Turin: Einaudi, 1963.
– *Socialismo e questione femminile in Italia: 1892–1922.* Milan: Mazzotta, 1974.
Pirandello, Luigi. Pirandello, Luigi. *Maschere nude.* Ed. Alessandro D'Amico. Vol. 3. Milan: Mondadori, 2004.
– *Novelle per un anno.* Ed. Mario Costanzo. Vol. 3, Tome 1. Milan: Mondadori, 1990.
– *On Humor.* Trans. Antonio Illiano and Daniel P. Testa. Chapel Hill, NC: U of North Carolina P, 1974.
– *Tutti i romanzi.* Vol. 1. Milan: Mondadori, 1973.
– *L'umorismo.* Ed. Salvatore Guglielmino. Milan: Mondadori, 1986.
Pompei, Manlio. 'La famiglia e il fascismo: Un'inchiesta da fare.' *Critica fascista* 11, no. 9 (1 May 1933): 163–6.
Pozzi, Antonia. *Breath: Poems and Letters.* Ed. and trans. Lawrence Venuti. Middletown, CT: Wesleyan UP, 2002.
Procacci, Giuliano. *Storia degli Italiani.* Rome-Bari: Laterza, 1998.
Prosperi, Carola. *L'estranea.* Milan: Treves, 1915.
Puccini, Sandra. 'Può la femminista essere madre? Appunti sulla tesi della Macciocchi.' *Paese Sera.* 26 April 1979: 9.
Ramondino, Fabrizia. *Althénopis.* Turin: Einaudi, 1981.
Ravera, Camilla. *Breve storia del movimento femminile in Italia.* Rome: Editori Riuniti, 1978.
Ravera, Lidia. *Bambino mio.* Milan: Bompiani, 1979.
Re, Lucia. 'Fascist Theories of "Woman" and the Construction of Gender.' In Pickering-Iazzi, *Mothers of Invention* 76–99.
Recent Demographic Developments in Europe. Strasbourg: Council of Europe Press, 1999.

Reich, Jacqueline. 'Fear of Filming: Alba de Céspedes and the 1943 Film Adaptation of *Nessuno torna indietro.*' In Gallucci and Nerenberg 132–52.
Rich, Adrienne. *Of Woman Born: Motherhood as Experience and Institution.* New York: Norton, 1995 [1976].
Roccella, Eugenia. 'Ma la pancia è della donna.' *Il Mondo.* 1 August 1974: 7.
Rosa, Giovanna. *Cattedrali di carta: Elsa Morante romanziere.* Milan: Il Saggiatore, 1995.
Ruddick, Sara. *Maternal Thinking: Towards a Politics of Peace.* Boston: Beacon, 1989.
Ruinas, Stanis. *Scrittrici e scribacchine d'oggi.* Rome: Accademia, 1930.
Russell, Rinaldina, ed. *Italian Women Writers: A Bio-bibliographical Sourcebook.* Westport, CT: Greenwood, 1994.
Rutter, Itala T.C. 'Women as Subject: Theory and Micropolitical Practices in Italian Feminist Texts.' In Benedetti et al. 19–29.
Saint-Point, Valentine de. *Manifeste de la femme futuriste, suivi de Manifeste futuriste de la Luxure, Amour et Luxure, le Théâtre de la Femme, Mes débuts chorégraphiques, La Métachorie.* Ed. Jean-Paul Morel. Paris: Mille et Une Nuits, 2005.
Salvatorelli, Luigi, and Giovanni Mira. *Storia d'Italia nel periodo fascista.* Turin: Einaudi, 1964.
Santacroce, Isabella. *Zoo.* Rome: Fazi, 2006.
Santoro, Anna. *Narratrici italiane dell'ottocento.* Naples: Federico & Ardia, 1987.
Sanvitale, Francesca. *Madre e figlia.* Turin: Einaudi, 1980.
Saracinelli, Marisa, and Nilde Totti. '"L'almanacco della donna italiana: Dai movimenti femminili ai Fasci.' In Addis Saba, *La corporazione delle donne* 73–126.
Sarfatti, Margherita. *I vivi e l'ombra.* Milan: Mondadori, 1934.
Sarogni, Emilia. *La donna italiana 1861–2000: Il lungo cammino verso i diritti.* Milan: Il Saggiatore, 2004 [1995].
Scaraffia, Lucetta. 'Devozioni di guerra: Identità femminile e simboli religiosi negli anni quaranta.' In Bravo, *Donne e uomini* 135–60.
Scattigno, Anna. 'La figura materna tra emancipazionismo e femminismo.' In D'Amelia 273–99.
Serao, Matilde. *Mors tua...* Milan: Treves, 1926.
– *Parla una donna: Diario feminile di guerra, Maggio 1915 – Marzo 1916.* Milan: Treves, 1916.
– 'Scuola normale femminile.' In *Il romanzo della fanciulla: Le virtù di Checchina.* Naples: Liguori, 1985.
Sereni, Clara. *Casalinghitudine.* Turin: Einaudi, 1987.
– *Il gioco dei regni.* Florence: Giunti, 1993.

Soldani, Simonetta, ed. *L'educazione delle donne: Scuole e modelli di vita femminile nell'Italia dell'Ottocento*. Milan: Franco Angeli, 1991.
Spackman, Barbara. *Fascist Virilities: Rhetoric, Ideology, and Social Fantasy in Italy.* Minneapolis and London: U of Minnesota P, 1996.
Suleiman, Susan Rubin. 'Writing and Motherhood.' In Shirley Nelson Garner et al., eds., *The (M)other Tongue: Essays in Feminist Psychoanalytic Interpretation.* Ithaca and London: Cornell UP, 1985. 352–77.
Tamaro, Susanna. 'Sotto la neve.' In *Per voce sola*. Milan: Baldini & Castoldi, 1994.
Tomasello, Giovanna. 'La donna nella *Nuova colonia.*' In Stefano Milioto, eds., *La Donna in Pirandello*. Agrigento: Edizioni del Centro Nazionale di Studi Pirandelliani, 1988. 57–63.
Urbancic, Anne. '"L'invasore' di Annie Vivanti.' In Ada Testaferri, ed., *Donna: Women in Italian Culture*. Ottawa: Dovehouse, 1989. 121–30.
Urso, Simona. *Margherita Sarfatti: Dal mito del Dux al mito americano*. Venice: Marsilio, 2003.
Valentini, Chiara. *Le donne fanno paura*. Milan: Il Saggiatore, 1997.
Vegetti Finzi, Silvia. *Mothering: Toward a New Psychoanalytic Construction*. Trans. Kathrine Jason. New York: Guilford, 1996.
Vené, Gian Franco. *Mille lire al mese: Vita quotidiana della famiglia nell' Italia fascista*. Milan: Mondadori, 1988.
Venuti, Lawrence. 'Versions of Antonia Pozzi.' In Pozzi xi–xxiii.
Verga, Giovanni. 'Nedda.' In *Tutte le novelle*. Milan: Mondadori, 1993. Vol. 1, 5–29.
– 'Vagabondaggio.' In *Tutte le novelle*. Milano: Mondadori, 1993. Vol. 2, 5–32.
Viganò, Renata. *L'Agnese va a morire*. Turin: Einaudi, 1950.
Viganò, Valeria. *Il piroscafo olandese*. Milan: Feltrinelli, 1999.
– *Prove di vite separate*. Milan: Rizzoli, 1992.
Vivanti, Annie. *I divoratori*. Milan: Mondadori, 1910.
– *L'invasore*. Milan: Quintieri, 1915.
– *Marion, artista di caffé-concerto*. Ed. Carlo Caporossi. Palermo: Sellerio, 2006.
– *Mea culpa!* Mondadori, Milan, 1937. [1927].
– *Racconti americani*. Ed. Carlo Caporossi. Palermo: Sellerio, 2005.
– *Vae Victis!* Milan: Quintieri, 1924 [1917].
– *Zingaresca*. Milan: Mondadori, 1918.
Weber, Alison. *Teresa of Avila and the Rhetoric of Femininity.* Princeton, NJ: Princeton UP, 1990.
Wellek, René. 'The Fall of Literary History.' In *The Attack on Literature and Other Essays*. Chapel Hill, NC: U of North Carolina P, 1982. 64–77.
Wood, Sharon. *Italian Women's Writing, 1860–1994*. London and Atlantic Highlands, NJ: Athlone, 1995.

Zaczek, Barbara. 'Narrating a Partisan Body: Autobiographies of Carla Capponi and Giovanna Zangrandi.' *Quaderni d'Italianistica* 2 (2003): 71–85.
Zanardi, Cinzia. 'Foreword.' In Vegetti Finzi vii–viii.
Zancan, Marina, ed. *Alba de Céspedes*. Milan: Mondadori, 2001.
– , ed. *Alba de Céspedes*. Milan: Mondadori, 2005.
– *Il doppio itinerario della scrittura: La donna nella tradizione italiana*. Turin: Einaudi, 1998.

Index

abortion, 9, 142n52, 142n59, 146n56
Addis Saba, Marina, 135n31, 137n83, 138n96, 138n4 (chap. 3)
affidamento, 118–19
Aguirre D'Amico, Maria Luisa, 134n20
Airoldi Naimer, Fulvia, 134nn17–18
Albalisa, 141n50
Aleramo, Sibilla, 6, 15, 20, 66, 67, 87, 127n24, 129nn50–1, 130n61; *Una donna*, 28–32
Amoia, Alba della Fazia, 125n11, 131n86
Angelone, Matilde, 129n48, 129n54, 130n56
Ariès, Philippe, 124n3
Arslan, Antonia, 18, 125n11, 126nn19–20, 127n31

Baccini, Ida, 14, 125n10
Badinter, Elisabeth, 13, 124n3
Banti, Anna, 57, 126n23, 136nn56–7
Barbagli, Marzio, 147n9
Bardini, Marco, 139n21
Bassanese, Fiora, 130n63
Beauvoir, Simone de, 25, 128n36
Bebel, August, 21

Benedetti, Laura, 137n88, 137n92
Benjamin, Jessica, 5, 123nn9–10
Bergman, Ingmar, 95
Bernard, Jessie, 123n5
Bernardini, Adelaide, 30
Bini, Daniela, 134n18, 134n20
Bini, Giorgio, 125n8
Birnbaum, Lucia Chiavola, 138n9
Bono, Paola, 140n37, 140n40, 143n11, 147nn13–14
Booth, Wayne, 119, 144n19
Borio, Maria di, 32
Borla, Laura, 146n6
Bravo, Anna, 123n13, 123n15, 124n2, 138n7
Breschi, Danilo, 133n13
Brosio, Valentino, 25
Buttafuoco, Annarita, 130n57, 130n58

Caldwell, Leslie, 124n26, 133n6, 134n21, 135n28, 147n15
Calvino, Italo, 75, 138n5
Cannistraro, Philip, 135n40
Cappa Marinetti, Benedetta, 51
Capuana, Luigi, 23
Carducci, Giosuè, 127n32

Carletti, Sandra, 139n17
Casartelli Cabrini, Laura, 48, 134n25
Casati law, 13, 124n5
Casini, Gherardo, 133n13
Castellani, Renato, 140n40
Cavarero, Adriana, 90, 124n27, 142n55
Cecchi, Carlo, 139n29
Cerati, Carla, 10, 87, 100–2, 141n45, 144n18, 144nn20–1
Chodorow, Nancy, 7, 29, 129nn52–3
Christian iconography, 11
Cialente, Fausta, 77–8, 139nn18–19
Colebrook, Claire, 123n3
Colombi, Marchesa (Maria Antonietta Torriani), 14, 131n87
Comencini, Cristina, 108–10, 129n45, 145nn43–4, 146n47
Conti, Bruna, 129n54, 130n60
Conti Odorisio, Ginevra, 74, 138n3, 140n37
Croce, Benedetto, 42, 74, 132n95
Cutrufelli, Maria Rosa, 138n9

Daly, Brenda, 123n8, 143n4
D'Annunzio, Gabriele, 39–40
De Céspedes, Alba, 6, 137nn88–91, 137n93, 138n94, 139n17, 146n5; *Nessuno torna indietro*, 67–72
De Felice, Renzo, 138n1
De Giorgio, Michela, 125n13, 125n15, 130n71, 131n88
Degli Esposti, Piera, 108, 145nn40–1
De Grazia, Victoria, 49, 132n2, 133n5, 133n9, 134n22, 134n24, 135n28, 135nn30–1, 136n58, 138n96, 138n4 (chap. 3)
Deledda, Grazia, 9, 26, 33–5, 39, 51, 130nn63–4, 131n83, 131n85
De Libero, Giuseppe, 58

De Mauro, Tullio, 124n5
demography, 3, 116–17
D'Héricourt, Madame, 21
divorce, 9
Diotima, 7
Doganiere, Il, 46, 52, 62
Dolmetta, Adolfo, 63, 136n72, 137n84
Dombroski, Robert, 27, 128n42
Donati, Italia, 125n9
Drigo, Paola, 9, 137nn76–81; *Maria Zef*, 64–8
DuPlessis, Rachel, 38, 131n82

Echegaray, José, 123n5
Eliot, T.S., 139n26

Fabbretti, Nazareno, 89
Fallaci, Oriana, 9, 89, 142n53, 142nn57–8, 142n62, 142nn64–5; *Lettera a un bambino mai nato*, 89–93
Fascism: demographic policies, 8, 44; literature, 45–6; advertising, 72–3
Fattorini, Emma, 123n14
feminism, 84
Ferrante, Elena, 10, 104–7, 108, 144nn31–2, 145nn34–38
Ferrero, Guglielmo, 22, 127n30
Fiorensoli, Maria Paola, 140n40
Fiumi, Maria Luisa, 51, 59, 136n62
Forgacs, David, 138n6
Franchi, Anna, 15
Frateili, Arnaldo, 51, 133n11
Frenquellucci, Chiara, 28
Frese Witt, Mary Ann, 128n40
Freud, Sigmund, 143n11

Gallop, Jane, 142n61
Gallucci, Carole, 137n86, 137n92

Garboli, Cesare, 82, 83, 139n29, 140n35
Gargiulo, Alfredo, 28
Gatt-Rutter, John, 92, 142n54, 142n63
Gavioli, Davida, 144n17
Giacosa, Giuseppe, 30, 130n55
Gianini Belotti, Elena, 35, 125n9
Ginzburg, Natalia, 77–8, 139nn15–16
Giocondi, Michele, 124n20, 136n69, 137n87
Giordanelli, Tudy, 143n2
Giorgio, Adalgisa, 123n11, 124n25, 143n4, 144n25, 144n29, 145n39, 146n49, 147n19
Girard, René, 33, 130nn65–6
Gorjux, Wanda, 132n3
Graf, Arturo, 30
Gramsci, Antonio, 40
Grasso, Laura, 142n1
Graziosi, Mariolina, 133n7
Grillenzoni, Carlalberto, 47
Guida, Patrizia, 134n23

Hansen, Elaine, 119–20, 124n28, 147n19
Hirsch, Marianne, 10, 94, 143nn4–5, 143n11
Horney, Karen, 143n11

Industrial Revolution, 12
Interlandi, Telesio, 136n71
Invernizio, Carolina, 12, 124n1
Irigaray, Luce, 108, 142n55, 143n11
Isidori Frasca, Rosella, 138n97

Jacopone da Todi, 52, 135n42

Kalay, Grace Zlobnicki, 79, 139n24, 139n27

Kemp, Sandra, 140n37, 140n40, 143n11, 147nn13–14
King, Martha, 128n40
Klein, Melanie, 143n11
Kroha, Lucienne, 27, 128n38, 129n44, 129n54

Lagorio, Gina, 9
Lara, Contessa, 14
Lazzaro-Weis, Carol, 147n22
Lilli, Laura, 86
Livi-Bacci, Massimo, 137n82
Lloyd, Genevieve, 96, 143n7
Loffredo, Ferdinando, 44
Lombardo, Ester, 48, 135n27
Lombroso, Cesare, 22, 127nn29–30
Lombroso, Gina, 27, 30, 58, 129nn46–7, 136n60
Longo, Gisella, 133n13
Lonzi, Carla, 85, 139n28, 140nn38–9
Luti, Giorgio, 137n76

Macciocchi, Maria Antonietta, 87, 124n17, 129n54, 133n7, 141n48
Mack Smith, Dennis, 74
Madesani, Palmiro, 26
Mafai, Miriam, 138n8
Magli, Ida, 95, 143n6
Magnani, Anna, 75, 140n40
Majno, Ersilia, 31
Manacorda, Mario Alighiero, 124n6
Mantegazza, Paolo, 19, 126n17, 127n29
Manzini, Gianna, 9, 46, 133n14, 134n15
Manzoni, Alessandro, 80–1, 140nn30–1
Maraini, Dacia, 87, 121, 141nn43–4, 145nn40–1
Marcellini, Marcello, 13, 124n4

164 Index

Marchesini, Daniele, 124n5
Marotta, Giuseppe, 76, 138nn12–13
Marotti, Maria Ornella, 125n11, 146n52
Martone, Mario, 144n30
Masina, Giulietta, 140n40
Matteotti, Giacomo, 47
Mazzoni, Cristina, 108, 125n16, 127n29, 131n80, 142n60, 145n42, 147n16
Meldini, Piero, 124n18, 132n3, 133n8, 134n20, 136n59, 137n85
Minghelli, Giuliana, 142n61
Mira, Giovanni, 135n47
Molino Colombini, Giulia, 21
Monnier, Alain, 123n1
Morandini, Giuliana, 14
Morante, Elsa, 7, 9, 78–84, 124n29, 139nn22–3, 139n26, 140n32, 140n36; *La Storia*, 9, 79–81
Morino, Alba, 129n54, 130n60
motherhood: and Catholicism, 6, 35, 76; and intellectual ability 22–3; and working women, 40; and feminism, 84–8
Muraro, Luisa, 97, 119, 124n27, 143n10
Mussolini, Benito, 8, 43, 45, 51, 132n1, 133n4, 135n46, 136n61, 137n76

Nardi, Isabella, 5, 123n4, 123n7, 126n20
Neera (Anna Radius Zuccari), 8, 122, 125n12, 125n14, 125n16, 126n18, 127n23, 127n28, 147n24; *L'indomani*, 15–18; *Le idee di una donna*, 19, 121; *Confessioni letterarie*, 23
Negri, Ada, 8, 14, 41–2, 52, 54, 59, 60, 124n7, 132nn92–4, 135nn43–4, 136n49

Neiger, Ada, 130n70
Nerenberg, Ellen, 137n86

Offen, Karen, 133n13
Ortese, Maria, 81, 140n34

Pancrazi, Pietro, 136nn74–75
Panizza, Letizia, 125n11
Papini, Giovanni, 55, 136n52
Parati, Graziella, 136n73, 140n37, 147n16, 147n21
Pascoli, Giovanni, 4–5, 123n5
Pertile, Lino, 133n10, 135n45
Pesce Gorini, Edvige, 51
Piano, Maria Giovanna, 130n67
Piazza, Marina, 117, 147n10
Pickering-Iazzi, Robin, 50, 124n19, 132n96, 135n32, 137n76, 138n96
Pieroni Bortolotti, Franca, 127nn26–7, 132n90
Pirandello, Luigi, 30, 70, 128n41, 128n43, 131n82, 134n16, 134n18, 137n92; *Suo marito*, 25–8, 109; *L'umorismo*, 26; *La nuova colonia*, 46–7
Pompei, Manlio, 54, 136n48
Pozzi, Antonia, 7, 115, 146nn1–2
Procacci, Giuliano, 135n41
Prosperi, Carola, 18, 126nn21–2
Puccini, Sandra, 141n49

Ramondino, Fabrizia, 10, 102–4, 106, 108, 124n23, 144nn26–8
Rasy, Elisabetta, 95
Ratta, Amedeo, 137n84
Ravera, Camilla, 132n89
Ravera, Lidia, 88, 141n51
Re, Lucia, 135n29
Reddy, Maureen T., 123n8, 143n4
Reich, Jacqueline, 138n95

Rich, Adrienne, 7, 28, 110, 129n49, 146n48
Roccella, Eugenia, 86, 141n42
Rosa, Giovanna, 140n33
Rossellini, Roberto, 75
Rousseau, Jean-Jacques, 13
Ruddick, Sara, 55, 91, 120, 136n50, 142n56, 142n60, 143n9, 147n20
Ruinas, Stanis, 50–2, 59, 135nn33–8, 136n64
Russell, Rinaldina, 125n11
Rutter, Itala, 140n37

Saint-Point, Valentine de, 55, 131n81, 136n51
Salvatorelli, Luigi, 135n47
Santacroce, Isabella, 145n35
Santoro, Anna, 125n11
Sanvitale, Francesca, 10, 110, 144n17, 146nn50–1, 146nn53–5, 146nn57–9
Saracinelli, Marisa, 134n25, 135n26
Sarfatti, Margherita, 52, 135n40, 135n42
Scaraffia, Lucetta, 138n10
Scattigno, Anna, 124n22, 143n3
Scola, Ettore, 49
Serao, Matilde, 14, 55–8, 136nn53–4
Sereni, Clara, 98–100, 102, 144nn14–16
Showalter, Elaine, 98
Spackman, Barbara, 133n4
Spellman, Elizabeth, 94
Suleiman, Susan, 109, 129n45, 145n46
Sullivan, Brian, 135n40

Tamaro, Susanna, 115, 146n4
Tomasello, Giovanna, 134n19
Totti, Nilde, 134n25, 135n26
Trivulzio di Belgioioso, Cristina, 14

Urbancic, Anne, 130n74
Urso, Simona, 135n40

Valentini, Chiara, 147n12
Vegetti Finzi, Silvia, 94, 120, 142n1, 144n23, 147n18
Vené, Gian Franco, 125n15
Venuti, Lawrence, 146nn1–2
Verga, Giovanni, 41, 132n91, 137n93, 146n5
Viganò, Renata, 75, 138n7
Viganò, Valeria, 117, 120, 124n24, 147n10, 147n23
Vivanti, Annie, 9, 14, 127n32, 128nn33–4, 128n37, 130nn73–7, 131nn78–9, 136n66, 136n68, 136n73, 146n5; *I divoratori*, 23–5; *Vae Victis!* 35–9; *Mea culpa!* 60–4

Weber, Alison, 96, 143n8
Wellek, René, 7, 123n12
West, Rebecca, 140n37, 147n16, 147n21
women, legislation, 75–6
Wood, Sharon, 125n11

Zaczek, Barbara, 138n7
Zanardi, Cinzia, 115, 146n3
Zancan, Marina, 130nn58–9, 137n88

www.ingramcontent.com/pod-product-compliance
Lightning Source LLC
Chambersburg PA
CBHW020416080526
44584CB00014B/1348